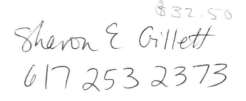

Public Policy
toward
Cable Television

AEI Studies in Telecommunications Deregulation
J. Gregory Sidak and Paul W. MacAvoy, series editors

TOWARD COMPETITION IN LOCAL TELEPHONY
William J. Baumol and J. Gregory Sidak

TOWARD COMPETITION IN CABLE TELEVISION
Leland L. Johnson

REGULATING BROADCAST PROGRAMMING
Thomas G. Krattenmaker and Lucas A. Powe, Jr.

DESIGNING INCENTIVE REGULATION FOR
THE TELECOMMUNICATIONS INDUSTRY
David E. M. Sappington and Dennis L. Weisman

THE FAILURE OF ANTITRUST AND REGULATION
TO ESTABLISH COMPETITION IN
LONG-DISTANCE TELEPHONE SERVICES
Paul W. MacAvoy

UNIVERSAL SERVICE:
COMPETITION, INTERCONNECTION, AND MONOPOLY
IN THE MAKING OF THE AMERICAN TELEPHONE SYSTEM
Milton L. Mueller, Jr.

TELECOMMUNICATIONS COMPETITION:
THE LAST TEN MILES
Ingo Vogelsang and Bridger Mitchell

VERTICAL INTEGRATION IN CABLE TELEVISION
David Waterman and Andrew A. Weiss

PUBLIC POLICY TOWARD CABLE TELEVISION:
THE ECONOMICS OF RATE CONTROLS
Thomas W. Hazlett and Matthew L. Spitzer

Public Policy toward Cable Television

The Economics of Rate Controls

Thomas W. Hazlett
Matthew L. Spitzer

The MIT Press
Cambridge, Massachusetts
London, England
and
The AEI Press
Washington, D.C.
1997

Published by

The MIT Press
Cambridge, Massachusetts
London, England

and

The AEI Press
Washington, D.C.

Library of Congress Cataloging-in-Publication Data

Hazlett, Thomas W.
    Public policy toward cable television : the economics of rate
controls / Thomas W. Hazlett, Matthew L. Spitzer.
        p.   cm. — (AEI studies in telecommunications deregulation)
    Includes bibliographical references and index.
    ISBN 0-262-08253-5 (cloth)
    1. Cable television—Government policy—United States.   2. Cable
television—Rates—United States.   3. Cable television—
Deregulation—United States.   4. Competition—United States.
I. Spitzer, Matthew L. (Matthew Laurence), 1952– .   II. Title.
III. Series.
HE8700.72.U6H39   1997
384.55'51'0973—dc21   97-20449
                                                                     CIP

Printed in the United States of America

To our friends at the Federal Communications Commission who helped us, and to our critics at the Federal Communications Commission who inspired us.

Contents

Foreword

DRAMATIC ADVANCES IN COMMUNICATIONS and information technologies are imposing severe strains on a government regulatory apparatus devised in the pioneer days of radio and are raising policy questions with large implications for American economic performance and social welfare. Before the passage of the Telecommunications Act of 1996, one was compelled to ask, Is federal and state telecommunications regulation impeding competition and innovation, and has that indeed become its principal if unstated function? Is regulation inhibiting the dissemination of ideas and information through electronic media? Does the licensing regime for the electromagnetic spectrum allocate that resource to its most productive uses? Now that the 1996 act is in place, is it likely to correct any of those ill effects?

Thomas W. Hazlett and Matthew L. Spitzer examine the effect of rate regulation in cable television with a focus on the impact of price controls on consumer welfare. This work is one of a series of research volumes addressing those questions commissioned by the American Enterprise Institute's Telecommunications Deregulation Project. The AEI project is intended to produce new empirical research on the entire range of telecommunications policy issues, with particular emphasis on identifying reforms to federal and state regulatory policies that will advance rather than inhibit innovation and consumer welfare. We hope that research will be useful to legislators and public officials at all levels of government, and to the business executives and, most of all, the consumers who must live with their policies. The volumes have been written and edited to be accessible to readers with no specialized knowledge of communication technologies or economics; we hope they will find a place in courses on regulated industries and communications policy in economics and communications departments and in business, law, and public policy schools.

Each volume in the Telecommunications Deregulation Project has been discussed and criticized in draft form at an AEI seminar involving federal and state regulators, jurists, business executives, professionals, and academic experts with a wide range of interests and viewpoints, and has been reviewed and favorably reported by anonymous academic referees selected by the MIT Press. I wish to thank all of them for their contributions, noting, however, that the final exposition and conclusions are entirely the responsibility of the authors of each volume.

I am particularly grateful to Paul W. MacAvoy, Williams Brothers Professor of Management Studies at the Yale School of Management, and J. Gregory Sidak, F. K. Weyerhauser Chair in Law and Economics at AEI, for conceiving and overseeing the project's research and seminars, and to Frank Urbanowski, Terry Vaughn, and Victoria Richardson of the MIT Press for their support and steady counsel in seeing the research to publication.

CHRISTOPHER C. DEMUTH
President, American Enterprise Institute
for Public Policy Research

Preface

THIS EXAMINATION OF RATE REGULATION in cable television is intended for policymakers, journalists, telecommunications industry analysts, and academic economists. We have tried to write a book that will be accessible to the wide range of individuals who have an interest in the subject matter. Some readers may want to focus on the sections describing the actual reaction of the cable market to price controls; others may want to read more about the scholarly debate and the theoretical issues raised by the regulation of cable television service. Readers not conversant with the terminology of that subject area may want to refer to the glossary.

We wish to thank seminar participants at the U.S. Department of Justice, Simon Fraser University, the University of California, Los Angeles, and the University of California, Davis, for comments on an earlier draft. Seminars delivered at the American Enterprise Institute in October 1994 and May 1995 were a source of exceptionally valuable feedback and guidance. Lorraine Egan and Kim Yasuda provided excellent computer and research work. Inputs that further benefited this research effort were graciously supplied by Nick Allard, Robert Bramson, Tim Brennan, Robert Crandall, Rich Esposto, Harold Farrow, George Ford, Harold Furchtgott-Roth, Daniel Ginsburg, Joe Guliano, Michael Katz, William Lehr, Paul MacAvoy, Gail MacKinnon, Chip Mahla, Mark Nathanson, Joe Pavalone, Robert Pepper, Ken Robinson, Richard Sexton, Greg Sidak, Robert Sieber, Jacob Sullum, Adam Thierer, John Wohlstetter, and Martin Morse Wooster. The somewhat magical assistance of Lynn Evans is duly noted. The usual disclaimer applies. The American Enterprise Institute and the Institute of Governmental Affairs at the University of California, Davis, provided support for this study, which is gratefully acknowledged. The authors remain solely responsible for its content.

THOMAS W. HAZLETT
MATTHEW L. SPITZER

About the Authors

THOMAS W. HAZLETT is a professor at the University of California, Davis, where he teaches economics and public policy in the Department of Agricultural and Resource Economics. He also directs the Program on Telecommunications Policy at the Institute for Governmental Affairs. From 1991 to 1992, Mr. Hazlett served as chief economist at the Federal Communications Commission, and from 1990 to 1991 he was a visiting scholar at the Columbia University Graduate School of Business. He has written numerous scholarly articles on competitive and regulatory issues in the cable and broadcast television industries.

MATTHEW L. SPITZER is the William T. Dalessi Professor of Law and director of law and economics programs at the University of Southern California. Mr. Spitzer specializes in law and economics and in broadcast regulation. His recent research has focused on content control in broadcasting. Among his publications are *Seven Dirty Words and Six Other Stories: Controlling the Content of Print and Broadcast* and "Experimental Law and Economics." Mr. Spitzer teaches administrative law, broadcast regulation, and economic analysis of law. Before joining the USC faculty, he taught at Northwestern University.

1

Introduction

THE EFFECTIVENESS of price regulation in constraining market power has been a subject of inquiry by economists for over three decades. Since the provocative 1962 paper by George Stigler and Claire Friedland,[1] the rate regulation of monopolies, natural or franchised, has been challenged by investigators who ask, What can regulators regulate? In its formative years, that challenge seemed a heavy one, prompting scholars such as Milton Friedman to judge regulation categorically ineffective in a dynamic world:

> When technical conditions make a monopoly the natural outcome of competitive market forces, there are only three alternatives that seem available: private monopoly, public monopoly, or public regulation. All three are bad so we must choose among evils. Henry Simons, observing public regulation of monopoly in the United States, found the results so distasteful that he concluded public monopoly would be a lesser evil. Walter Euken, a noted German liberal, observing public monopoly in German railroads, found the results so distasteful that he concluded public regulation would be a lesser evil. Having learned from both, I reluctantly conclude that, if tolerable, private monopoly may be the least of the evils.[2]

That skepticism over the effectiveness of regulation dominated economic research in the years following Stigler and Friedland's question[3] and may have at least partially motivated the deregulation of several sectors in

---

1. George J. Stigler & Claire Friedland, *What Can Regulators Regulate? The Case of Electricity,* 5 J.L. & ECON. 1 (1962).

2. MILTON FRIEDMAN, CAPITALISM AND FREEDOM 28 (University of Chicago Press 1962).

3. Sam Peltzman, *George Stigler's Contribution to the Economic Analysis of Regulation,* 101 J. POL. ECON. 818 (1993).

the 1970s and 1980s.[4] The U.S. cable television industry has witnessed a remarkable and seemingly unique policy cycle since the mid-1980s, with rate controls being lifted in the Cable Communications Policy Act of 1984, reimposed in the Cable Television Consumer Protection and Competition Act of 1992, and once again phased out in the Telecommunications Act of 1996.

This volume, in examining the effect of rate regulation in cable television, focuses particularly on the impact of price controls on consumer welfare. The traditional, textbook view—challenged by Stigler and Friedland—is that in an industry where price is set above marginal cost, price ceilings may reduce monopoly price markups and thereby expand output. Presumably, that increased volume lowers deadweight loss from monopolistic output restriction and is the aim of proconsumer regulation. What the literature on economic regulation has established, however, is that imposing controls on any industry is a complicated affair, and it is proper to question whether regulators can in fact achieve their announced goals.

We find that rate regulation in cable television has affected consumers in a number of significant ways, though not always in accord with common expectations or popular conclusions. Deregulation following the Cable Act of 1984 led not to a "fly-up" in rates, for example, but to price increases driven by (and commensurate with) quality upgrades in the cable television "package." Reregulation following the Cable Act of 1992, after a "false start" in 1993, did effectively constrain cable rates by about 8 to 10 percent in 1994. The reregulation of cable, however, was accompanied by a dramatic drop in viewer ratings for basic cable program services, which suggests a loss of quality in the eyes of consumers.

The most dramatic evidence of the failure of rate regulation to lower rates is found in the output data, which indicate that subscribership was neither restricted by cable deregulation nor expanded by reregulation. The strong support given to regulation by competitors to cable, including broadcasters and local telephone companies, and the vocal opposition to rate regulation expressed by programming interests further buttress the hypothesis that rate regulation has not lowered quality-adjusted cable rates. That failure of regulation is all the more striking in light of the overwhelming evidence that cable operators enjoy considerable amounts of market power, price substantially above average cost, and realize excess returns.

---

4. Roger G. Noll, *Comments and Discussion* (discussing Sam Peltzman, *The Economic Theory of Regulation After a Decade of Deregulation*), Brookings Papers on Econ. Activity: Microecon. 48 (1989).

2

The Recent Debate over Cable Rate Regulation

IN BOTH NEWS STORIES and popular discourse, it has been an article of faith that the deregulation of cable television rates on December 29, 1986, unleashed a price spiral that harmed consumers. It was commonly assumed in the years that followed that reregulation would produce corresponding consumer benefits, as long as regulators took the task of rate regulation seriously.[1] Such commentary was supported by reports of substantial cable rate increases, abysmal service, or both, and by three General Accounting Office surveys that showed cable rates rising much more quickly than the general inflation rate during the deregulation period (roughly 1987–1992).[2] Senator Daniel Inouye (D-HI), chairman of the Senate Communications Subcommittee, argued for the reregulation bill that became the 1992 Cable Act (S. 12) in words that would become commonplace in the congressional debate: "The GAO report demonstrates that S. 12 is needed now more than ever. Cable rates for the most popular basic cable tier of programming have increased 61 percent since deregulation went into effect in

---

1. *See, e.g.*, Jube Shiver, *Rising Rates Bring Cable Firms Static from Public*, L.A. TIMES, Mar. 17, 1989, at IV:1, 7; Mary Lu Carnevale, *Soaring Cable-TV Prices Could Usher in Reregulations*, WALL ST. J., Aug. 3, 1989, at B1; Paul Farhi, *Reregulating Cable: A Political Response to a Wired Nation*, WASH. POST, Jan. 22, 1992, at A1; *To Stop the Cable Gouging*, N.Y. TIMES, Jan. 28, 1992, at A20.

2. GENERAL ACCOUNTING OFFICE (GAO), TELECOMMUNICATIONS: NATIONAL SURVEY OF CABLE TELEVISION RATES AND SERVICES, GAO/RCED-89-193 (Aug. 3, 1989); GAO, TELECOMMUNICATIONS: FOLLOW-UP NATIONAL SURVEY OF CABLE TELEVISION RATES AND SERVICES, GAO/RCED-90-199 (June 13, 1990); GAO, TELECOMMUNICATIONS: 1991 SURVEY OF CABLE TELEVISION RATES AND SERVICES, GAO/RCED-91-195 (July 17, 1991).

1986. . . . During the same 4 1/2-year period, the cost of consumer goods rose by only 17.9%."[3]

Press accounts of rising cable rates made regulation a front-burner policy issue. The range of price increase estimates varied, but the theme was constant, as described in a review of press coverage of the 1992 Cable Act by *Baltimore Sun* reporter Carl Gannon:

> Sixty percent[,] said the Los Angeles Times. But the New York Times put this figure at 50 percent. U.S. News said 61 percent, but put the year [of deregulation] at 1986, not 1987. Gene Kimmelman, the consumer advocate, said 56 percent.
>
> And no matter what the numbers, this same phrase kept coming up again and again: Cable rates had risen at "triple the rate of inflation."[4]

If excessively rapid rate increases owing to cable's deregulated status were the agreed-upon source of the problem, the prevailing conclusion both in the news reports and in congressional debate was that the introduction of competition into local cable markets—though the preferred remedy for cable's monopoly pricing—would prove viable only in the long run. In the short run, rate regulation would be necessary to limit cable's market power. Michael Kinsley succinctly summarized the prevailing sentiment: "The [reregulation] bill also would take steps to promote genuine competition, which everyone agrees is superior to regulation if it can be made to happen."[5] Senator Lloyd Bentsen (D-TX) explained that the regulatory measure was reluctantly enacted:

> In sum, the pending legislation is necessary to satisfy the Government's compelling obligation to protect the rights of consumers where market forces are insufficient. I would prefer not to create a new system of Federal regulations—but, history tells us that where competition does not exist, the rights of consumers will ultimately be trampled upon. Thus, enacting this legislation is an appropriate action for Congress to take—until effective competition takes root in the cable industry.[6]

---

3. CONG. REC. S562 (daily ed. Jan. 29, 1992). The law itself contains findings implied by the GAO studies: "Pursuant to the Cable Communications Policy Act of 1984, rates for cable television services have been deregulated in approximately 97 percent of all franchises since 1986. . . . The average monthly rate has increased almost 3 times as fast as the Consumer Price Index since rate deregulation." Cable Television Consumer Protection and Competition Act of 1992 § 2.

4. Carl Gannon, *To the Editor: Did Your Cable Rates Go Up?*, 1 FORBES MEDIACRITIC 38 (1994).

5. TRB from Washington, *Remote Control,* NEW REPUBLIC, April 23, 1990, at 4.

6. CONG. REC. S591 (daily ed. Jan. 29, 1992). The most ardent public lobbyist for the

As is evident in that discussion, Stigler and Friedland's question seems not to have permeated the mass consciousness: there is no troubled equivocation over the issue of what, exactly, regulators can regulate. Indeed, the burden of proof is not upon those who seek regulation to lower prices, but upon those who would assert competition as an alternative short- or long-term policy. As we shall see, where head-to-head rivalry does exist in cable, rates are substantially lower in quality-adjusted terms. The evidence is just the reverse for regulation, which appears to raise effective prices to consumers. That the possibility of robust competitive rivalry in that historically monopolistic market is routinely discounted may not be curious, but it is noteworthy that price regulation is seen as the default position for those announcing opposition to monopoly pricing.

That faith in the ability of rate regulation to deliver consumer benefits appears to have held steady despite the fluidity of the predictions made regarding the magnitude of consumer savings. During the congressional debate over the 1992 Cable Act, advocates of the bill repeatedly referred to the estimate, credited to the Consumer Federation of America, that cable subscribers would save $6 billion each year.[7] (That figure implied that basic cable charges would fall by one-half, and the typical subscriber's overall bill by 30 percent; see table 2-1.) When the Federal Communications Commission announced its rules implementing the rate regulation measure on April 1, 1993, however, the projected savings were set at $1 billion.[8] Then, in its February 1994 reconsideration of the rules, the commission estimated consumer rate savings at $3 billion annually.[9] In early 1994 two other estimates were made of the benefits allegedly delivered to cable subscribers

---

1992 act, Gene Kimmelman of the Consumer Federation of America, made the same point: "Regulation is only an interim solution until cable competition emerges. But this short-term protection could save consumers $6 billion per year and is an essential first step." Gene Kimmelman, *Help Cable Customers by Regulating the Rates,* USA TODAY, June 15, 1991, at 5A.

7. "Lawmakers routinely try to claim the moral high ground by invoking the Consumer Federation of America, and they frequently quote its estimate that the measure will save cable consumers $6 billion a year." Edmund Andrews, *Cable Bill Advocate Divides and Conquers,* N.Y. TIMES, Sept. 28, 1992, at D6.

8. "FCC officials said the action should produce $1 billion in rate cuts for consumers." *FCC Angers Cable Firms, Aids Networks,* WALL ST. J., Apr. 2, 1993, at B1, 7.

9. "[FCC chairman Reed Hundt] predicted the rollback would affect roughly 90% of all cable systems and would result in a $3 billion savings to consumers: 'It's one of the greatest consumer savings in the history of American business regulation.'" Kim MacAvoy, *FCC Promises Price Drop for Most Subs,* BROADCASTING & CABLE, Feb. 28, 1994, at 7.

Table 2-1
Consumer Savings Estimates from 1992 Cable Act

Date	Estimated Total Savings ($ billions)	Estimated Annual Savings ($ billions)	Estimated Savings/ Sub./Mo. ($)	Source
Sept. 1992	NA	6.00	9.00	Consumer Federation of America
Apr. 1993	NA	1.00	1.45	FCC
Feb. 1994	NA	3.00	4.25	FCC
Mar. 1995	2.8	1.77	2.54	FCC
May 1995	3.5	2.10	4.00	FCC

Notes: See appendix for explanation of estimates. NA = not applicable. Savings/sub./mo. = savings per subscriber per month.

during the first year of regulated rates. The cable television industry produced a study setting revenue losses at $2 billion during 1993.[10] At the same time, Commissioner Andrew Barrett of the FCC claimed that a February 1994 survey showed consumer savings of $1 billion—as promised when the rules were enacted the previous year.[11]

The confusion in quantifying consumer savings is indicative of the nature of the beast: regulating cable rates is a complex task. Rates are changing in 11,000 cable systems, but so are basic and expanded packages, à la carte offerings, premium channels, and pay-per-view. Moreover, programs carried on existing networks are coming and going; even old shows are changing in the value viewers attribute to them. Marketing efforts are shifting, and capital investment plans are in flux. Billing arrangements may be altered, customer-premises equipment made friendlier or cheaper. Cable firms may offer nonvideo services—local access to computer and telephone networks, or home security services, for example—obscuring simple product market definitions. Between the cable industry and the FCC, it is a challenge for reporters to discern basic economic facts, let alone to develop

10. January 1994 Paul Kagan Associates study, *cited in* Federal Communications Commission, Separate Statement of Commissioner Andrew Barrett, Re: Implementation of the Cable Television Consumer Protection and Competition Act of 1992—Rate Regulation: Fourth Order on Recons., Fourth Rep. and Order (Feb. 22, 1994), at 4.

11. *Id.*

a coherent storyline. The latter task may seem overwhelming. Indeed, after the first year of reregulation, articles began appearing that questioned whether anyone had predicted what was going to happen under rate regulation.[12] Even those attempts at journalistic introspection missed the rich economic story told by rate regulation.

THE ECONOMIC LITERATURE

As in the popular press, the debate over the effects of cable rate regulation in the economics literature has been uncompelling regarding the question of regulatory effectiveness. Analytical work by economists on cable television regulation has been spurred by both the 1984 and the 1992 cable acts and has generally taken two investigative paths: examinations of the market power exercised by cable television systems in local video markets and cross-sectional studies using data before 1987 to assess the efficacy of cable regulation in suppressing rates.

The market power investigators contrast cable rates or cable system values in a way that sheds light on some key variables but fails to isolate the impact of regulation or deregulation on consumers. For instance, Steven Wildman and James Dertouzos regress cable rates against a vector of variables and find that prices are somewhat constrained by the existence of a greater number of over-the-air broadcast television signals.[13] That suggests that cable television and broadcast television are, at some level, substitutes, as the historical wiring pattern of cable operators (who first went into areas where broadcast signals were weakest) also indicates. Yet their study does not allow us to conclude that the presence of a given number of off-air television competitors eliminates market power.[14] Nor does it purport to address the efficiency of rate regulation.

---

12. See, *e.g.,* Gannon, *supra* note 4; Kirk Victor, *Beware of the Soothsayers,* NAT'L J., Dec. 4, 1993, at 2912.

13. Steven Wildman & James Dertouzos, Competitive Effects of Broadcast Signals on Cable, Attachment to Comments of National Cable Television Association in Federal Communications Commission filing: MM Dkt. Nos. 89-600 and 90-4 (1990).

14. An interesting aspect of the Wildman and Dertouzos results is that while cable rates appear to decline with the addition of marginal television signals up to a total of five in the market, beyond that number the price of cable service tends to increase (although that result is not statistically significant). The intuition is straightforward: in a market with fewer than the five network affiliates (CBS, NBC, ABC, Fox, PBS), cable demand tends to decline with the addition of stations; as additional (generally UHF) stations are added to the over-the-air mix, cable becomes a complement to broadcast television viewing, and demand for retransmission service increases.

Robert Crandall estimates the own-price elasticity of demand for cable systems across the United States and finds a range between -1.6 and -3.4, with an average of -2.2.[15] Although his estimates indicate that, for the marginal subscriber, there are good substitutes for cable television service, a rational monopolist would be expected to institute a pricing policy to achieve exactly that result. Consider the Lerner index, a formula showing the profit-maximizing elasticity for a price-searching firm: $(P - VC)/P = 1/\eta$, where η = absolute value of the elasticity of demand, P = price, and VC = variable cost. Because the average ratio of variable costs to revenues for U.S. cable systems was 53.9 percent in 1992,[16] the index implies that a profit-maximizing monopolist would raise price until it encountered an elasticity of -2.17.[17] Pricing along the elastic portion of the demand curve does not imply that market power is absent or that regulation could not reduce prices for consumers.

Robert Rubinovitz, in a Justice Department paper widely cited during congressional debate over the 1992 Cable Act,[18] estimated that about 57 percent of the price increases since the year-end 1986 cable deregulation were attributable to operating cost increases of cable systems; the other 43 percent were attributable to market power.[19] It is true, by assumption, that

---

15. Robert Crandall, Elasticity of Demand for Cable Service and the Effect of Broadcast Signals on Cable Prices, Attachment to TCI Comments to the FCC, MM Dkt. No. 90-4 (1990). Crandall's results are also described in BRUCE M. OWEN & STEVEN S. WILDMAN, VIDEO ECONOMICS (Harvard University Press 1992).

16. PAUL KAGAN ASSOCIATES, CABLE TV FINANCIAL DATABOOK, June 1993, at 36. That gives the cash flow ratio as 46.1 percent. That is defined as earnings before interest, taxes, depreciation, and amortization, or revenues minus operating costs.

17. Setting the price equal to $1 and variable cost to $.539 yields $1/\eta = .461/1$, so $\eta = 2.17$.

18. Robert N. Rubinovitz, *Market Power and Price Increases for Basic Cable Service Since Deregulation,* 24 RAND J. ECON. 1 (1993); citations are to an earlier draft, ROBERT N. RUBINOVITZ, MARKET POWER AND PRICE INCREASES FOR BASIC CABLE SERVICE SINCE DEREGULATION (U.S. Department of Justice, Antitrust Division, Economic Analysis Group Discussion Paper No. 91-8, Aug. 6, 1991). Typical of the congressional debate was the statement of Sen. Donald Riegle (D-MI) in support of S. 12: "I strongly support efforts to regulate cable. . . . The fact that most cable companies hold a monopoly over cable users provides them with the opportunity to raise rates in excess of that which would be allowed in a competitive market. A study conducted by an economist from the Department of Justice confirms this. That study found that at least 45 to 50 percent of the price increases since the mid-1980's were due to the cable industry's market power." CONG. REC. S14614 (daily ed. Sept. 22, 1992).

19. That finding is not surprising. As noted, the average cash flow ratio in the cable industry is about 46.1 percent. PAUL KAGAN ASSOCIATES, CABLE TV FINANCIAL DATABOOK, June 1993, at 36.

perfectly competitive firms cannot charge more than marginal cost; hence, a finding that cable firms charge above marginal cost may be considered tantamount to proving market power. Yet significant sunk costs must be invested in creating cable distribution systems, and firms that did not charge above marginal cost would realize negative profits.[20] If we use the FCC's finding that the cost of capital for cable system construction is 11.25 percent[21] and assume a useful fifteen-year life span and an initial capital cost of $619 per subscriber,[22] the typical cable system must recoup $7.13 monthly to amortize its investment. In 1992 that amounted to about 22 percent of the typical subscriber's bill. Prices in excess of long-run marginal costs are thus not prima facie evidence of supracompetitive profits.[23]

Beyond the assumption that prices in excess of marginal costs are attributable to market power, the Rubinovitz study does not reveal what consumers gained from price controls. As Rubinovitz is alert to note, the fact that nominal cable rates increased after deregulation does not end the matter; quality may have shifted upward, leaving consumers better off, worse off, or not much affected, on net: "[T]he cause of these price increases is not obvious."[24] He specifically cites the increase in quality in the cable marketplace after deregulation, and criticizes earlier studies for not accounting for such quality changes. Yet he does not explore whether the increasing cable quality (which he does find) was worth the surcharge that cable systems (with market power) were able to collect. The welfare of consumers under regulation or deregulation is not considered: consumers may prefer higher prices for higher quality in the marketplace after deregulation, even if they pay twice the marginal cost for added services.

---

20. That assumes, of course, that average total cost is above marginal cost, which seems appropriate in the cable television industry.

21. In the Matter of Implementation of Sections of the Cable Television Consumer Protection and Competition Act—Rate Regulation, Buy-Through Prohibition, Third Report and Order, MM Dkt. Nos. 92-266 and 92-262 (adopted Feb. 22, 1994; released Mar. 30, 1994). The commission later reopened that question in response to the cable companies' argument that the cost of capital was higher. If true, that would increase the monthly carrying costs.

22. ALBERT K. SMILEY, DIRECT COMPETITION AMONG CABLE TELEVISION SYSTEMS (U.S. Department of Justice, Antitrust Division, Economic Analysis Group Discussion Paper No. 86-9, June 5, 1986); Thomas W. Hazlett, *Duopolistic Competition in Cable Television: Implications for Public Policy*, 7 YALE J. ON REG. 65 (1990).

23. Although other evidence establishes quite conclusively that such is the case (see below).

24. RUBINOVITZ, *supra* note 18, at 3.

Adam Jaffe and David Kanter note that the popular preoccupation with nominal price increases is analytically troublesome.[25] Examining basic prices following deregulation, the authors comment:

> This price increase does not, however, demonstrate the existence of monopoly pricing. Prices for premium services have decreased slightly (in nominal terms), and there is general agreement that the regulatory regime enforced a cross-subsidization from premium to basic services. Also, quality may have improved overall, and franchisors (who are now prohibited from negotiating over prices) may be increasing their demands for nonprice concessions.[26]

Although we are dubious about two of those assertions (concerning pay-to-basic cross-subsidies and franchiser demands), Jaffe and Kanter are correct in pushing the analysis beyond a one-period examination of nominal prices. In dealing with the market power issue, they go on to note: "Just as the run-up in basic prices does not prove the existence of market power, the existence of inter-media competition does not disprove it."[27]

Jaffe and Kanter present evidence that cable systems generally rose in value after deregulation, but that the overall trend, when decomposed, was due to the increase in rural cable systems' sale prices. Systems located in major television markets did not increase in value. Those results depend upon the authors' premise that the effects of the 1984 Cable Act were capitalized into market transactions during the period *following* its passage in October 1984, a questionable assumption given that cable rate deregulation had been moving through Congress since 1979.[28] They conclude that greater

---

25. Adam B. Jaffe & David M. Kanter, *Market Power of Local Cable Television Franchises: Evidence from the Effects of Deregulation*, 21 RAND J. Econ. 226 (1990).

26. *Id.* at 227.

27. *Id.*

28. Jaffe and Kanter write that "[t]he earliest public draft of what eventually became the Cable Franchise Policy and Communications Act of 1984 . . . was proposed as a compromise between the National League of Cities, the U.S. Conference of Mayors, and the National Cable Television Association in November 1983." *Id.* at 229. That is misleading, at best. According to the legislative history of the Cable Telecommunications Policy Act of 1983, precursor legislation to the 1984 Cable Act, the first such measure (S. 622) was introduced on March 12, 1979, by Senators Barry Goldwater, Harrison Schmitt, Larry Pressler, and Theodore Stevens, while a competing measure (S. 611) was introduced on the same day by Senators Ernest Hollings, Howard Cannon, and Theodore Stevens. During the spring of 1979, hearings were held on both bills on all or part of twenty-two days, during which 171 witnesses were heard. *See* Cable Telecommunications Policy Act of 1983: Report, Together with Minority Views, Senate Subcommittee on Commerce, Science, and Transportation on S. 66, To Amend the Communications

competition is offered to cable television systems in major markets, presumably by over-the-air television and other entertainment outlets. Even if that conclusion is true, their previous admonition still stands: the existence of inter-media competition establishes not the absence of market power, but only that profitability is greater in some areas than in others. Moreover, the existence of—or changes in—cable system profitability are not perfectly correlated (negatively or positively) with consumer welfare.[29]

Although other studies attempt to examine the issue of price controls more directly, the results, unfortunately, are mixed. In a cross-sectional study of sixty-six cable systems (six of which were locally deregulated) before federal deregulation, Mark Zupan found that rate regulation was associated with a large price reduction: 34 percent.[30] Such cross-sectional studies are problematic in that, under a regime in which the municipality may regulate but chooses not to, the deregulation dummy variable is difficult to inter-

---

Act of 1934 (Apr. 27, 1983). Of further interest is that the "compromise" over the 1984 Cable Act came about only because the legislation backed by the National Cable Television Association had been making substantial progress; as early as September 1981 the *New York Times* reported that "[i]n some city halls, the deregulation proposal approved by the Senate Commerce Committee is causing more consternation than the recent round of budget reductions. . . . The legislation, which the Commerce Committee approved last month without hearings and which is strongly supported by the industry, says that no level of government 'may establish, fix or restrict the rates charged' for the use or sale of cable television." John Herbers, *Cities Fight to Keep Grip on Cable TV,* N.Y. TIMES, Sept. 1, 1981, at A14. *See also Cities Fight Move to Curb Local Cable TV Regulation,* NAT'L J., Sept. 5, 1981, at 1599–1600. The so-called compromise on the final bill was widely seen as a capitulation by the municipalities, which were losing several court challenges to their franchise authority and being rebuffed in various FCC rulings; the cities finally saw the legislation as a last-ditch effort to salvage some federal endorsement of the local franchising process. Indeed, in an amazing twist, the NCTA actually withdrew its support for the 1984 act before its passage, because cable interests felt they had substantially achieved deregulation without legislation. The municipalities ended up lobbying hard for the passage of "deregulation," a position they had expressed opposition to from the outset but, as defined in the 1984 act, had become the best they could do. *See* Cynthia Pols, *Cable Bill Essential This Year,* 7 NATION'S CITIES WKLY., Aug. 20, 1984, at 1, 6.

29. Further complicating the issue is that Robin Prager, *The Effects of Deregulating Cable Television: Evidence from the Financial Markets,* 4 J. REG. ECON. 347 (1992), finds that cable systems did not increase in value during the window when rate deregulation (in the 1984 act) was news. Systems appear to have appreciated only later (1986–1988). She attributes that result to a lag in the capital market's understanding of the effect of deregulation.

30. Mark A. Zupan, *The Efficacy of Franchise Bidding Schemes in the Case of Cable Television: Some Systematic Evidence,* 32 J.L. & Econ. 401 (1989).

pret. Is the cable company's price schedule truly unregulated if the locality could control it but elects not to? And given that the government has decided to allow an "unregulated" rate to be charged, is the observed rate truly a free market price?[31]

John Mayo and Yasuji Otsuka, examining 1982 data for approximately 1,300 cable systems in price regressions, used information from existing (presumably regulated) systems to predict what prices unregulated firms would charge.[32] Their results indicated that rates were constrained to below-monopoly price levels. The study was flawed in its assumption that all systems were rate regulated in 1982. The General Accounting Office has found that about one-fourth of cable systems were decontrolled before federal preemption of local controls in the 1984 Cable Act (see chapter 5). Thus, the authors' data set, in which regulated and unregulated systems were mixed up together, may account for the curious empirical result that the constraining effects of franchise regulation were higher for premium channel prices, which have never been regulated by local (or other) governments, than for basic cable rates. The authors attribute that to the possibility of reputational effects—what FCC-watchers have called "regulation by raised eyebrow." But why informal regulation should be more binding than formal regulation is not obvious. And if informal rate regulation, backed up by the possibility of franchise revocation or nonrenewal, is more effective than explicit controls, why should formal rate deregulation have a significant impact at the margin?

In any event, other studies have empirically estimated just the reverse result. In Robin Prager's 1990 study of 221 cable systems using 1984 (before deregulation) data, an estimated price equation found that systems operating under local franchise regulation charged rates that were above deregulated system rates by a statistically significant amount.[33] In a slightly different context, but coming to the same conclusion regarding the effectiveness of franchise regulation, Philip Beutel examined 27 randomly selected cable franchise auctions occurring between 1979 and 1981.[34] Those data revealed that companies that committed to charging higher prices had

---

31. See Thomas W. Hazlett, *A Reply to Regulation and Competition in Cable Television*, 7 YALE J. ON REG. 141, 143 (1990).

32. John W. Mayo & Yasuji Otsuka, *Demand, Pricing, and Regulation: Evidence from the Cable TV Industry*, 22 RAND J. ECON. 396 (1991).

33. Robin Prager, *Firm Behavior in Franchise Monopoly Markets*, 21 RAND J. ECON. 211 (1990).

34. Philip Beutel, *City Objectives in Monopoly Franchising: The Case of Cable Television*, 22 APPLIED ECON. 1237 (1990).

a higher probability of winning the franchise award. Beutel's explanation was that municipal regulators were interested not only in keeping prices low for consumers but also in distributing rents to key constituencies in the form of cross-subsidies. To the extent that projected price schedules and promised commitments were accurate assessments of future actions by the franchisee, municipal franchising agents selected, on average, the higher-priced, higher-rent package.[35]

Although the existing studies provide much interesting evidence, they do not confront the actual effects of federal deregulation and reregulation on consumers. At least two factors complicate that question: the regulation-deregulation dichotomy is tainted as long as regulation remains the option of the municipal government, on the one hand, and increased profitability does not necessarily emanate from decreased consumer surplus, on the other. In fact, two studies that have attempted to examine most directly deregulation's effect on consumer welfare have both found that rate regulation did not spur output and that, therefore, controls must not have constrained the quality-adjusted price. Thomas Hazlett finds that result for California's deregulation in the early 1980s;[36] John Woodbury and Kenneth Baseman find that for the federal deregulation in the late 1980s.[37]

---

35. Estimates of the size of the cross-subsidies involved in local cable regulation are found in Thomas W. Hazlett, *Private Monopoly and the Public Interest: An Economic Analysis of the Cable Television Franchise,* 134 Univ. Pa. L. Rev. 1335 (1986), and Mark A. Zupan, *Non-price Concessions and the Effect of Franchise Bidding Schemes on Cable Company Costs,* 21 Applied Econ. 305 (1989).

36. Thomas W. Hazlett, *The Demand to Regulate Franchise Monopoly: Evidence from CATV Rate Deregulation in California,* 29 Econ. Inquiry 275 (1991). In that instance, deregulation was achieved at the discretion of the cable system operator; sample selection bias would thus tend to exacerbate price increases associated with rate deregulation. Still, no evidence of quality-adjusted rate increases was found.

37. John R. Woodbury & Kenneth C. Baseman, Assessing the Effect of Cable Rate Deregulation (Oct. 10–11, 1990) (paper presented at the American Enterprise Institute conference on network industries). That research was contracted for by the National Cable Television Association and became embroiled in public controversy after being used in Commerce Department estimates of the impact of rate regulation in the summer of 1992. Paul Farhi, *House Probing Cable TV Cost Data,* Wash. Post, Aug. 29, 1992, at A7. In fact, the results of the Woodbury-Baseman study appear quite consistent with the economic evidence available from the reregulation (post-1992 experience). Interestingly, the National Cable Television Association has now officially abandoned its pre–1992 Cable Act previous position supported by the Woodbury and Baseman paper following passage and implementation of the act. It then claimed that regulation was highly effective in constraining cable rates.

CABLE RATE CONTROLS, WELFARE, AND RENTS

In 1982 Eli Noam anticipated the direction rate control on cable television service would take:

> With a century of regulation as a guide, one can confidently expect that rate setting will be used by regulators in an attempt to promote some types of programs over others. For example, in order to encourage the showing of programs that are socially desirable from the regulator's perspective, lower rates for their access may be instituted. Cross-subsidies are common in other areas of regulation, and it would be surprising if they would not also evolve quickly in the rate regulation of cable.[38]

Rate controls may be important even if they do not lower prices below monopoly levels. That is, local franchise regulators may employ rate controls either to lower price toward marginal cost (as in the traditional, public interest view) or to promote certain cross-subsidies,[39] or to achieve some combination thereof. In other words, regulators may use controls as low-cost (nonlitigious) contract enforcement devices, where the contract in question encompasses both the explicit franchise agreement and implicit political understandings tied to the franchise award.

The enforcement of franchise terms is a classic and continuing problem for local governments dealing with cable monopolists,[40] and city governments have repeatedly professed the view that rate regulation is a means to an end: cable franchise discipline. The leading trade association for municipal regulators, the National League of Cities, initially told its members to oppose the 1984 Cable Act's rate deregulation from that perspective: "The National League of Cities is leading the fight against the [rate deregulation] changes in the bill. Without control over rate increases, cities would lose their efforts to force cable firms to provide adequate service, said Cynthia Pols, the league's legislative counsel."[41]

---

38. Eli M. Noam, *Towards an Integrated Communications Market: Overcoming the Local Monopoly of Cable Television,* 34 FED. COMM. L.J. 209, 220 (1982).

39. Those familiar with the economic theory of regulation may expect that price controls would be used to set price floors in the interests of the "regulated" industry. Because cable franchises are typically monopolies, they may set their own "price floors" without collusion and do not, therefore, gain directly from regulation-imposed rate controls. There is evidence that legislators and cable industry incumbents have considered rate regulation as a quid pro quo for legal entry restrictions, but this story is entirely consistent with the cross-subsidy view of price controls.

40. *See* Oliver E. Williamson, *Franchise Bidding for Natural Monopoly—In General and with Respect to CATV,* 7 BELL J. ECON. 73 (1976).

41. *Cities Fight Move to Curb Local Cable TV Regulation,* NAT'L J., Sept. 5, 1981, at 1600. Alan Beals, executive director of the National League of Cities, also explained

Two study groups appointed by the California legislature to analyze the impact of state deregulation of cable television systems in 1979 officially delineated that view. In both the 1982 and the 1984 reports, the analysis concluded that price increases under deregulation had been "innocuous," but that a large problem had developed: cable systems were increasingly unresponsive to municipal requests to abide by franchise terms. The proposed solution was that the legislature authorize new "financial sanctions . . . [to be] applied to rate-deregulation systems as enforcement mechanisms."[42] It is revealing that the California League of Cities had, like its national counterpart, opposed rate deregulation in 1979 with the argument that "periodic rate hearings are the only practical method a local government has to insure that cable companies live up to the promises they made in the original franchise."[43]

The cable industry has long held a symmetric view. As congressional reregulation rumblings began, a leading cable industry analyst wrote: "Cable's legislative headaches are a by-product of the Cable Act. Rate deregulation curtailed local leverage, thereby forcing franchising authorities to threaten more drastic action in order to extract commitments."[44] By 1990 that view of price controls had become conventional wisdom. In reporting on the effects of deregulation, the General Accounting Office described rate regulation as follows:

> When cable television first developed as a means of providing better television reception, many cities and a few states began regulating the basic rates charged to cable subscribers. The regulation of basic rates was a condition of the local government's grant of a franchise or license. The franchise permitted the cable system to construct and operate cable facilities and systems, and to use local streets and rights-of-way to connect cable subscribers. The franchise agreement could also be used by the locality to prevent cable op-

---

why municipalities should oppose rate deregulation: "All city officials should make every effort to meet with their Representatives on cable legislation. . . . At these meetings, stress the impact of H.R. 4103 [the 1984 Cable Act] on your cable franchise. . . . Point out that, if passed, H.R. 4103 will end nearly all rate regulation in your communities; that it will break commitments made during the franchise process; and that it will virtually guarantee franchise renewal." Alan Beals, *The Cable TV Issue: Where We Are, What We Must Do*, NATION'S CITIES WKLY., Jan. 30, 1984, at 1, 7.

42. California Public Broadcasting Commission, *The Impact of 699* (April 1982).

43. Lee Margulies, *Pending Bill Pulls Plug on Fee Controls*, L.A. TIMES, June 19, 1979, at VI-12. The article also quoted Bill Keiser, general legislative counsel to the League of California Cities, as saying that "[i]t [rate deregulation] is the biggest stick we have, and if you lose it, it makes it much more difficult to force compliance with the terms of the franchise." *Id.*

44. PAUL KAGAN ASSOCIATES, CABLE TV FRANCHISING, May 31, 1989, at 1.

erators from charging unreasonably high basic rates for what was seen as an essential service in these areas. In addition, cities viewed the ability to deny or delay a requested rate increase as a useful tool to enforce other provisions of a franchise agreement, such as the obligation to provide service to all residents of the service area.[45]

Economic analysis has tended to overlook that bargaining dynamic. For example, Kathleen Carroll and Douglas Lamdin assert, when looking at cable operator stock prices, that "[t]he traditional [public interest] view would predict that share values would increase upon news of rate deregulation and decrease with news of rate reregulation."[46] That perspective omits the possibility that rate deregulation could increase profits of incumbent monopolists by raising enforcement costs of local franchisers, thereby effectively relaxing cross-subsidy requirements without raising prices charged consumers.

A two-dimensional view of cable rate regulation is clearly inadequate: market power may well be exercised even if supracompetitive profits do not flow solely to the cable franchisee. Rents may be transferred to other interest groups in the form of cross-subsidies, or rent-seeking expenditures may be incurred to procure or retain the monopoly franchise. It has been shown repeatedly that such cross-subsidies within the franchise arrangement are common in cable markets.[47] As we have seen, Noam goes so far as to offer that it would be remarkable if such cross-subsidies did not emerge from the rate regulation regime.[48]

---

45. GAO, Telecommunications: Follow-up, *supra* note 2, at 12.

46. Kathleen A. Carroll & Douglas J. Lamdin, *Measuring Market Response to Regulation of the Cable TV Industry*, 5 J. Reg. Econ. 385, 387 (1993).

47. Williamson's classic 1976 article, *supra* note 40, is a good example of that, while Peter Edwards offers an even more elaborate description of rent-seeking for the cable franchise. *See* Peter D. Edwards, Cable Television Franchising: A Case Study of Minneapolis, Minnesota (1985) (Communications Media Center, New York Law School). Hazlett, *supra* note 35, reports various such quantifications, including an Ernst & Whinney tabulation that the typical cable franchise in the early 1980s was required to devote 22 percent of total costs to uneconomic (that is, cross-subsidized) services. Zupan, *supra* note 35, divided such costs into capital and operating categories, finding 26 percent in the former and 11 percent in the latter. Beutel, *supra* note 34, also reports econometric findings that reveal large cross-subsidies embodied within cable franchise agreements.

48. In addition to saving on cross-subsidy expense, cable franchisees may benefit from deregulation in two ways that do not entail higher rates for consumers: (1) lessened transaction costs in evading controls (retiering, changing network investment strategies, shifting marketing efforts, and so on); (2) elimination of a source of business risk.

The economic theory of regulation has, in its most recent rendition, led us to look for distributional coalitions emerging victorious in regulatory competitions. Such coalitions typically include the incumbent firms in the regulated industry but are not strictly limited to such. Thomas Gilligan, William Marshall, and Barry Weingast note: "[A] multiple-interest-group perspective is frequently necessary to understand the inception of regulation. Regulation, in many cases, appears not to follow the stylized pattern of a concentrated producer group against an undifferentiated, diffuse set of consumers."[49]

Whereas George Stigler posited that the regulated producer group would generally dominate the regulatory regime, Sam Peltzman (1976) generalized the model to include the possibility that consumer interests could receive some consideration in the trade-off between (regulated) price and profits received by consumers.[50] Added to that mix is now a second-stage trade-off, which follows the insight of Gilligan and his colleagues: once profits are created (or permitted) by regulators, they may be reassigned within the political process to maximize support for key public decision makers.[51] That approach incorporates the compelling view of regulation found in Richard Posner's 1971 essay with the rent-sharing realities of regulation found in more recent studies.[52]

A graphic representation may elucidate our two-stage analysis of price regulation (see figure 2-1). Beginning with the familiar price-profit trade-off, regulators must first establish an optimal output price for the regulated service (P^*) at or below the monopoly price ($P^* \leq P_m$), which, in turn, determines the profitability of the regulated industry ($\pi^* \leq \pi_m$). That decision is assumed to emanate from the support-maximizing behavior of regulators.

---

49. Thomas W. Gilligan, William J. Marshall & Barry R. Weingast, *Regulation and the Theory of Legislative Choice: The Interstate Commerce Act of 1887,* 32 J.L. & Econ. 35, 60 (1989).

50. George J. Stigler, *The Theory of Economic Regulation,* 2 Bell J. Econ. Mgmt. Sci. 3 (1971); Sam Peltzman, *Towards a More General Theory of Regulation,* 19 J.L. & Econ. 211 (1976).

51. Gilligan, Marshall & Weingast, *supra* note 49.

52. Richard A. Posner, *Taxation by Regulation,* 2 Bell J. Econ. & Mgmt. Sci. 22 (1971). The Gilligan, Marshall, and Weingast study concluded that the Interstate Commerce Act of 1887 was the product of an interindustry compromise, rather than one of pure producer capture. Similarly, Hazlett found that the Radio Act of 1927 was a rent-sharing political solution predicated on blocking new entry into broadcasting. Thomas W. Hazlett, *The Rationality of U.S. Regulation of the Broadcast Spectrum,* 33 J.L. & Econ. 133 (1990).

Figure 2-1
Price Controls and Rent Distribution

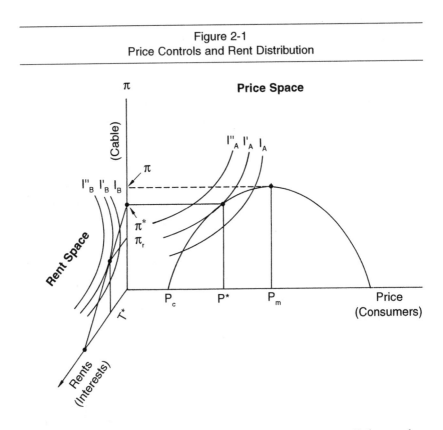

As such, it may well take consumer interests into account, as Peltzman has modeled the problem, with the A family of isosupport curves determining (in their tangency with the profit hill) a support-maximizing optimum for the regulator in what we call "price space."

Yet the relevant regulatory trade-offs are complicated by the existence of other competing social interests (noncable, nonconsumer) that are apt to influence political decision making. We can best think of those third-party interests as potential recipients of cross-subsidies, rents accruing from profits generated by the regulated firm. Hence, there is another family of isosupport curves in "rent space," here simplified to two dimensions. It is now apparent that the regulator has a two-stage optimization problem and that there is interactivity: all potential claimants for rents in the second stage (cable versus interests) will actively bid to raise price toward P_m during the first stage (cable versus consumers), thus relaxing the budget constraint.

If it is true that rate regulation helps police the optimal political distribution of rents, then rate deregulation (reregulation) could increase (decrease) profits at any given price level. That would imply a move along the budget constraint in rent space toward (away from) π^*. In general, the political equilibrium will involve some transfer (T^*) of the rents created in price space, such that $\pi_r \leq \pi^*$. When researchers view changes in the profitability of cable systems as prima facie evidence of changes in the prices charged consumers, they are implicitly assuming that rate controls do not affect rent-sharing. If controls affect cross-subsidies, that will be unwarranted.

Rate regulation imposes at least three additional burdens on cable firms even when, on average, quality-adjusted rates to consumers are not reduced. First, the cross-subsidy burden increases, because the "tax" authorities have acquired a new tool to impose penalties for nonpayment. Second, transaction costs rise, because evasive reactions are costly. Third, risk rises: regulatory approvals are neither free, as just noted, nor certain. The cost of capital rises under rate regulation.[53]

Theoretically, then, rate deregulation will unambiguously increase cable company profitability (and reregulation will decrease it), but whether a loss suffered by cable companies will result in any economic benefit to their subscribers is not clear. For the public to gain from controls on cable rates, the companies will have to lower service prices *and* avoid a corresponding decline in product quality. Given the extra costs imposed by rate regulation (transaction inefficiencies, capital costs, and rent seeking), agency problems in the regulatory structure, and supplier incentives to evade controls, the impact of rate controls may be either positive or negative on actual customers. Therefore, we must study the direct effect on consumers and not infer it from the observation that cable companies oppose rate controls and are financially worse off under them.

---

53. Regulated industries that are known for low-cost capital are those in a rate-of-return world. Cable rate controls are more like price caps (as discussed below). Moreover, "deregulation" of rates has not meant deregulation of entry barriers—the source of much risk for competitive businesses.

3

Market Power in Multichannel Video Markets

THE ISSUE OF RATE REGULATION must be considered in its institutional context. In local cable markets, sole operators dominate the distribution of multichannel video services to the home. As of June 30, 1995, there were an estimated 59.45 million cable television subscribers, 2.51 million authorized backyard satellite dish subscribers,[1] and 690,000 wireless cable subscribers.[2] An April 1992 survey of fifty U.S. markets in which cable companies compete head-to-head found that the overbuilders (second entrants) involved in such competitions passed about 932,750 homes, or just over 1 percent of the 89.4 million homes passed by cable in 1992.[3] (On a subscriber basis, counting both incumbents and overbuilders, the total competitive subscriber count of 1.17 million is about 2 percent of the 1992 total.)[4] It is clear that incumbent cable operators dominate local video markets; they face only modest direct rivalry either from cable competitors or from challengers using alternative (wireless) technologies such as direct satellite transmission or microwaves.[5]

---

1. Authorized means that such households were subscribing to scrambled cable programming services. That total includes direct broadcast satellite subscribers to services such as USSB, DirecTV, and Primestar.

2. PAUL KAGAN ASSOCIATES, MARKETING NEW MEDIA, June 19, 1995, at 4.

3. PAUL KAGAN ASSOCIATES, CABLE TV FRANCHISING, Apr. 30, 1992, at 4; PAUL KAGAN ASSOCIATES, CABLE TV FINANCIAL DATABOOK, June 1993, at 7. That is the largest sample of competitive cable systems of which we are aware, including that surveyed by the FCC in 1992 and 1993. For the definition of *homes passed*, see the glossary.

4. PAUL KAGAN ASSOCIATES, CABLE TV FRANCHISING, *supra* note 3.

5. In December 1995 the FCC put the market share of all nonmonopoly providers of multichannel video services at 9 percent. FCC, Annual Assessment of the Status of

Yet the source of such dominance is not readily apparent. Cable firms that establish secure market positions could be efficient competitors that defeat their rivals by providing superior product, by charging low prices, or by doing both. Under those circumstances, entrants would be hard pressed to improve upon the choice that current subscribers face, and monopoly market share would be the efficient outcome for consumers. Here we explore the question of monopoly pricing, which, in raising the consumer's cost above the producer's opportunity cost, restricts output and results in social waste.

To gauge the degree to which cable operators actually exercise market power by engaging in monopolistic output restriction, we shall examine three categories of evidence: q-ratios, to investigate what levels of excess profitability are available, on average, to cable operators; price differences between competitive and monopolistic cable systems; and business cases, to explore whether average cable markets would support competitive entry, particularly, lower-priced competitive entry. The evidence strongly suggests that, at least since the mid- to late 1980s, cable operators price well above marginal and average costs and earn returns significantly above competitive levels.

q-RATIOS

In a competitive industry, buyers will be unwilling to pay much more to buy assets than they would to build them from scratch. The market value of a competitive business is thus generally approximated by the replacement cost of its physical assets. The q-ratio is an economic measure based on that logic and is defined as: q = market value/replacement cost of tangible assets. An industry earning just competitive profits would be expected to demonstrate a $q \approx 1$.

Selling prices for cable television systems have averaged about $2,000 per subscriber since the late 1980s (see table 3-1). Yet information from a variety of sources sets cable's capital costs at only about $600 per subscriber. In 1986, for example, Albert Smiley calculated the typical cable system capital cost as $619 per subscriber.[6] Historic book cost is even lower: as of 1988 the cable industry had invested about $450 per subscriber,

Competition in the Market for the Delivery of Video Programming, Second Report, CS Dkt. No. 95-61 (Dec. 11, 1995).

6. That calculation is shown, with appropriate citations, in Thomas W. Hazlett, *Duopolistic Competition in Cable Television: Implications for Public Policy,* 7 YALE J. ON REG. 65, 98 (1990).

Table 3-1
Sales Prices for U.S. Cable Systems, 1982–1995

Year	No. of Systems	Total Subscribers	Dollar Value per Home Passed	Dollar Value per Subscriber
1982	212	934,071	486	922
1983	256	2,631,190	554	1,026
1984	295	3,023,144	520	948
1985	356	7,992,899	546	1,008
1986	620	6,797,164	733	1,339
1987	498	6,506,466	946	1,723
1988	596	7,596,344	1,162	2,003
1989	379	5,951,353	1,255	2,291
1990	105	531,207	1,277	2,049
1991	111	4,523,433	961	1,795
1992	97	1,876,754	1,023	1,765
1993	96	3,852,668	1,258	2,160
1994	64	7,504,177	1,123	1,869
1995[a]	54	5,416,291	1,178	1,846

a. Through June.

Sources: Paul Kagan Associates, *Cable TV Investor,* Jan. 31, 1995, p. 18; Feb. 12, 1993, p. 6; July 31, 1995, p. 5.

undepreciated.[7] A variety of sources place the market value of cable systems

---

7. Bruce L. Egan & Douglas A. Conn, *Capital Budgeting Alternatives for Residential Broadband Networks,* in TELEPHONE COMPANY AND CABLE TELEVISION COMPETITION: KEY TECHNICAL, ECONOMIC, LEGAL AND POLICY ISSUES 135, 147 (Stuart Brotman ed., Artech House 1990). BRUCE L. EGAN, INFORMATION SUPERHIGHWAYS: THE ECONOMICS OF ADVANCED PUBLIC COMMUNICATION NETWORKS 95 (Artech House 1991), lists "gross plant in service" for the cable television industry nationally of $21.872 billion in 1988. With 48,636,520 subscribers in 1988 (NATIONAL CABLE TELEVISION ASSOCIATION, CABLE TELEVISION DEVELOPMENTS, Apr. 1993, at 2-A), that comes out to $449.70 per subscriber. Cable industry executives verify such capital cost/subscriber numbers in the trade press. Then–Tele-Communications, Inc., senior vice president (and industry technology expert) John Sie stated in 1988 that the industry's efficient "tree-and-branch" architecture allowed it to wire a market with coaxial cable for just $350 per home passed (Paul Kagan Associates, CABLE TV FRANCHISING, Sept. 27, 1988, at 2). (At 58.3 percent penetration, that translates into $600 per subscriber.) At just that time, cable system sales were averaging

at 2.5 to 6 times capital costs.[8] By comparison, the average q-ratio for the firms listed on the New York Stock Exchange in February 1990 was .85.[9]

We can cross-check those numbers by using capital cost data given in Paul Kagan Associates' 1993 *Cable TV Financial Databook*. It lists capital expense per cable plant mile of $31,000 and estimates a national coverage of 1,090,000 miles.[10] The databook also finds an average plant age of 57.89 percent—the ratio of useful life that is left, or undepreciated. Smiley gives the cost of a head-end (the central receiving point of a cable television system), including start-up costs, as $1.2 million, and the National Cable Television Association estimates that there are 11,460 head-ends.[11] Smiley allows $120 for the cost of a converter (including the drop and installation cost), but current costs for a state-of-the art converter may be higher. We assume $200 for the cost of subscriber-specific (customer-premises) equipment, including (nonrecoverable) installation charges. At year-end 1993, there were 57.2 million cable subscribers in the United States. The total cost of new capital, nationwide, would then amount to: ($31,000)(1,090,000) + (11,460)($1,200,000) + (56,300,000)($200) = $58.98 billion. If 57.89 percent of that capital is undepreciated, it has a net book value of $34.14 billion. On the market value (numerator) side of the q-ratio, the average selling price of a cable subscriber in 1993 was $2,124. That figure implies a nationwide market value of about $121.49 billion. Dividing the replacement cost of capital into the market value of capital assets yields a q of 3.56.[12]

$1,153 per home passed (and $1,997 per subscriber). *Cable System Sales Comparison, April–June, 1988,* Cable TV Investor, July 31, 1988, at 4.

8. Hazlett, *supra* note 6; Paul W. MacAvoy, Tobin's q and the Cable Industry's Market Power, Attachment to Comments of United States Telephone Association to the Federal Communications Commission, MM Dkt. No. 89-600 (Feb. 28, 1990), at 27.

9. FCC, In the Matter of Competition, Rate Deregulation and the Commission's Policies Relating to the Provision of Cable Television Service, MM Dkt. No. 89-600 (July 26, 1990), at 38. The document is also known as the 1990 FCC Cable Report.

10. Paul Kagan Associates, Cable TV Financial Databook, June 1993, at 9.

11. Albert K. Smiley, Direct Competition Among Cable Television Systems (U.S. Department of Justice, Antitrust Division, Economic Analysis Group Discussion Paper No. 86-9, June 5, 1986); National Cable Television Association, Cable Television Developments, Apr. 1994, at 1-A.

12. The FCC used q-ratio analysis in its September 1994 Report on the Status of Video Competition (Annual Assessment of the Status of Competition in the Market for the Delivery of Video Programming, First Report, CS Dkt. No. 94-48, 9 F.C.C. Rcd. 7442, Sept. 28, 1994). The results, discussed below, show that cable market power was substantial even after the advent of rate regulation and direct broadcast satellite (DBS) competition.

An industry q-ratio of 3 is exceptionally high. In a review of q-ratios in twenty industries, Lawrence Katz and Lawrence Summers estimate industry rents for the time period 1960–1985 (including the subset period 1981–1985).[13] The highest industry q found during the entire sample period, 3.24, was for the scientific instruments sector. (The next highest was 1.9, in printing.) The economic intuition behind that finding is that in a sector with relatively high expenditures on research and development, selection bias will be present because only survivors will be counted. Overall, the average q-ratio during the 1960–1985 time frame was 1.28; in the 1981–1985 period, .85.

In the 1990 FCC Cable Report,[14] the commission listed a number of reasons why q-ratios might overstate the monopoly power of cable operators. They included such factors as capitalization of entrepreneurial foresight, high riskiness, and returns to monopsony power. Interestingly, none of those factors compromises the evidence of excess profits in the cable industry. Entrepreneurship can hardly explain industry averages when no selection bias (via survivorship) is extant. In the cable industry, hypothetical cable systems have been evaluated ex ante at monopolistic q-ratios: in June 1987 a pro forma financial model by Deloit, Haskins and Sells capitalized a typical (hypothetical) cable system with physical assets accounting for 40 percent of assets and "franchise and goodwill" at 60 percent,[15] implying that $q = 2.5$.

Survivorship bias cannot provide an efficiency explanation for high q-ratios unless relatively inefficient firms exit the market—something not seen in cable, where systems always sell at or above book value and bankruptcy is even much rarer than competition. Whereas a market in which potential monopolists race for position (as in Schumpterian profit seeking) yields supracompetitive returns only to innovative survivors that enhance consumer welfare, the race in the cable industry has been for municipal franchises. That involves classic rent-seeking inefficiency, as local governments sponsor excess-demand competitions to extract off-budget payments.[16] Although transfers have been the object of such political

---

13. Lawrence F. Katz & Lawrence H. Summers, *Industry Rents: Evidence and Implications,* BROOKINGS PAPERS ON ECON. ACTIVITY: MICROECON. 209, 214 (1989).

14. FCC, *supra* note 9.

15. PAUL KAGAN ASSOCIATES, CABLE TV FINANCIAL DATA FACTBOOK, June 1987, at 218.

16. Thomas W. Hazlett, *Competition vs. Franchise Monopoly in Cable Television,* 4 CONTEMP. POL'Y ISSUES 80 (1986); Thomas W. Hazlett, *Private Monopoly and the Public Interest: An Economic Analysis of the Cable Television Franchise,* 134 U. PA. L. REV. 1335 (1986).

competitions, no net social welfare enhancement has resulted.[17] Such a situation is the sine qua non of monopolistic market structure. That survivorship filtering process increases, rather than mitigates, the economic distortion associated with the cable industry's local market power.

In terms of risk, the volatility of returns is taken into account by market investors, who set values on assets by their bids; high riskiness would lower the market estimate of value itself and is not a reason for additionally discounting q-ratio data. Doing so would double discount for risk. And attributing cable qs to monopsony power simply subdivides the market power pie; this division does nothing to diminish the market power estimate indicated by high qs. Indeed, it raises the specter of a double-edged monopoly position. Attempts to explain away the cable industry's exceptionally high q-ratio are thus uncompelling.

So substantial are cable's monopoly profits that the industry has gone to court to protect its right to depreciate such capitalizations for tax purposes. And it has succeeded: in 1990 the U.S. Tax Court ruled in favor of the claim of Tele-Communications, Inc. (TCI) that it should be able to depreciate not just the physical assets of cable systems it purchases but also the intangible value of each cable franchise.[18] The tax court specifically rejected the IRS argument that such values should be attributed to goodwill and instead identified them as pure rents: "When a business is conducted pursuant to a de facto monopolistic franchise granted it by a governmental body and it has no bona fide competition, it cannot have any goodwill separate and distinct from the value of its monopolistic franchise."[19] According to the *Wall Street Journal,* "Intangible assets can comprise as much as 80% of the purchase price [of cable systems]."[20]

Buttressing the q-ratio evidence of cable market power are the extraordinarily high levels of debt to book value in the sector. Before regulators imposed restrictions on highly leveraged transactions in late 1989, banks were willing to lend cable television systems between $1,300 and $1,500 per subscriber to finance system sales—more than double the cost of physical capital. Even with the severe tightening of credit in the 1990–1991 market-

---

17. In fact, rent-seeking expense adds to social cost, as does the subsidization of services that are not worth their opportunity cost to consumers. That is typically the case with subsidies offered by potential cable franchises bidding for monopoly licenses.

18. TCI is the largest U.S. cable operator, serving about one-fourth of the U.S. market.

19. Tele-Communications, Inc. and Subsidiaries *v.* Commissioner of Internal Revenue, 95 T.C. No. 36 (Nov. 7, 1990), at 1.

20. Kevin Salwen, *Public Franchises Could Get Boost from Tax Ruling,* WALL ST. J., Nov. 9, 1990, at B10.

place, lenders were advancing up to $700 per subscriber;[21] when a severely illiquid market limits borrowing to about 100 percent of physical capital, the suspicion is excess returns. For the industry as a whole, cable company debt averaged $630 per subscriber by 1988, or twice its net book investment;[22] by year end 1989 it stood at $821 per subscriber.[23] Debt per mile of plant was $44,716, approximately double plant costs, and the debt–cash flow ratio in 1989 was 6.61.[24]

COMPETITIVE PRICING DIFFERENTIALS

Duopolistic competition in cable television markets further demonstrates that supracompetitive pricing obtains in sole-supplier markets. Several statistical investigations of the effect of head-to-head competition on cable prices (regressing price against a vector of explanatory variables, including a dummy for the presence of duopolistic competition) have revealed similar results. In 1985 Douglas Webbink's study for the Federal Trade Commission determined that cable prices were $1.18 per month lower in "overbuilt" markets.[25] For a package consisting of basic cable plus one premium service, Hazlett found monthly rates about $1.82 lower under duopoly than monopoly.[26] Those studies used data from the early 1980s; as cable rates have risen, more recent research shows that the competitive price discount (in percentage terms) has risen as well, implying that market power has increased over time. In 1991 economists Stanford L. Levin and John B. Meisel, in similar cross-sectional analysis, found that "[c]ustomers of competitive cable systems pay between $2.94 and $3.33 less for [basic] service, and this basic service typically includes more channels."[27] Competitive basic cable prices thus appeared to be 22 to 30 percent cheaper than monopoly rates. A 1993 study by Willis Emmons and Robin Prager buttressed those

21. Kathy Clayton, *Where There's Smoke,* CABLE WORLD, Oct. 29, 1990, at 36.

22. Egan & Conn, *supra* note 7, at 148.

23. PAUL KAGAN ASSOCIATES, CABLE TV FINANCIAL DATABOOK, June 1990, at 54.

24. On plant costs and on debt–cash flow ratio, *see id.* and Smiley, *supra* note 11.

25. Douglas Webbink, The Impact of Regulation and Competition on Cable TV Service Prices, Channels, and Pay Tier, (May 2, 1985) (Bureau of Economics, Federal Trade Commission).

26. Hazlett, *Competition vs. Franchise Monopoly, supra* note 16, at 91.

27. Stanford L. Levin & John B. Meisel, *Cable Television and Telecommunications: Theory, Evidence, and Policy,* TELECOMM. POL'Y 519, 525 (Dec. 1991).

results. Using 1989 data, they estimated the competitive price discount at between 17 and 22 percent.[28]

The evidence from those estimated price equations is buttressed by additional surveys that compare the prices charged by a sample of competitive cable systems with those of monopoly systems, revealing consistent and significant price discounts in competitive markets. Hazlett found the basic cable package plus one premium channel 23.5 percent less expensive for nineteen duopoly firms than for twenty-four monopoly firms; writing for *Consumers' Research,* John Merline noted that basic cable prices for fifty-five competitive systems in twenty-six cities were 18.5 percent below prices in twenty-six monopoly systems, while more channels were featured in the competitive systems on average (40 versus 33).[29] In 1990 the FCC surveyed a number of competitive systems and found that their per-channel rates were 34 percent below monopoly system prices.[30] The commission was led to conclude that "direct cable competition has resulted in reduced per-channel rates for cable service."[31]

Data from Paul Kagan Associates further indicate the price-lowering effects of head-to-head rivalry. In an April 1992 survey of 103 systems competing in fifty separate cable markets, the average revenue per subscriber (for the full package, basic plus pay services) was $25.08,[32] with an average of forty channels offered on the basic package. The average monthly revenue per subscriber for all U.S. cable systems in 1992 was $32.12, which implies that competitive systems were pricing their products about 21.9 percent lower (see table 3-2). Because competitive firms carry a higher number of channels on average, the per-channel rate differences are even larger.[33]

---

28. Willis Emmons & Robin Prager, The Effects of Market Structure and Ownership on Prices and Service Offerings in the U.S. Cable Television Industry (June 22, 1993) (paper presented to the Western Economic Association's 68th Annual Conference).

29. Thomas W. Hazlett, *Cabling America: Economic Forces in a Political World, in* FREEDOM IN BROADCASTING 208, 219 (C. Veljanovksi ed., London Institute of Economic Affairs 1989); John Merline, *How to Get Better Cable TV at Lower Prices,* CONSUMER'S RESEARCH 10 (Mar. 1990).

30. FCC, *supra* note 9, at app. H-2.

31. *Id.* at 53.

32. Paul Kagan Associates break down the data into "incumbent" and "overbuilder" categories. The figures used here are equally weighted averages of the two.

33. The February 1993 FCC cable system survey also found that competitive systems carry a higher number of channels than do monopoly systems. FCC, FCC CABLE RATE SURVEY DATABASE (Feb. 24, 1993).

Table 3-2
Competitive versus Monopolistic Cable Systems

	Sample Size (subscribers, millions)	Mean Revenue per Month ($)	Mean Basic Rate ($)[a]	Mean Basic Channels (no.)[a]	Basic Price per Channel ($)
Monopoly (11,354 systems)	54.89	32.12	19.08	35	.55
Competitive (103 systems)	1.13	25.08	17.49	40	.44
Competitive Difference (%)		−21.90	−8.30	14.30	−19.80

a. On most popular tier of basic programming.

Sources: Paul Kagan Associates, *Cable TV Franchising,* Apr. 30, 1992, p. 4; General Accounting Office, "1991 Survey of Cable Television Rates and Services" (July 1991), p. 5; National Cable Television Association, *Cable Television Developments,* Oct. 1992, p. 1-A.

More recent FCC survey data have, when subjected to regression analysis, suggested that basic rates charged by private cable systems engaged in head-to-head competition with another private cable system were 22.1 percent lower than rates charged by monopoly systems on a per-channel basis.[34] That differential was estimated in a price equation that adjusted for other factors such as the number of system subscribers and the number of satellite channels carried.[35] (When the competitive dummy subsample was extended to include municipal systems and private systems competing with municipals, the price difference increased to about 27.9 percent.) The same survey data were reworked in the FCC's February 1994 rate regulation rulemaking, and a somewhat different model placed the competitive price

34. FCC, In the Matter of Implementation of Sections of the Cable Television Consumer Protection and Competition Act—Rate Regulation, Report and Order and Further Notice of Proposed Rulemaking, MM Dkt. No. 92-266 (adopted Apr. 1, 1993; released May 3, 1993).

35. *Id.,* app. E, at 12–13. The competitive sample used for the dummy variable included forty-six competitive franchises. These were referred to as type B systems.

differential at 16.0 percent. (When the competitive subsample was limited to municipally owned cable systems and private firms competing with municipals, the price differential jumped to 37 percent.)

There have been numerous surveys and econometric studies comparing competitive (duopolistic) with monopolistic cable rates (see table 3-3). Every inquiry finds competitive cable prices significantly lower.[36] Bolstering those results is the fact that unmeasured, nonprice aspects of competitive supply are also more consumer-friendly than service characteristics found in monopoly markets.[37] Indeed, narrative accounts regularly report that customer service in competitive markets is superior.[38]

Incumbent cable companies respond dramatically to new cable rivals. When an entrant begins constructing a competing system, the incumbent typically cuts prices just in those areas (literally, the blocks) where the competitor has placed its lines.[39] Prices have been sharply lower in areas where rivalry has been in evidence, a good sign that prices before entry were above competitive levels.[40] When the giant TCI faced direct head-to-head competition from tiny Alsea River Cable in Waldport, Oregon, in the 1980s, for example, it dropped prices just in that locality and the immediately surrounding area. According to the Eugene, Oregon, newspaper, TCI charged

---

36. In a legal challenge to the FCC's implementation of rate regulation, cable television operators argued that, using the FCC's 1992 data for monopoly and "overbuilt" systems, no statistically significant price reduction was found for systems of over 5,000 subscribers. As the D.C. Circuit Court of Appeals noted, however, the result is dubious because it reduces a small sample into a tiny one; there is no theoretical reason to do so, and including size as a regressor makes truncating the data unwarranted. Time Warner Entertainment Co. *v.* Federal Communications Commission, 1995 WL 33 D928 (D.C. Cir.), at 10–11.

37. Jennifer Fearing & Charles Lubinsky, Qualitative Differences in Competitive Cable Markets Prior to Rate Reregulation (Nov. 1995) (paper delivered at the annual meetings of the Southern Economic Association).

38. Mark Lewyn, *More Choice for Cable TV?* Bus. Wk., May 13, 1991, at 44–45; Daniel R. Levine, *Behind the Cable TV Rip-Off,* Reader's Digest, June 1992, at 53–57.

39. Some analysts characterize the price cutting as unsustainable over the long run, intended only to purge the market and allow higher prices to obtain. *See* Leland L. Johnson, Toward Competition in Cable Television 19–21 (MIT Press and AEI Press 1994).

40. In 1994 a Sacramento cable firm was found guilty of violating a 1941 California statute that prohibits the use of price discrimination to keep or attain a monopoly. Leza Coleman *v.* Sacramento Cable Television, Sacramento County Super. Ct. Case No. 524077 (filed Nov. 20, 1991; opinion delivered Apr. 11, 1994). *See also* Pam Slater, *Cable Firm Told to Pay $1 Million,* Sacramento Bee, June 8, 1994, at D6; Thomas W. Hazlett, *Predation in Local TV Markets,* 40 Antitrust Bull. 609, 614–25 (1995).

Table 3-3
Studies and Surveys of Competitive Pricing Differential in Cable

Study (Year)	Data Year	Method	Price Difference in Duopoly Markets (%)	Product Definition
Webbink (1985)	1984	OLS	−7.9	Basic cable adjusted for size and quality
Hazlett (1986b)	1982	OLS	−10.1	Basic cable adjusted for size plus one premium
Hazlett (1989)	1987	Survey	−23.5	Basic cable plus one premium
Merline (1990)	1990	Survey	−18.4	Basic cable
FCC (1990)[a]	1990	Survey	−34.4	Basic cable on price-per-channel basis
Levin & Meisel (1991)	1990	OLS	−22 to −30	Basic cable adjusted for size and quality
Kagan (1992)[b]	1992	Survey	−21.9	Entire service package (i.e., total revenue per subscriber)
FCC (1993)[c]	1992	Survey	−32.2	Basic cable on price-per-channel basis
FCC (1993) (app. E, at 30)	1992	OLS	−22.1	Basic cable price per channel adjusted for size and quality
FCC (1994)[d] (app. C, table A-1)	1992	OLS	−16.0	Basic cable price per channel adjusted for several variables
Emmons and Prager (1993)	1989	OLS, 2SLS, SUR	−17 to −22.1	Basic cable adjusted for size and quality

a. FCC Report, In the Matter of Competition, Rate Deregulation and the Commission's Policies Relating to the Provision of Cable Television Service, MM Dkt. No. 89-600 (July 26, 1990).

Table 3-3 (cont.)

b. Paul Kagan Associates, *Cable TV Franchising,* Apr. 30, 1992.

c. FCC, In the Matter of Implementation of Sections of the Cable Television Consumer Protection and Competition Act—Rate Regulation, Report and Order and Further Notice of Proposed Rulemaking, MM Dkt. 92-266 (adopted April 1, 1993; released May 3, 1993).

d. FCC, In the Matter of Implementation of Sections of the Cable Television Consumer Protection and Competition Act—Rate Regulation, Buy-Through Prohibition, Third Report and Order, MM Dkt. No. 92-266 and MM Dkt. No. 92-262 (adopted February 22, 1994; released March 30, 1994).

Notes: OLS = ordinary least squares; 2SLS = two-stage least squares; SUR = seemingly unrelated regressions.

$10.50 in the Waldport–Yachats–Seal Rock cable market for a twenty-six-channel monthly basic service in 1987. For the same package of services, TCI charged $15.45 in the neighboring Newport–Toledo–Otter Rock market. Premium channels were also cheaper in the competitive market. In Waldport, TCI charged $7.95 monthly for HBO, Showtime, or the Movie Channel; those channels cost subscribers $11.95 in the Newport market just a few miles up the coast.[41]

In a similar case, when Time Warner Cable faced competition in recent years in its Orlando, Florida, franchise, it reacted quickly. Time Warner responded to the "overbuilder" with a sharp form of price discrimination—slashing prices only to those homes that had access to the new cable supplier. In April 1992 the Time Warner system was charging $20.70 per month for basic cable and $11.90 per month for a premium channel on those streets where it enjoyed a monopoly; on those that had been wired by a competitor, it charged only $13.95 for basic and $8.95 for pay. Moreover, its monopoly prices for additional outlets and remote controls were $4.95 and $4.00, respectively; in competitive areas it charged just $.99 for the remote and gave away free additional outlets. Installation was $49.95 when monopolistic, but free when competitive.[42] In December 1992 Time Warner announced an agreement to purchase its competitor, Telesat Cablevision, and end the head-to-head competition altogether. The merger had not yet been com-

41. Larry Bacon, *Little Cable TV Company Prospering,* EUGENE REGISTER-GUARD, Nov. 24, 1987, at 1D, 2D.

42. PAUL KAGAN ASSOCIATES, CABLE TV FRANCHISING, Apr. 30, 1992, at 3.

pleted, however, when Time Warner withdrew its offer, blaming red tape associated with the Federal Trade Commission's evaluation of the proposed merger under the antitrust laws.[43] Although the 1992 Cable Act includes a provision making discriminatory pricing illegal,[44] the underlying market evidence speaks loudly about the market power enjoyed by cable incumbents that use incentives to fend off small, independent entrants into local markets.[45]

In Montgomery, Alabama, a local cable operator received a competitive franchise and began marketing its service in 1990. By 1995 it had enlisted some 9,200 households, 40 percent of homes passed. The incumbent cable supplier, TCI, reported losing some 3,700 customers to the entrant, which implies that total market penetration in the overbuilt submarket rose 23.9 percent (5,500/23,000). Given that systemwide cable penetration in Montgomery was about 65 percent before competition began, that penetration gain constitutes about a 36.8 percent increase in output—close to what a 20 percent effective price reduction would imply was an elasticity of demand equal to minus two.[46]

The price discounting that is persistently reported in competitive cable markets indicates that market power is exercised in monopoly situations; if other video services were close enough substitutes to cable television service, then prices would be fully constrained before additional cable entry. Instead, strong evidence exists that prices respond, and sharply, to competi-

---

43. A Time Warner official explained the decision to withdraw the offer: "As a result of what we consider to be burdensome, time-consuming and never-ending requests from the Federal Trade Commission for additional documentation, we determined it was no longer a fruitful use of our resources to go forward with the deal." T. Christian Miller, *Paperwork Sinks Sale of Telesat,* St. Petersburg Times, Mar. 8, 1994, at 1. On the aborted merger, the county attorney, Larry Haag, commented: "It's good news to us. We've opposed the sale all along due to the fact it would create a monopoly." *Id.* Later Telesat was purchased by another Florida cable competitor, Adelphia.

44. Sec. 623(e). The legislative history explains the provision as "intended to prevent cable operators from dropping the rates in one portion of a franchise area to undercut a competitor temporarily." S. Rep. No. 102-92, at 76 (June 28, 1991) (to accompany S. 12).

45. Interestingly, Telesat, an aggressive overbuilder, had become a leading target of the cable industry years earlier. The company filed a fascinating brief with the FCC detailing the lengths to which cable incumbents would go in efforts to raise the entrant's cost of competing. Comments of Telesat Cablevision, In the Matter of Competition, Rate Regulation and the Commission's Policies Relating to the Provision of Cable Television Service, MM Dkt. No. 89-600 (Mar. 1, 1990).

46. Debbie Narrod, *Overbuilds '95,* Cable World, May 1, 1995, at 46–49.

Table 3-4
Competitive Cable System Sales Prices, 1988–1991

Year	Sample Size (no. of systems)	Sample Size (sales, $ millions)	Dollar Value per Subscriber	Dollar Value per Subscriber (U.S. mean)	Percentage Discount vs. Monopoly
1988	9	35.905	1,649	1,953	18.5
1989	8	170.229	1,886	2,351	19.7
1990	2	7.325	1,638	2,047	20.0
1991	1	5.200	1,300	1,569	17.1

Source: Paul Kagan Associates, *Cable TV Franchising, News Roundup,* June 28, 1991.

tive entry. We conclude that rates were being set in excess of competitive levels when monopoly prevailed.[47]

COMPETITIVE SYSTEM SALES PRICE DIFFERENTIALS

Cable's market power is also evident when competitive cable systems are traded in capital markets. Over the 1988–1991 period, there were twenty recorded sales transactions involving cable companies in competitive (duopolistic) markets. The sales prices averaged 17 to 20 percent less, on a per-subscriber basis, than contemporary sales of cable systems in monopoly markets (see table 3-4). If cable systems in duopoly markets are worth less to buyers—on a per-subscriber basis—than cable systems in monopoly markets, that suggests that prices (and hence profits) in monopoly markets are higher than in more competitive situations.[48] To test the hypothesis for-

---

47. The alternative explanation is that we are experiencing a short-run disequilibrium in examining competitive prices—that incumbents are slashing prices in predatory attempts to deter overbuilding. (That was, amazingly, what cable operators asserted in *Time Warner, supra* note 36, at 8.) That cannot be a defense that absolves cable television of market power, however, for such predation makes sense only if supracompetitive returns are being exercised in the absence of competition.

48. It may also reflect a lower capital cost basis: if monopoly systems serve more subscribers over a given fixed capital investment, then future upgrades (rebuilding the cables and associated electronics) will be cheaper in a monopoly system than in a competitive system, *ceteris paribus*. That density factor, however, can be accounted for separately (that is, apart from market structure) by including either density (homes passed

mally that competitive systems sold for a lower price than did monopoly systems, we estimate a price (per-subscriber) equation using system sales price data during the 1988–1992 period.

We took sales prices from Paul Kagan Associates' *Cable TV Financial Databook* (1989–1993), which lists all U.S. cable sales in a given year. The dependent variable was the natural log of price per subscriber.[49] The estimation was via ordinary least squares. We took natural logs of the exogenous variables, except the three dichotomous variables. Independent variables included: *AGE*, age of the system at time of sale (in days); *SUBS*, number of subscribers; *CAP*, system channel capacity; *AIR*, number of locally available off-air television signals; *PEN*, cable system penetration rate; and *INC*, mean income in the community. There were three dummies: *COMP*, to indicate overbuild (1 = competitive; 0 = monopolistic); *NONMSO*, to indicate whether the buyer was a multiple system operator (1 = non-MSO buyer; 0 = MSO buyer); and *HLT*, highly leveraged transaction (1 = sale takes place after highly leveraged transaction restrictions enacted in October 1989; 0 = sale before). We summarize the results in table 3-5.

The estimated model indicates that newer systems and larger systems (either in terms of capacity or in terms of subscribers) have systematically higher market values, as do systems sold prior to the highly leveraged transaction restrictions. Those findings are consistent with anticipations. Most important, the coefficient on the competitive dummy is negative and highly significant. Interpreted as an elasticity,[50] it implies that, after adjusting for the variables included in the model, system sales prices per subscriber are about 13.6 percent less in markets where head-to-head competition is present. That price differential is statistically significant at the 99 percent level.[51]

---

per mile) or penetration (subscribers per homes passed) as independent explanatory variables. That is the approach we take.

49. We adjusted the data set because some sales prices were evidently misleading or misreported. (When systems under construction are sold, per-subscriber prices are confusing to interpret on a per-subscriber basis; also, when other assets are sold with the cable systems, prices assigned to the cable system are arbitrary.) Hence, we eliminated prices lower than one-half the mean or greater than twice the mean. That left a binding range of $921 to $3,667. The number of observations decreased from 390 to 358, and the mean of the dependent variable dropped from $2,101 to $1,862.

50. Elasticity, η, is calculated from the coefficient on the overbuild dummy, c_i, as $\eta_i = e^{c_i} - 1$.

51. That discount for duopoly systems is likely understated because many of the system sales were to a direct competitor. In this case, the target firm may share some of the capital asset premium the acquiring firm realizes in ending an overbuild. That would put the system sales price somewhere between the duopoly and the monopoly level.

Table 3-5
Regression Results: Competitive Cable System Sales Price Differential

Variable	Coefficient	Standard Error	t
AGE	−.042	.014	−3.04[a]
SUBS	.071	.008	9.12[a]
PEN	.039	.032	1.21
CAP	.049	.030	1.67[a]
AIR	.035	.024	1.46
INC	.146	.053	2.73[a]
COMP	−.147	.053	−2.78[a]
NONMSO	.021	.039	.53
HLT	−.086	.023	−3.74[a]
Constant	5.273		
R^2	.411		
No. of observations	358		
Degrees of freedom	348		

a. Significant at .95.

The steep discounts observed in competitive system sales are entirely consistent with all the other evidence, which indicates that market power is available to monopoly cable suppliers. Capital markets clearly anticipate that the profits in a market with just one cable provider will be higher—owing to a more generous price structure—than in markets with a greater degree of competition.

IS ENTRY FEASIBLE?

Despite the abundant evidence indicating supracompetitive pricing and excess profits within the cable television sector, it may be argued that such an equilibrium has developed because of a divisibility problem: it is only economically efficient for one firm to serve a given cable market.[52] That is,

52. This section is based on Thomas W. Hazlett, *Telco Entry into Video*, ANN. REV. COMM., 1994–95, at 212 (1995).

although prices would theoretically be lower under competition and are observed so in the infrequent instance where that occurs, there is no rational
way to squeeze multiple cable firms into competitive rivalry: the unit costs
would be so high that firms would either have to raise prices (to sustain the
"rivalry") or compete back to a winner-take-all monopoly market structure.

Typically, the arguments for competitive entry are made in conjunction with reference to an alternative or emerging technology. Without question, the dynamics of the telecommunications sector are impressive, and
new technologies or modes of organization drive much of the progress consumers have made. Yet the financial impact of such entrants is extremely
problematic to analyze *ex ante*; such entrants do not, typically, know their
true costs or their actual demands until long after they have run through a
maze of market tests. One way to sidestep much of the difficulty is to take
a very conservative approach to new entry in cable markets and to consider
only entry employing current off-the-shelf technology. That avoids much
of the arbitrariness inherent in assumptions regarding future conditions, as-
yet undiscovered services, and currently unobservable scope economies in
supply.

The following spreadsheet exercise involves two basic scenarios. In
the first, we ask, What rate of return (or net present value) does a firm
achieve when it overbuilds a cable incumbent in a market having average
density (ninety-three homes passed per mile[53]), average penetration (62
percent[54]), 1991 average revenue per subscriber per month ($29.93[55]), and
average cash flow margin (42.9 percent[56]), assuming the entrant achieves a
50 percent market share? Capital costs are taken from the 1986 work of
Smiley,[57] which suggested an average price per mile of $23,000 for plant,[58]
$1.2 million for head-end and start-up, and $120 converter/installation
charges (variable capital charge per subscriber). The 50,000-home market
size is assumed by Smiley and is therefore assumed here. Revenue growth
is assumed to be 5 percent per year, which is below the 1987–1990 experience, but about the pace of 1991–1993 growth. A fifteen-year life is assumed for all capital, and there is zero salvage value. (See table 3-6.)

In the benchmark case, there is no increase in penetration because of
competition; two rivals simply take 31 percent penetration apiece, at preentry

53. Paul Kagan Associates, Cable TV Financial Databook, June 1990, at 56.

54. That is the figure as of November 1991. National Cable Television Association,
Cable Television Developments, March 1992, at 1A.

55. *Id.* at 2A, 8A.

56. Paul Kagan Associates, *supra* note 53.

57. Smiley, *supra* note 11.

58. That assumed a 70–30 split between aerial and underground conduit.

Table 3-6
Assumptions for Baseline Scenario in Financial Simulation

Variable	Value	Rationale	Source
Market size	50,000 homes	Typical U.S. urban/ suburban cable market	Smiley (1986), p. 21
Cable penetration	62%	Nov. 1991 U.S. average	NCTA, *Cable TV Developments*, Mar. 1992, p. 1A
Market density	93 homes passed per mile	1989 U.S. average	Kagan, *Cable TV Financial Databook*, June 1990, p. 56
Revenue per subscriber per month	$29.93	1991 U.S. average	NCTA, *Cable TV Developments*, Mar. 1992, pp. 2A, 8A
Growth rate of subscriber revenues	5%	Industry projection	Kagan, *Cable TV Financial Databook*, June 1992, p. 7
Cash flow margin ([Revenue – Operating costs]/ Revenue)	42.9%	1989 U.S. average	Kagan, *Cable TV Financial Databook*, June 1992, p. 56
Cost of plant per mile	$23,000	Typical industry costs	Smiley (1986), p. 22
Cost of converters and drops per subscriber	$120	Typical industry costs	Smiley (1986), p. 22
Cost of head-end and start-up	$1,200,000	Typical industry costs	Smiley (1986), pp. 22–23
Cost of capital	12%	Typical industry costs	FCC, "Implementation of the Cable TV Consumer Protection and Competition Act—Third Report and Order," 1994 found cable's cost of capital to be 11.25%.

(1991) price levels. In such a world, the off-the-shelf cable entrant is able to attain an 18 percent rate of return. A current-period investment of $15.43 million has a net present value of $5.73 million. Contrary to theoretical assertions of natural monopoly, the market demand for cable is able to financially sustain two competitors at current (or recent) prices in the typical U.S. market. Varying assumptions for penetration and annual revenue growth indicate that a large number of U.S. cable markets are able—at current costs and demand levels—to support head-to-head rivals (see sensitivity analysis in table 3-7).

The "problem" with competitive entry is that prices are not likely to stay at preentry levels. The evidence presented above indicates that rates for the full cable package fall about 20 percent when duopolistic competition obtains. Price decreases are welfare improving, but may deter entry altogether, thus leaving monopoly prices intact. Interestingly, however, a second simulation model shows that the average U.S. cable market (in terms of density, revenue, penetration, and cash flow) would allow an entrant to earn a 16 percent return, even assuming a 20 percent decrease in price (revenue per subscriber) accompanied by a 20 percent increase in penetration.[59] In that scenario, the entrant again captures a 50 percent market share, which implies a single-firm penetration rate of 37 percent. Although revenue per subscriber falls by 20 percent, the cash-flow margin stays constant at the national average; that implies some degree of X-efficiency.[60] Again, we employ conservative assumptions regarding annual revenue growth (5 percent) and salvage value (0). Those results suggest that, given long-run, risk-adjusted capital costs of about 12 percent,[61] entry is financially viable in typical cable markets, even when prices significantly decline.

EXPERT ANALYSIS

A host of experts have also come to the conclusion that cable operators exercise considerable market power. Federal agencies that have studied the

---

59. That implies an arc elasticity of one (in absolute value terms) and sends market penetration from 62 percent to 74 percent. That is conservative, given actual experience in competitive cable markets. A much higher point elasticity is theoretically deducible at current prices by using the Lerner index or empirical estimates, as discussed above.

60. Harvey Leibenstein, *Allocative Efficiency vs. "X-Efficiency,"* 56 AM. ECON. REV. 392 (1966). That suggestion is plausible, because monitoring service quality would become easier. Firms that face direct competition can more cheaply ascertain when employees or business practices are not performing efficiently.

61. In February 1994 the FCC ruled that the cost of capital for cable companies was 11.25 percent.

Table 3-7
Rates of Return for Competitive Cable Entrants

Annual Revenue Growth (%)	Density (homes passed per mile)						
	53	73	93[a]	113	133	153	173
.00	.05	.09	.13	.16	.19	.21	.24
2.50	.07	.12	.15	.18	.21	.24	.26
5.00[a]	.10	.14	.18[b]	.21	.24	.26	.28
7.50	.12	.16	.20	.23	.26	.29	.31
10.00	.14	.19	.22	.26	.28	.31	.33
12.50	.16	.21	.25	.28	.31	.33	.36

a. Base-case assumption.

b. Base-case result.

state of competition in the cable market in recent years have unanimously agreed that significant entry barriers protect incumbent suppliers, a finding that is consistent only with the view that market power is currently exercised. The National Telecommunications and Information Administration concluded that municipal franchising was responsible for significant market power:

> The franchising process eliminates or seriously impedes entry by competitors, imposes substantial costs and delays on franchisees, cable subscribers and the public, which are not offset by countervailing benefits. The public would be better served by municipal efforts to provide a choice of cable service providers rather than extracting costly concessions from a sole cable franchisee. We therefore recommend that municipalities no longer grant exclusive franchises. Instead, municipalities should permit, even encourage, entry by competitive service providers.[62]

In the FCC's 1990 Cable Report, the evidence suggested supracompetitive pricing and profits:

> A careful examination of the characteristics of cable service and the characteristics and availability of rival distribution media suggests that cable systems do possess varying degrees of market power in local distribution. . . . Our conclusion regarding cable market power is supported by the q ratio

62. U.S. Dep't of Commerce, National Telecommunications and Information Administration (NTIA), Video Program Distribution and Cable Television: Current Policy Issues and Recommendations (Government Printing Office June 1988), at 30–31.

analysis. While the exact magnitude of the cable industry q ratio cannot be pinpointed precisely, the record shows that it is high enough to indicate the presence of some market power.[63]

The FCC has similarly criticized the franchising process as creating anticonsumer barriers to entry. In releasing the 1990 FCC Cable Report, Chairman Alfred Sikes recommended that "[l]egislation should be passed which limits municipal authority to erect or sustain entry barriers and which prohibits an 'unreasonable refusal to grant a second franchise.'"[64] That policy position stemmed from the commission's findings that "[d]espite some promising developments, . . . this proceeding reveals competing systems face several problems that can be eased by changing the franchise process. . . . While exclusive franchising is not the only impediment to the growth of second competitive systems, it is clear that the number of competitive systems would grow at a more rapid pace if local franchise authorities were unable to discourage or forbid such systems."[65]

A Federal Trade Commission report has echoed that conclusion, commenting in its 1990 study of cable competition:

> Restricting entry into cable markets can be justified only under a very restrictive set of conditions; namely, when the local cable market is a natural monopoly, and when this monopoly is not sustainable. Moreover, these criteria are best thought of as necessary, but not sufficient, conditions for insulating an incumbent from the threat of entry. When entry requires the creation of sunk assets, the incumbent might still be able to deter inefficient entry and cover its costs even when the conditions for sustainability are not satisfied. The resulting price may be well below that which would prevail if entry were restricted. . . .

63. FCC, *supra* note 9, at 42. The Justice Department concurred: "[G]iven the magnitude of the q ratios, and the likely size of any corrections that should be made to them, it is likely that the q ratios for cable firms are greater than should be expected in industries subject to effective competition. . . . The information before the Commission suggests strongly that neither conventional television broadcasts nor any of the alternative technologies presently available are close enough substitutes for basic and pay television services to prevent the providers of such cable services from exercising some degree of market power." U.S. Dept. of Justice, Filing on Effective Competition in Cable at the FCC, *cited in* S. Rep. No. 101-381, Cable Television Consumer Protection Act of 1990, at 11 (July 19, 1990).
64. Statement of Alfred C. Sikes, Federal Communications Commission, July 26, 1990.
65. FCC, *supra* note 9, at 72, 74.

The principal message of this section is that there is likely to be little merit in discouraging entry.[66]

All such critiques of the local franchising process rest upon the conclusion that cable operators possess significant market power. Otherwise, the entry barrier established by the local franchising authorities would be of no (economic) moment: perfect substitutes would constrain cable pricing to competitive levels even in the absence of a second cable entrant. In addition, long-run contracting institutions are insufficiently established to limit prices below monopoly levels as in the contestability sense of competition for the market (via long-term contracts). To identify the exclusive franchise as a monopoly problem is to establish the case that the behavior of the cable company is not so effectively policed by noncable video suppliers as it would be by another cable company, which points directly to a problem of local market power.

MARKET POWER SUMMARY

The conclusion is inescapable that cable television operators have, at least for the past several years, enjoyed economic rents: returns are easily in excess of the risk-adjusted cost of capital. Cable would thus appear to be a prime candidate for rate regulation that would lower consumer prices and expand the volume of sales. The industry exhibits marked tendencies toward monopolistic market structure, and the classic case for public utility–type regulation appears to prevail.

The learning of three decades of the regulation literature, however, raises the question: What can regulators regulate?[67] Even under the neces-

---

66. Comment of the Staff of the Bureau of Economics and the San Francisco Regional Office of the Federal Trade Commission, In the Matter of Competition, Rate Deregulation and the Commission's Policies Relating to the Provision of Cable Television Service, MM Docket No. 89-600 (Apr. 20, 1990), at 13–14.

67. The insight that government regulation is not an immaculate cure for market failure is, of course, much older than Stigler and Friedland's consideration of the question. Pigou wrote: "In any industry, where there is reason to believe that the free play of self-interest will cause an amount of resources to be invested different from the amount that is required in the best interest of the national dividend, there is a prima facie case for public intervention. The case, however, cannot become more than a prima facie one, until we have considered the qualifications which governmental agencies may be expected to possess for intervening advantageously." ARTHUR CECIL PIGOU, THE ECONOMICS OF WELFARE 331–32 (Macmillan, 4th ed. 1962) (1932).

sary conditions for possible welfare-enhancing price controls, the case for regulatory effectiveness has not been made. The sufficient condition for proconsumer regulation is that real-world institutions exist that can succeed in lowering quality-adjusted prices to consumers, thereby overcoming the natural tendencies of suppliers and demanders to find ways around controls. The finding that prices rise above competitive levels is an interesting backdrop to the rate regulation discussion, but proof of regulatory effectiveness can come only from evidence that price controls outperform unregulated markets from the perspective of subscribers. The cable television marketplace has fortuitously given us multiple switches in regulatory regimes to observe. We turn now to an empirical evaluation.

4

Price Controls and Cable Television

> Price really has no meaning except in terms of an assumed quality of
> service; price is a ratio, with money in the numerator and some physical
> unit of given or assumed quantity and quality in the denominator. Price
> regulation alone is meaningless.
>
> —Alfred E. Kahn, *The Economics of Regulation*

IN THE CASE OF PRICE CONTROLS on a firm where marginal costs
are constant and market power is exercised, a reasonable approximation of
local cable markets in the United States, the unregulated price will be set
above marginal cost.[1] In such an environment, price controls hold out the
theoretical possibility of enhancing welfare by lowering market price and
expanding the volume of sales past the point where marginal revenue equals
marginal cost. To the extent that controls are binding in such a market,
however, the supplier may have an incentive either to exploit whatever market power is available by *lowering* product quality or to withdraw from the
rate-regulated market. The first opportunity arises when regulatory authorities imperfectly monitor the substitution of lower-cost inputs for those of
higher cost; the second arises when there is an "adjacent" market that is
unregulated, allowing the seller to shift sales there, absorbing some transactions costs but freeing itself of regulatory constraint.

Thus, the seller will avail itself of such options whenever the expense
(incurred by the supplier) of such a strategy is exceeded by the cost of
complying with price regulation. That is relevant to the cable television

---

1. Epigraph: ALFRED E. KAHN, THE ECONOMICS OF REGULATION 21 (MIT Press 1988).

market in that each regulated system supplies services that can be altered by operator expenditures, while each system simultaneously sells in unregulated markets—for premium and pay-per-view services, for instance[2]— that invite additional entry (investment or marketing effort) to the degree that price controls on basic cable services impose revenue losses on the operator. There, the regulation of price does not directly lead firms to lower the quality of their product overall, but just that of the regulated package. Price regulation does, however, lead to marketing inefficiencies undertaken to evade regulatory constraints. The higher marginal costs that result may raise effective price.

The underlying logic in either instance is that a firm may partially evade price controls by changing the product that is controlled.[3] In most instances, however, transactions costs and factor mobility constraints will limit such reactions. Moreover, regulators will monitor product quality as part of the price-control effort, precisely owing to the incentive structure that such controls yield. Policymakers generally understand that price controls cannot be successfully implemented without some practical or imposed constraint on product quality (for example, the existence of significant sunk investments or aggressive regulatory oversight). The package of services on which the price control is levied must be "sticky" with respect to quality, or else the "controlled" product will simply metamorphose into a new, quality-depreciated, "decontrolled" product.[4] When resources are mobile but imperfectly so, the incentive for suppliers to depreciate quality will obtain but will be muted to some degree.[5]

Rent controls in residential housing markets offer the classic illustration of that problem. Policymakers have long known that municipalities

---

2. In 1992 U.S. cable operators, on average, derived 57.5 percent of total revenues from basic cable, while the remaining 42.5 percent was from other sources, largely unregulated under the 1992 act. National Cable Television Association, Cable Television Developments, June 1993, at 8-A.

3. Of course, the firm could market a higher-quality, "new and improved" package, but price ceilings would not permit that route of escape. Price floors, however, do have the well-known effect of improving product quality, as suppliers attempt to deliver more product to the customer to circumvent the minimum price restrictions. The preregulation airline industry was an example of that form of nonprice competition.

4. Donald J. Boudreaux & Robert B. Ekelund, *The Cable Television Consumer Protection and Competition Act of 1992: The Triumph of Private over Public Interest,* 44 Ala. L. Rev. 355 (1993), present a nice theoretical model explaining how cable operators will shift quality in response to price controls.

5. For inputs that are sunk in the short to medium term, depreciation of product quality can occur in the form of deterred investment; suppliers elect simply to let old (depreciated) capital provide services for a longer period of time.

instituting rent controls must monitor a host of second-order adjustment margins. Those margins concern quality depreciation of rental units and attempts to sell housing services in adjacent, unregulated markets. The first concern has spawned rules concerning appropriate maintenance and enforcement of housing codes. The second has prompted regulations circumscribing nonprice (or extralease) bidding for apartments (for example, key money, bribery, discrimination). Rules attempting to prevent housing units from "escaping" have been at least partially effective. Most notable are laws limiting the ability of landlords to withdraw rental units from the market altogether. Condominium or cooperative conversion laws are notably strict in communities with stringent rent controls.

THE CABLE TELEVISION PRODUCT

The apartment market has at least one very large difference when compared with the cable television market: the relative fixity of apartment services.[6] Once the structural investment is sunk, the housing services flowing from a building cannot be instantly depreciated by curtailing operating costs.[7] Physical plant can be depreciated in response to regulation, but only over a substantial time frame. Cable television services, however, entail both the transport function over cables (sunk similarly to housing structures)[8] and the provision of video programming. Only the former is directly analogous

---

6. While cable plant is largely sunk, cable operators provide program services over fixed infrastructure. In general, operating expenses (excluding amortization, depreciation, or interest charges) constitute about 54 percent of cable revenues. PAUL KAGAN ASSOCIATES, CABLE TV FINANCIAL DATABOOK, June 1993, at 36. That is far above the proportionate operating costs of apartment owners.

7. In his 1974 article, *A Theory of Price Control*, 17 J.L. & ECON. 53 (1974), Steven Cheung used the rent control market to establish what he believed to be a general paradigm for price (or other) regulation. The theory revolves around how buyers and sellers will attempt to claim or dissipate the economic rents that become, in essence, common property when binding controls create excess demand. That Cheung focused on apartment rent controls led him to overlook the straightforward point that a supplier (landlord) can reclaim lost property rights by withdrawing costly inputs. That avoidable costs are such a small portion of the apartment supply function apparently kept that insight hidden. It can be included in his property rights framework, however, by noting that, where $VMP > MC$, the withdrawal of an input is a wasteful rent-seeking dissipation: to recoup some of the rents lost from price controls, suppliers are willing to forgo socially efficient expenditures.

8. Cables depreciate far more rapidly. A twenty-year-old apartment house is often thought of as "new"; a twenty-year-old cable system is obsolete. That is another important difference between the two markets in examining the impact of price regulation.

to the rent control example; the program menus comprise inputs that are highly mobile.

Not only is quality difficult to measure[9] and, hence, monitor, but cable regulators are legally constrained from seeking to influence programming quality by both federal regulations and the U.S. Constitution. Since the late 1970s cable operators have won a series of landmark cases establishing their First Amendment rights as "electronic publishers." The courts have barred local officials from exercising authority over what channels are carried or their content. Operators' status as constitutionally protected publishers received a large boost in 1993 when it was extended to a telephone company attempting to compete in cable. The federal court decision found that Bell Atlantic, a supplier of local telephone exchange services, had a First Amendment right to provide transport of video signals and to own the programming that was provided directly to subscribers.[10] There are certainly strong public policy reasons for leaving that First Amendment barrier in place. Eli Noam has considered the issue in the context of constraining cable's market power:

> The emergence of rate regulation would cause no cheer. Historically, rate regulation is easiest to administer where the product can be clearly defined and quantified and where the industry is relatively stable; the provision of water or electricity are good examples. Rate regulation is much more difficult when it deals with complex and variable mixtures of services or where the regulated industry is extremely dynamic in its development as is the case with cable television.[11]

---

9. The difficulty in measuring cable program quality has forced economists who have undertaken that task to employ measures such as "total channels offered to subscribers" as a proxy. *See* Yasuji Otsuka, The Effects of Regulation on Social Welfare: Evidence from the Cable TV Industry (Nov. 1993) (paper presented at the meetings of the Southern Economic Association). That such an approach is fraught with danger is obvious to anyone who has used a cable television remote control. Not only are not all channels created equally, but rate regulation (or franchise regulation) can systematically bias the use of that quantitative measure of quality.

10. Chesapeake and Potomac Telephone Company of Virginia *v.* United States, E.D. Va., No. 92-1751-A (Aug. 24, 1993), 42 F.3d 181 (4th Cir. 1994); *remanded for consideration of mootness,* 116 S. Ct. 1036 (1996), *vacated* No. 93-2340 (4th Cir. Apr. 17, 1996).

11. Eli M. Noam, *Towards an Integrated Communications Market: Overcoming the Local Monopoly of Cable Television,* 34 Fed. Comm. L.J. 209, 219 (1982). It is curious that Noam, writing in 1982, talked about the "emergence of rate regulation." Of course, that was during a period when local governments were perfectly free to engage in rate regulation, and most of them professed to do so. Those close to the industry (including, apparently, Noam, a highly knowledgeable analyst) never seriously considered regula-

Public regulation of private business is fraught with difficulty under the best of circumstances, and economists have, for at least three decades, continually returned to the simple question, What can regulators regulate? In the cable market, regulators are asked to control market prices without any substantial ability to regulate legally the content of the unit being sold.[12]

Another potentially important aspect of cable rate regulation is institutional. Historically, cable television systems have not been regulated on a rate-of-return basis, as have public utilities. Instead, pre-1984 franchise agreements (generally controlled by municipalities but in some cases involving state regulatory authorities) typically included a starting price schedule, along with a provision that the franchisee must receive permission to raise rates. A city council (or other legislative or regulatory body) would vote to approve or disapprove price increases requested by firms. That procedure did not involve elaborate fact finding with respect to a system's underlying cost base. Even the 1992 federal reregulation (which mandates the FCC to create rate guidelines, to be enforced by localities in conjunction with the commission) sets rate caps rather than rate-of-return formulas.[13]

---

tion an effective tool for consumers. In fact, M. L. Greenhut and colleagues conveyed what they believed to be the conventional wisdom on the subject when they wrote: "[I]t is well-known that regulation of rates has had little effect on monopoly prices, as most rate-increase requests have been granted." M. L. GREENHUT, GEORGE NORMAN & CHAO-SUN HUNG, THE ECONOMICS OF IMPERFECT COMPETITION: A SPATIAL APPROACH, 372 (Cambridge University Press 1987) (footnote omitted).

12. That constraint on regulatory monitoring has been discussed before. A 1990 Federal Trade Commission report identified the statutory problem associated with nonprice attributes of cable television in municipal franchising proceedings by noting: "The 1984 Cable Act . . . may make it more difficult for local governments to threaten non-renewal. Section 626(c)(1) limits the criteria that the government may use in deciding to not renew an operator's franchise. This decision may not be based on the prices charged by the operator, nor on 'the mix, quality, or level of cable services or other services provided over the system.' The fact that cities cannot use them in renewal decisions likely vitiates the usefulness of the franchise bidding process as a regulatory mechanism." Comment of the Staff of the Bureau of Economics and the San Francisco Regional Office of the Federal Trade Commission, In the Matter of Competition, Rate Deregulation and the Commission's Policies Relating to the Provision of Cable Television Service, MM Dkt. No. 89-600 (Apr. 20, 1990), at 34. The report cites to First Amendment case law in cable, and those decisions continue as precedents even as the 1984 Cable Act has been largely repealed. Ironically, the FTC recommended giving localities more discretionary authority over cable services without noting the potential dilemma regarding either abridgments of the First Amendment or wasteful cross-subsidy requirements.

13. The FCC allows systems to charge higher-than-capped prices via a cost-of-service showing, as a safety-valve measure. Such procedures are expressly created as special-case exemptions from the general rules.

The institutional structure is fundamentally different, then, from the cost-plus environment created by rate-of-return regulation, and that has given rise to the overinvestment incentives described as the Averch-Johnson effect.[14]

The Cable Television Package

Cable program services are delivered in three broad groupings: basic services, premium services, and pay-per-view.[15] The most popular basic package contained an average (nationwide) of thirty-five channels in the General Accounting Office's 1991 survey of cable rates.[16] Those include the locally available off-air (broadcast) signals (such as ABC, NBC, CBS, Fox, PBS, and the independents) as well as cable-only networks (such as CNN, ESPN, Discovery, A&E, USA, and MTV).[17] That basic package is the product that has been regulated or deregulated as dictated by public policy. Premium services (such as HBO, Showtime, or Disney) are delivered on an à la carte basis, and they have been explicitly exempted from price regulation since the 1970s.[18] Pay-per-view also falls into this unregulated category.

Basic Tiers

Within the "basic package" are varying tiers of service. "Limited basic" has characteristically included a bare-bones menu of off-air broadcast signals and local origination–public access programming (sometimes including C-SPAN). That level of service has historically constituted a very small portion of the market; a 1994 FCC survey showed just 3.4 percent of cable customers subscribed to such service in April 1993, although reregulation in 1993 raised that percentage to 13.4 percent as of September 1993.[19] The

14. Harvey Averch & Leland L. Johnson, *Behavior of the Firm Under Regulatory Constraint,* 52 AM. ECON. REV. 1053 (Dec. 1962).

15. Advertising, home security, digital music, alternative telephone access, home shopping, and other services are also delivered by cable systems, but the three major categories of basic, pay, and pay-per-view accounted for about 90 percent of the industry's total revenue in 1992. PAUL KAGAN ASSOCIATES, CABLE TV FINANCIAL DATABOOK, June 1993, at 7.

16. GENERAL ACCOUNTING OFFICE, TELECOMMUNICATIONS: 1991 SURVEY OF CABLE TELEVISION RATES AND SERVICES, GAO/RCED-91-195 (July 17, 1991).

17. Broadcast stations that are distributed nationwide to other cable systems (such as WOR, WGN, or WTBS) are called "superstations" and are generally counted as cable networks.

18. They were also exempted from price controls in the 1992 Cable Act.

19. FCC, CABLE SERVICES BUREAU, FCC CABLE REGULATION IMPACT SURVEY, CHANGES IN

1992 Cable Act refers to that limited menu simply as "basic cable." Such terminology is confusing, however, because what is commonly (outside the act) referred to as "basic cable service" typically includes a much larger complement of cable-only networks. The act refers to such packages as "cable programming tiers."[20] They do not include premium channels or pay-per-view.

Retransmission and Customer Service

In terms of identifying product quality, two final components of the cable television package are important. The first component is the quality of broadcast signal retransmission. Because the typical cable household will spend at least half of its viewing hours watching broadcast signals, one may assume that the increased signal quality of off-air channels received over wireline systems will account for some of the service for which consumers pay. (That is also implied by the fact that cable penetration rates are generally highest in areas in which off-air signals cannot be easily received via rooftop antennas.) The second component is the quality of service the cable company provides. It can provide faster, more reliable technical service appointments, have fewer signal interruptions, and answer its customer service telephone lines more quickly. Both elements of product quality are real, yet exceptionally difficult to measure quantitatively. We shall not analyze them separately here. We shall, however, implicitly account for them in analyzing consumer choices that determine output changes in the marketplace.

Cable systems have been able to adjust product quality in response to price controls.[21] Cable programming is a highly mobile input, and the system sending television viewing products may change its program menu at low (but not zero) transactions cost. That menu may be changed by retiering, by adding to or subtracting from the total number of networks offered, or by shifting marketing expenditures in order to favor different services. In addition, cable networks (upstream input suppliers) may themselves respond to changing system demands by adjusting the quality of programming on a given channel.

CABLE TELEVISION RATES BETWEEN APRIL 5, 1993–SEPTEMBER 1, 1993: REPORT AND SUMMARY 14 (Feb. 22, 1994). Many systems collapsed their "expanded" basic into the lowest tier, thus raising the percentage subscribing to that package.

20. The easiest way to think of the basic package is to use the term *limited basic* to describe what is usually described in the 1992 act as "basic" and to call the full package "expanded basic," which the act refers to as "cable programming services."

21. See the model in Boudreaux & Ekelund, *supra* note 4.

Here we shall examine observable consumer effects in the wake of three major switches in the cable rate regulation regime: California rate deregulation in 1979; national rate deregulation in 1984; and national rate reregulation in 1992. But before proceeding to any of the specifics, we must first introduce a general framework for analyzing the consumer welfare effects of cable television rate controls.

EVALUATING THE ECONOMIC EVIDENCE ON RATE
DEREGULATION/REREGULATION

When binding rate controls are imposed on cable operators, a number of consequences are predictable: systems will tend to shift desirable basic programming to unregulated tiers or à la carte status; systems will tend to reduce program expenditures and offer lower-quality program services on regulated tiers; and systems will tend to shift marketing efforts toward unregulated services. The reverse should be observed when rate controls are eliminated. The key question for policy analysis is, What is the net effect of such changes on consumer welfare?

The empirical analysis in this book is straightforward. We assess how rate regulation of cable systems affects consumer welfare by focusing on two aggregate variables observable in the cable television industry: price and output. We also examine ancillary evidence, including interest group support of (or opposition to) various regulatory rules. The baseline for our analysis is the economic intuition that, in the event that price controls "work," price and output will move in opposite directions following a regime switch. If price is effectively constrained, cable penetration will rise;[22] if rates are permitted to go up, penetration should fall.[23]

The logic of the output test is derived with the help of an assumption that linear demand curves shift parametrically in response to quality changes, as in figure 4-1. Starting at (p_0, q_0), or point A, imagine a positive demand shift—say, from D_0 to D_1—accompanied by a price increase from p_0 to p_1. Clearly, if $q_1 > q_0$ obtains, then consumer surplus is greater at the higher price. (In other words, $p_1BF > p_0AE$.) Alternatively, were quantity to decline owing to a shift in demand, as at point C, the change in consumer surplus would be negative ($p_0AE > p_2CG$). In either case, $\partial CS/\partial q > 0$.

---

22. Penetration, subscribers/homes passed, is a measure of output adjusted for system size.

23. Indeed, state telephone regulators routinely use penetration measures to gauge compliance with rate regulation in local exchange service. We are indebted to Ken Robinson for that observation.

Figure 4-1
Demand Shifts with Price Changes

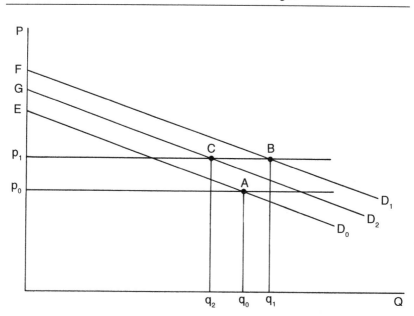

Some evidence suggests that during the deregulation period demand curves do shift in roughly parallel fashion, in that inframarginal customers value quality changes as much (in dollar terms) as do marginal buyers. We derive that conclusion from viewing share data that show changes at the penetration margin correlated with changes in viewership among those already receiving cable program services. That assumption rules out product quality changes that skew toward (or away from) new customers. If the cable package were to change substantially, increased penetration could result from a much lower-priced, much lower-quality service. Such a situation could result in a much flatter demand curve and thus violate the parallel shift assumption. Such disruptions in product quality should be detectable, once again, by examining viewer share data.

If the standard view is that rate regulation lowers prices to consumers, the following alternative hypotheses emerge:

$$H_0 \Rightarrow p_u > p_r \text{ and } q_u < q_r$$
$$H_1 \Rightarrow p_u \leq p_r \text{ and } q_u \geq q_r,$$

where

p_u = real, quality-adjusted, unregulated price,
p_r = real, quality-adjusted, regulated price, and
q = quantity demanded (= quantity supplied).[24]

It follows that terminating an effective rate regulation regime will produce the following marketplace evidence:

$\Delta p > 0$ and $\Delta q < 0$, thereby supporting H_0.

A successful (proconsumer) rate regulation instituted in place of market pricing implies:

$\Delta p < 0$ and $\Delta q > 0$, again supporting H_0.

Those joint hypothesis tests follow from the idea that price and quantity are inversely related along a given demand curve. Although demand curve shifts will likely be involved in transitions from regulated to unregulated status, and vice versa, the output test should still consistently gauge the consumer welfare effects of price controls, as seen above. That is:

$\partial CS/\partial p < 0$; $\partial CS/\partial q > 0$, where CS = consumer surplus.

If we see rate deregulation and reregulation as reverse experiments in cable rate control, we may examine changes in subscription prices and quantities demanded following both experiences to gain a richer mix of evidence. In a newly deregulated environment, the null hypothesis—the view that regulation effectively constrains prices to consumers—is that, *ceteris paribus*, price rises and quantity demanded decreases. With reregulation, price should decline and output should grow.

The model developed here is entirely compatible with the analytical framework that the FCC has advocated for the evaluation of cable television rate regulation. FCC chairman Reed Hundt, after taking office in late 1993, repeatedly suggested that output, as measured by subscriber penetration, was the key variable to watch. For instance, in defending the February 1994 rulemaking that raised the competitive price differential (and therefore the FCC-mandated rate rollbacks) to 17 percent, Hundt was reported by the *Washington Post* as saying that

---

24. There is no excess demand under rate controls as long as $p_r > MC$. That condition characteristically obtains in cable television markets; there are no classic shortages as would be evidenced by queuing.

the 17 percent in price reductions ordered by his agency will enable cable companies to attract customers who until now have been scared away by the cost of monthly service. Cable subscriptions, he noted, have "plateaued" at about 60 percent of the nation's households, and lower prices will help operators "break through" to more customers.

"The question begged is why does the telephone industry have 100 percent penetration and cable only 60 percent, and I would suggest that price has something to do with it."[25]

CALIFORNIA'S RATE DEREGULATION, 1979

A 1979 California statute provided for the decontrol of cable rates at the discretion of the local operator.[26] In AB699 the California Cable Television Association procured that pricing freedom in a compromise with "public access" lobbyists. In exchange for a nominal fee, any cable system within the state could elect to escape existing municipal rate controls (although systems with penetration above 70 percent[27] were then supposed to raise rates no higher than the statewide average). The money paid went to a foundation to subsidize local origination–public access programming on cable systems throughout the state.

Over the 1980–1985 period, only about one-fourth of California's cable systems elected to pay the modest fee of fifty cents per subscriber per year to deregulate. The California state legislature appointed two official study groups to analyze the episode, and both concluded that price increases emanating from deregulation were "innocuous." Ironically, the studies nonetheless dubbed the reform a failure because too few systems had deemed regulation sufficiently onerous to pay to escape it. (As a result, funds gathered for the program subsidy foundation were disappointingly low.) Moreover, the availability of the deregulation safety valve had made it more difficult for local governments to enforce cable franchise terms. Greater reneging on agreements by the cable firms was cited as the chief economic outcome.

The data support those findings. The mean annual price increase for systems jumping into deregulated status minus the same year mean annual

---

25. Paul Farhi, *FCC Head Defends Cuts in Cable Fees,* WASH. POST, Apr. 6. 1994, at D1.

26. This section relies on Thomas W. Hazlett, *The Demand to Regulate Franchise Monopoly: Evidence from CATV Rate Deregulation in California,* 29 ECON. INQUIRY 275 (1991).

27. The logic was that systems with high penetration were located in areas where cable was more of a necessity.

increase of nonderegulated systems, weighted by system subscriber size and summed across all six years, was 10.22 percent (statistically significant at the 99 percent level). In that the deregulated sample is likely to be biased in favor of firms anxious to raise prices, the price changes associated with that sample appear modest. More interesting, perhaps, is the fact that output, as measured by penetration, increased in the deregulated systems (by a statistically insignificant amount) relative to same-year nonderegulated systems.[28] Because a regime switch from effectively regulated prices to unregulated prices would be accompanied by a restriction of output, these results are highly suggestive.

They imply that, while prices increased in the newly deregulated systems, quality of service was increasing commensurately.[29] Because output did not contract in systems escaping price controls relative to other systems, the market evidence suggests that regulation was not effectively constraining prices. If it had, unit sales would have fallen as prices increased. Although the price increases were visible, declining penetration was not. The alternative explanation is that price controls had lowered service and quality elements of the cable television package. When controls were removed, quality improved to offset price increases, and output stayed the same or increased.[30] Penetration changes (or the lack thereof) suggest that cable operators adjusted quality in response to regulation.[31]

That economic appraisal is quite faithful to the public arguments made on behalf of AB699 in 1979. The legislature was told that local government

28. Differences in the price changes of newly deregulated firms over a two-year period reveal a mean rate increase of just 5.58 percent. Penetration results are similar to the one-year experience.

29. Direct measurements of the quality of cable service (for example, cable channel ratings for California cable systems) are not available.

30. That does not mean that the rate controls were meaningless or foolishly imposed by the political system. Their importance lay in helping local officials and interest groups enforce the rent distribution schemes that had been part of the original franchise agreements. All else equal, firms would rather price in an unconstrained environment and charge a high monopoly price for a high-quality cable package. They will, if constrained by price controls, however, charge a low monopoly price for a low-quality cable package. But that is a second-best alternative for cable suppliers, as indicated by revealed preference.

31. Price and quantity demanded (of cable service) increased together owing to an increase in demand, and we assert that demand increased because quality increased. An alternative explanation, however, is that a decline in broadcast program quality increased the demand for cable. But that shift would have presumably affected all California viewers, not just those in the few markets where systems deregulated (which were interspersed with nonderegulated systems across the state). Such an explanation is therefore uncompelling.

rate regulation was creating a drag on upgrades in cable system capacity and delaying the carriage of new satellite networks then becoming widely available. Such channels more than tripled in number between 1978 and 1980. On the operative quality margin, cable operators faced a choice between depreciating existing plant versus expanding channel capacity and delivering many more signals. The existence of local rate controls added a regulatory tax on the decision to expand; even when rate increases were granted, the process of asking for the necessary permission could impose significant costs. Those might include subsidizing local origination–public access services and providing other nonremunerative amenities.[32] Legal representation, litigation costs, and campaign contributions may also have been part of the expected cost of rate increase requests. Moreover, the process itself imposed additional uncertainties on long-term cash flow analysis, thereby increasing business risk and raising the cost of capital.

Because constraining future returns blunts the incentive to commit specific capital, it is clear that in a dynamic industry rate caps may retard investment and growth. Regulatory oversight of such margins is severely challenged, in that the output restriction is never directly observed: it consists of efficient investments, or products, not made. That is analogous to a reverse Averch-Johnson effect: whereas the rate-of-return–regulated firm overinvests to obtain a guaranteed profit on a larger capital base, price caps with ineffective quality monitoring lead to underinvestment.

FEDERAL RATE DEREGULATION, 1984

Federal rate deregulation came in the Cable Communications Policy Act of 1984,[33] which preempted local, state, or federal rate controls in any community where the FCC found "effective competition" to exist. In April 1985 the FCC ruled that such was the case whenever three over-the-air broadcast

---

32. Those were routinely characterized as "bells and whistles" and were provided to gain favor with franchising officials. They were part of a regulatory quid pro quo, with monopoly franchises issued to firms that agreed to such cross-subsidy arrangements. Peter D. Edwards, Cable Television Franchising: A Case Study of Minneapolis, Minnesota (1985) (Communications Media Center, New York Law School); Thomas W. Hazlett, *Competition vs. Franchise Monopoly in Cable Television,* 4 CONTEMP. POL'Y ISSUES 80 (1986); Thomas W. Hazlett, *Private Monopoly and the Public Interest: An Economic Analysis of the Cable Television Franchise,* 134 U. PA. L. REV. 1335 (1986); Mark A. Zupan, *Non-price Concessions and the Effect of Franchise Bidding Schemes on Cable Company Costs,* 21 APPLIED ECON. 305 (1989); Philip Beutel, *City Objectives in Monopoly Franchising: The Case of Cable Television,* 22 APPLIED ECON. 1237 (1990).

33. 47 U.S.C. § 521.

television systems were available.[34] That ruling removed price controls on about 96.5 percent of U.S. cable systems, serving about 99 percent of all U.S. subscribers.[35]

The 1984 act, though popularly referred to as "deregulatory" in nature, did not open up local cable markets to competition. Quite the reverse: the measure added three significant entry barriers. First, it shored up the incumbent firms' hold on monopoly franchises by creating the first federal mandate that all cable systems be licensed by local governments; in a significant number of localities, free entry had been the rule.[36] Second, it increased the incumbent firms' property rights in the cable franchise and made revocation or nonrenewal much more difficult. Finally, the measure codified the FCC's 1970 telephone company–cable television cross-ownership ban. Because the local exchange companies were the likeliest large-scale competitors in local multichannel video markets and the FCC was soon to advocate a reversal of its policy,[37] the act's entry constraint was likely binding.

Although the term *rate deregulation* is literally accurate, labeling the policy reform an unqualified "deregulation" would be something of a misnomer. Rate controls were, for all practical purposes, eliminated for existing suppliers. At the same time, the 1984 Cable Act subjected potential entrants to stiffer regulatory burdens in gaining access to the market by requiring operators formally to obtain municipal franchises. In essence, the act created a haven from competition for cable industry incumbents. That is

---

34. "We now conclude that the existence of three or more off-the-air broadcast signals in the cable market provides viewers with adequate programming choices and presents an effective constraint on the market power of a cable system in the provision of basic service." FCC, In the Matter of Amendment of Parts 1, 63, and 76 of the Commission's Rules to Implement the Provisions of the Cable Communications Policy Act of 1984: Report and Order, MM Dkt. No. 84-1296 (adopted Apr. 11, 1985; released Apr. 19, 1985), at 32–33.

35. GENERAL ACCOUNTING OFFICE, TELECOMMUNICATIONS: FOLLOW-UP NATIONAL SURVEY OF CABLE TELEVISION RATES AND SERVICES, GAO/RCED-90-199 (June 13, 1990), at 63.

36. No national accounting of cable franchises is available. But a 1982 survey of Pennsylvania cable systems by Pennsylvania State University categorized systems by "franchise/no franchise" status. It found that 15.9 percent of cable systems within the state fell into the latter category. D. Allen & D. Kennedy, Municipal Regulation of Cable Television in the Commonwealth of Pennsylvania (1982) (Pennsylvania State University, Institute of Public Administration), at 3–11.

37. Telephone Company–Cable Television Cross-Ownership Rules: Further Notice of Inquiry and Notice of Proposed Rulemaking, 3 F.C.C. Rcd. 5849 (1988).

not how deregulation, in the sense of bringing new competition to an industry, is generally perceived.[38]

By the mid-1980s the cable industry was blessed with a regulatory environment characterized by five elements:

First Amendment rights to select programming. The government's ability to regulate program content was severely constrained, as even "must-carry" rules (the FCC policy that required cable companies to include all local broadcast signals on their basic packages, one of the last vestiges of broadcaster protection) were found unconstitutional by federal courts as an infringement upon the cable company's right to be an "electronic publisher."[39]

No rate regulation. The 1984 Cable Act preempted municipal regulation of basic cable rates, and rate regulation of premium channels (including what is now called pay-per-view) has never been allowed. The deregulation in the 1984 Cable Act was phased in: 5 percent rate increases were permitted for 1985 and 1986, followed by full rate decontrol as of December 29, 1986.

A secure property right in the cable franchise. The 1984 act shifted the burden of proof in franchise renewals: municipalities would henceforth have formally to prove that franchise terms had been violated to deny an incumbent's franchise renewal. Moreover, firms would have to be given explicit notice of, and then a reasonable opportunity to correct, whatever circumstances were responsible for threatening the good standing of the operator.

Franchise burdens for new entrants. The 1984 act required cable systems to be licensed by local governments, a requirement cable incumbents soon used to good advantage. When faced by competitors in local markets, cable associations went to state legislatures for passage of so-called level playing field laws, which created significant new regulatory hurdles for

---

38. That situation has been a source of misunderstanding in the economics literature. Kathleen A. Carroll & Douglas J. Lamdin, *Measuring Market Response to Regulation of the Cable TV Industry,* 5 J. REG. ECON. 385, 397 (1993), write that a firm lobbying *for* deregulation (as embodied in the 1984 Cable Act) is *"prima facie* evidence against the capture theory view." The regulated cable industry was not arguing for competition in supporting passage of the act; the industry gained both fewer regulatory obligations for itself and heightened regulatory barriers for its competitors. Hence, the 1984 Cable Act could hardly be a better example of a law that furthered the interests of the regulated industry.

39. Quincy Cable TV, Inc. *v.* FCC, 768 F.2d 1434 (D.C. Cir. 1985), *cert. denied,* 476 U.S. 1169 (1986).

entrants. Potential competitors were forced to show that admitting a second cable firm would be in the public interest. The model statute, passed in Florida in 1987, was directly aimed at stopping an aggressive competitor, Telesat, from gaining additional franchises.[40]

Codification by the 1984 Cable Act of the FCC's 1970 telephone company–cable television cross-ownership ban.[41] Telephone companies were prohibited from locally offering video service to the public in which they had any significant ownership interest.[42]

The resulting marketplace was an optimal policy outcome for incumbent cable operators: secure property rights in monopoly franchises, no regulatory constraint on product or pricing choices, and entry barriers against potential entrants, including an outright ban on integrated telephone company–cable television suppliers. It is little wonder that the president of the National Cable Television Association hung a framed copy of the 1984 Cable Act on his office wall.[43]

---

40. "The Florida state legislature, under intense pressure from the state's franchised cable operators, has passed a law aimed at reducing the instances of second companies overbuilding all or part of existing cable systems. The measure, dubbed the 'Level Playing Field Act' by Florida operators, is the first of its kind and could become a model for operators seeking government protection from selective overbuilding in other states, according to industry officials." John Wolfe, *Florida Operators Gain Weapon in Fight Against Overbuilders,* CABLEVISION, June 15, 1987, at 50–51. The law did become a model and was enacted in several other states in the ensuing years. *See also* Comments of Telesat Cablevision, In the Matter of Competition, Rate Regulation and the Commission's Policies Relating to the Provision of Cable Television Service, MM Dkt. No. 89-600 (Mar. 1, 1990); Thomas W. Hazlett & George S. Ford, The Fallacy of Regulatory Symmetry: An Economic Analysis of the "Level Playing Field" in State Cable TV Franchising Statutes (Nov. 1995) (paper presented at the meetings of the Southern Economic Association).

41. Applications of Telephone Common Carriers for Section 214 Certificates for Channel Facilities Furnished to Affiliated Community Antenna Television Systems, Final Report and Order, 21 F.C.C.2d 307 (1970), *recons. in part,* 22 F.C.C.2d 746 (1970), *aff'd sub nom.* General Telephone Co. of the Southwest *v.* United States, 449 F.2d 846 (5th Cir. 1971). The cross-ownership ban was codified in 47 U.S.C. § 533(b).

42. The local exchange companies were given the opportunity to apply to the FCC for permission to build conduit facilities upon which others could offer video programming to the public on a tariffed basis. The FCC calls that arrangement "video dialtone" service. Telephone Company–Cable Television Cross-Ownership Rules, Second Report and Order, Recommendation to Congress, and Second Further Notice of Proposed Rulemaking, 7 F.C.C. Rcd. 5781 (1992).

43. "Hanging in [NCTA president James] Mooney's office is a copy of the Cable Communications Policy Act of 1984, which deregulated cable, enriched cable operators

FEDERAL REREGULATION, 1992

Ironically, the overwhelming policy successes enjoyed by the cable industry exposed it to new political risks. Spurred by customer complaints concerning poor service, high prices, and monopoly arrogance, Congress began considering the reimposition of rate controls on cable by 1988 and came close to enacting legislation in October 1990. By October 1992 a bill that included the reregulation of cable television rates was enacted over President Bush's veto—the only instance of a congressional override during the Bush administration.

The Cable Television Consumer Protection and Competition Act of 1992 was a comprehensive measure. Its mandates included:[44]

The reregulation of basic cable. The 1992 act placed controls back on "basic" and "cable programming services"—expanded basic tiers (that is, everything up to à la carte or pay-per-view offerings), except in those markets where a head-to-head multichannel video competitor was operating.[45] The FCC was also directed to define what constituted "unreasonable" rate levels, to limit prices charged to "reasonable" levels with the assistance of municipal authorities and a consumer complaint process, and to define the terms of regulation. The commission chose to define reasonable rates as those that would obtain in a head-to-head competitive (duopolistic) cable market. In April 1993 the commission decided to require cable systems to roll back basic prices up to 10 percent, on a per-channel basis, with equipment rental rates to be set at amortized cost.[46] In February 1994 the com-

---

and contributed to the cable programming boon of the 1980's. It is a tribute to Mooney's legislative prowess. The act is the only major amendment to the Communications Act of 1934—the basic charter of communications law. Mooney would like to keep it that way." Harry A. Jessell, *Mooney: Rereg No Sure Thing,* BROADCASTING, May 4, 1992, at 15.

44. *See also* Nicholas W. Allard, *The 1992 Cable Act: Just the Beginning,* 15 HASTINGS COMM. & ENT. L.J. 305 (1993); Nicholas W. Allard, *Reinventing Rate Regulation,* 46 FED. COMM. L.J. 63 (1993).

45. That was defined as a market in which the smaller firm was capable of serving at least 50 percent of the homes in the franchise area and did, in fact, serve at least 15 percent. Competitors included wireless cable or direct broadcast satellite firms. Other exemptions from regulations were offered to cable firms that served less than 30 percent of the homes in the franchise area or competed with a municipally owned cable system. The overwhelming majority of systems did not qualify for those exemptions.

46. FCC, In the Matter of Implementation of Sections of the Cable Television Consumer Protection and Competition Act—Rate Regulation, Report and Order and Fur-

mission, on reconsideration, announced that it was changing the required rate rollback to 17 percent.[47]

The establishment of retransmission consent for broadcasters. Since the 1976 Copyright Act, broadcasters had been uncompensated by cable operators retransmitting their signals. That was reversed. When the property rights switch officially began in October 1993, however, cable companies generally refused to pay a fee to broadcasters, and the great majority of retransmission deals were consummated with no more than in-kind consideration such as cross-promotion marketing agreements or new basic cable network carriage deals.[48]

The alternative option for broadcasters of "must carry." This measure allowed a station to voluntarily forgo any retransmission fees in exchange for (mandatory) carriage on local cable systems.[49] Most smaller, nonnetwork television broadcasters selected this option.

The enactment of modest procompetition reforms. Included in the act were measures promoting program access for competitive video providers, uniform pricing by local cable systems (which had been discriminatorily underpricing new entrants), and a directive to cities requesting that they issue competitive franchises. Some reforms were effectively undermined by others, however (for example, the elimination of monetary damages against municipalities that unreasonably refused to grant competitive cable licenses).

---

ther Notice of Proposed Rulemaking, MM Dkt. No. 92-266 (adopted Apr. 1, 1993; released May 3, 1993).

47. FCC, In the Matter of Implementation of Sections of the Cable Television Consumer Protection and Competition Act—Rate Regulation, Buy-Through Prohibition, Third Report and Order, MM Dkt. Nos. 92-266 and 92-262 (adopted Feb. 22, 1994; released Mar. 30, 1994).

48. For instance, Fox-owned television stations dropped retransmission consent claims in exchange for cable company agreements to carry (and pay a license fee for) a new basic cable network from Fox, fX.

49. Although "must-carry" rules had previously been struck down on constitutional grounds by federal courts (see above), the U.S. District Court of Appeals (D.C. Circuit) surprised many industry analysts by approving the "must-carry" rules. Turner Broadcasting System, Inc. v. FCC, No. 92-2247 (D.C. Cir. Apr. 8, 1993). The U.S. Supreme Court has, in fact, overruled the D.C. Circuit decision in a 1994 opinion, remanding the matter to a lower court (114 S. Ct. 2445 (1994)). The Court did not find that cable operators have quite the degree of First Amendment protection afforded newspapers, but found that they had more standing than do broadcasters. Because the opinion was decided by a 5-4 majority, with one of the five being a retiring associate justice, the matter may still not be fully resolved. Linda Greenhouse, *Justices Back Cable Regulation,* N.Y. TIMES, June 28, 1994, at C1, C4; Paul M. Barrett, *Justices Order FCC to Justify Cable-TV Rules,* WALL ST. J., June 28, 1994, at A2, A20.

No change in the 1984 telephone company–cable television cross-ownership ban.

Institution of at least twenty-four FCC rulemakings and reports. Issues included interior wiring rules, horizontal concentration, vertical integration, controls on indecent or obscene programming, tier buy-through provisions, customer service, small cable system regulatory exemptions, cost-of-service adjustments to price regulations, and so on.

Rate Regulation under the 1992 Act

The process by which cable rates were regulated under the 1992 act was complex. The administrative structure created by Congress relied heavily on the FCC to determine exactly how rate controls would be instituted and what ancillary regulations would be needed. The act itself gave only the bare outlines.

The act mandated two levels of rate regulation: the first for basic service, the second for all higher tiers of cable programming services. The first level of service was to be regulated primarily by local governments, although the FCC was instructed to create regulatory guidelines and to officially certify local franchising authorities before they were allowed to carry out rate regulation.[50] Regulation of higher tiers was to be conducted directly by the FCC in response to complaints filed by local citizens or by the certified regulatory boards. The FCC was required to regulate if, upon such formal complaint, local cable rates were found "unreasonable." The act listed at least six factors the FCC should take into account in defining "unreasonable."

On April 1, 1993, the FCC announced that it would freeze prices for all tiers of basic cable at their levels (plus inflation) as of September 30, 1992, effective April 5, 1993. Further, it ordered rate rollbacks by September 1, 1993, of up to 10 percent.[51] Rate caps for programming were instituted on a per-channel basis. Each system was to determine, according to its size and number of channels, "benchmark rates" for its basic program-

---

50. If the local franchising authority failed to achieve certification, the FCC was required to regulate cable rates there pursuant to individual customer complaints. There are approximately 33,000 local franchising authorities and 11,000 cable television systems in the United States.

51. The commission addressed a host of other issues. The Report and Order was 521 typewritten pages, single spaced. The Notice of Proposed Rulemaking in December 1992 had inspired comment from 176 parties and reply comments from 121. One round of filings to the commission weighed over forty pounds. Allard, *Reinventing, supra* note 44.

ming services according to tables published by the commission. The system would then be allowed to charge either the benchmark rate or 90 percent of its per-channel rate as of September 30, 1992 (adjusted for inflation up to the present). That format applied to both basic and programming services.[52]

The 10 percent (maximum) rate rollback was based on the FCC's estimation of the difference between monopoly and competitive cable prices, but the commission had employed a curious definition of what constituted a competitive cable system. The 1992 act left it to the FCC to define its own rate-rollback standard, but did—in another context—define a cable system facing "effective competition"[53] in three ways. Type A comprised systems serving under 30 percent of the homes in their franchise areas. Type B comprised systems serving markets in which a second multichannel video operator could serve at least 50 percent of the households and did serve at least 15 percent. Type C comprised systems that were municipally owned or were private systems competing with a municipally owned system that passed 50 percent of the homes in the franchise area.

The FCC elected to borrow that statutory definition of effective competition and to estimate a price equation of the following form:

$$LNP_i = \alpha + \beta_1(ABC)_i + \beta_2(RECIPSUB)_i + \beta_3(LNCHAN)_i \\ + \beta_4(LNSAT)_i + \varepsilon_i,$$

where "LNP = natural logarithm of the composite price per channel for up to three tiers of service, weighted and adjusted to exclude franchise fees and include equipment and other subscriber charges; ABC = 1 if the community unit belongs to one of the categories comprising the statutory definition of 'effective competition,' . . . and = 0 otherwise; RECIPSUB = 1/number of households subscribing to the cable system; LNCHAN = natural logarithm of the number of channels in use in the tiers of service examined; and LNSAT = natural logarithm of the number of satellite-delivered channels in the tiers of service examined."[54]

---

52. Equipment charges, such as monthly fees for remote controls, additional outlets, converter boxes, and so on were also controlled, but the rate benchmarks were binding on the overall package, including equipment rental. Hence, if equipment charges were reduced, operators could raise monthly subscription charges as long as the new rate, overall, fell under the benchmark rate.

53. The act exempted a system from rate regulation if it were found to be effectively competitive. That was the context in which "effective competition" was defined within the act.

54. FCC, *supra* note 46, app. E, at 12.

The commission estimated that price equation with data from 377 cable franchises, of which 79 were type A, 46 type B, and 16 type C. There, "effective competition" included all three types of systems (A, B, and C), and the dummy coefficient β_1 equaled $-.0939$ (significant at 99 percent) and was interpreted as an elasticity. The commission rounded that up to 10 percent, which it determined was the percentage price discount associated with competition. That decision was controversial, and the FCC solicited a further round of public comment,[55] although it decided not to change its standard before implementing the September 1993 rate controls. When run as separate dummy samples in the FCC's model, the three distinct definitions of competition produce coefficients of 9.2 percent (A), -22.1 percent (B), and -38.7 percent (C), all of which are statistically significant at 99 percent. In other words, the A group demonstrated prices *above* those typically found in monopoly systems. The inclusion of those systems diluted the price-lowering impact of actual head-to-head competition such that only about a 10 percent differential was observed.[56] Widespread criticism in the press followed the September "rollbacks," however, and prompted Congress to urge the FCC to reconsider the figure of 10 percent once again.[57] In February 1994 the commission did so and issued new regulations based on a "revised competitive differential of 17 percent."[58]

---

55. One of the authors submitted an affidavit in those proceedings. Affidavit of Thomas W. Hazlett, In the Matter of Implementation of Sections of the Cable Television and Consumer Protection and Competition Act of 1992, Rate Regulation, MM Dkt. No. 92-266 (accompanying joint comments of Bell Atlantic, GTE, and NYNEX) (June 17, 1993).

56. Of course, there are substantial reasons to exclude A systems from the definition of "effectively competitive." First, many of them are simply systems that have failed to construct cable plant covering an entire franchise area. Because the 30 percent subscribership proportion is defined as "subscribers divided by homes in franchise area," a system can qualify, even with normal penetration, just by having a sufficient number of homes in the franchise area that are not passed by cable. Second, the economics are counterintuitive: a system can be declared "effectively competitive" by having prices so high, service so poor, or both that it signs up a small proportion of its potential market. That has been sarcastically designated "the bad actor exemption." *Id.*

57. Paul Farhi, *FCC Rethinks Cable TV Rules with Eye Toward Price Cuts,* WASH. POST, Jan. 25, 1993, at A1, 19.

58. FCC, Executive Summary, Implementation of Sections of the Cable Television Consumer Protection and Competition Act of 1992, Report and Order and Further Notice of Proposed Rulemaking, MM Dkt. No. 93-266 (Feb. 22, 1994), at 2.

Rate Re-Reregulation, February 1994

On February 22, 1994, the FCC, on reconsideration of the 521 pages of rate regulations it had issued in April 1993, redefined its price caps. The key issues concerned the estimation of the competitive pricing differential: which competitive dummy sample was to be employed and which variables were to be included in the estimated price equation. The commission ruled that the influence of type A systems should be diminished in the competitive sample and that additional variables should be added to its regression. The recrafted model found that the difference between competitive and monopoly prices was higher: "Under the Commission's revised benchmark regulations, noncompetitive cable systems that have become subject to regulation will be required to set their rates at a level equal to their September 30, 1992 rates minus a revised competitive differential of 17 percent."[59] That revised rulemaking called for a new round of rate rollbacks, which the commission later announced would be instituted July 14, 1994.

The commission's new price equation was estimated in the form:

$$LRS = \alpha + c_0 A1 + c_1 OVL + c_2 C + c_3 MSO + \beta_0 LMS + c_4 RSS + c_5 RTC + c_6 PNB + c_7 PAO + c_8 PRM + c_8 PT2 + c_9 PTC + \beta_1 LIN + \varepsilon,$$

where

LRS = natural log of monthly regulated revenue per subscriber,
$A1$ = dummy for systems with subscribers/homes passed less than .3,[60]
OVL = proportional variable measuring degree of competitive overlap in B systems—continuous from 0 to 1,
C = dummy for municipal systems, or private systems competing with a municipal,
MSO = dummy for system owned by multiple system operator,
LMS = natural log of number of systems owned by an MSO,
RSS = reciprocal of system subscribers,
RTC = reciprocal of the average total channels,
PNB = reciprocal of nonbroadcast channels,
PAO = proportion of additional outlets,
PRM = proportion of remotes,
$PT2$ = proportion of tier 2 subscribers,

59. *Id.* Rates were allowed to rise from their levels on September 30, 1992, by a cost-of-living adjustment before being rolled back the mandated percentage.

60. Systems that served fewer than 30 percent of the homes in their franchise area but more than 30 percent of homes passed were eliminated from the A subsample.

PTC = proportion of tier changes, and
LIN = natural log of median income.

The key coefficient estimates involved the competitive variables. Having redefined the low-penetration[61] subsample, A1, to exclude systems that appeared to have low subscribership owing to factors entirely unrelated to competition, the estimate for c_0 virtually disappeared. The estimate for c_1, however, was $-.174$, implying an elasticity of $-.1597$.[62] (The estimated c_2 was $-.231$, implying an elasticity of $-.2063$.[63]) The commission concluded that the estimated coefficient on the *OVL* variable, representing the presence of private system overbuild competition, was the appropriate measure of the competitive price differential. That estimate of 16 percent was inflated to 17 percent,[64] which became the new benchmark for the second round of rate rollbacks.[65]

---

61. As noted above, while penetration is defined as subscribers/homes passed, the A category is defined by subscribers/homes in franchise area. The FCC found that 37 percent of the A systems actually had penetration greater than .3 and were therefore excluded from the analysis.

62. The elasticities, *d*, are estimated as $d_i = e^{c_i} - 1$.

63. Because C systems are both competitive (*OVL*) and municipal (or municipal competitors), their rates would be about 37 percent (16 percent + 21 percent) below monopoly levels.

64. The commission's rules included an appendix with a long explanation of its statistical calculations estimating the difference in competitive versus monopoly prices, but the FCC fudged the final number. The commission stated that the estimated 37 percent price differential between noncompetitive systems and type C cable systems (municipally owned or private systems in competition with a municipal) was "[a]rguably . . . the most accurate measure of the competitive differential because government-operated entities may be presumed to charge reasonable rates." FCC, In the Matter of Implementation of Sections of the Cable Television Consumer Protection and Competition Act—Rate Regulation, Second Order on Reconsideration, Fourth Report and Order, and Fifth Notice of Proposed Rulemaking, MM Dkt. No. 92-266 (adopted: Feb. 22, 1994; released: Mar. 30, 1994) ¶ 31. Yet the commission goes on to select 17 percent as the appropriate differential, "guided by the 16 percent figure estimated from our data on overbuilds." It explains how it got from 16 percent to 17 percent as follows: "We moved upward from 16 percent to reflect our conclusion that cable operators in an overbuild situation are likely over time to develop a tacit understanding of rate levels that may limit the intensity of rate competition. However, we did not depart upward as far as we might have, despite the evidence relating to municipal systems, on account of concerns about the interpretation of the data in our municipal subsample and on account of our consideration of low penetration systems. Furthermore, we were guided by our belief that consumer welfare is best served by financially sound cable operators." *Id.* ¶ 32.

65. The cable industry expressed outrage at both the substance and the form of the

Politics, rather than economic analysis, produced the commission's oscillating iterations on the appropriate competitive price differential. In fact, the econometric estimation was done *after* the issue had been decided by the three FCC commissioners.[66] Commissioner Andrew Barrett, in a separate statement attached to the regulations, openly admitted that, regardless of the regression model results, "[b]ased upon my own analysis, we believe that the new competitive differential of 17% as compared to the September 1992 rate levels represents the highest point of what we consider to be an acceptable range for this policy determination. . . . We have consistently emphasized the need to consider the effect of the cable rate regulations on industry investment."[67] Conversely, chairman Reed Hundt made it clear that if he had his way, the second rate rollback would have been an additional 16–18 percent, not 7 percent.[68]

The pressure driving the commission to up the regulatory ante was apparent. Congress, badly embarrassed by the negative publicity surrounding enactment of rate controls in 1993, leaned heavily on the commission—and particularly its newly confirmed chairman, Reed Hundt—to atone for what was popularly seen as a regulatory fiasco.

Hence, the commission not only increased the rate rollback mandate but tightened up on other margins, as well. For example, the February 1994

---

re-reregulation. After the rulemaking's technical appendix was released, a prominent industry analyst, Thomas P. Southwick, actually titled his weekly column in *Cable World*: "LAR = 2.04 + .07(MSO) + .0097(LMS) + 8.14(RSS) − 1.45(RTC) + .253(PNB) + .103(PAO) + .172(PRM) + .057(PT2) + .353(PTC) + .069(LIN)." His column began: "It's difficult to imagine what kind of people think that the above formula and similar equations included in the FCC's rate regulations can provide the perfect answer to how much every single cable system can charge every single cable subscriber in the world." Thomas P. Southwick, *LAR = 2.04 + .07(MSO) + .0097(LMS) + 8.14(RSS) − 1.45(RTC) + .253(PNB) + .103(PAO) + .172(PRM) + .057(PT2) + .353(PTC) + .069(LIN)*, CABLE WORLD, Apr. 25, 1994, at 20.

66. Susan Ness and Rachelle Chong had yet to join the commission. The three commissioners who enacted the February 22, 1994, rules were Reed Hundt, Andrew Barrett, and James Quello.

67. FCC, Re: Separate Statement of Commissioner Andrew C. Barrett, Implementation of the Cable Television Consumer Protection and Competition Act of 1992—Rate Regulation, Fourth Order on Reconsideration, Fourth Report and Order (Feb. 22, 1994), at 3. *See also* Paul Farhi, *FCC to Cut Cable TV Rates Again,* WASH. POST, Feb. 22, 1994, at A1, A6. A trade journal observed: "[FCC chairman Reed] Hundt was said to have pushed for a 26- to 28-percent rollback, but was rebuffed by fellow commissioners James Quello and Andrew Barrett, who voted last summer for the original 10-percent rollback." *Cable Execs See Telco Fingerprints All over New FCC Rate Rollbacks,* CABLE WORLD, Feb. 28, 1994, at 4.

68. *Cable Execs, supra* note 67.

rulemaking announced a declining rate cap formula, forcing future cable prices down by an annual productivity factor. Analogous to utilities' price caps, which leave profits unregulated but require prices to fall over time,[69] the framework appears to achieve symmetry with other regulatory structures in telecommunications. Yet it operates in a dramatically different direction: forcing price caps on unregulated operators who are simultaneously program content suppliers yields a host of transitional and compliance issues not of immediate consequence in natural gas, electricity, or telephony.[70]

The regulatory pendulum began swinging back toward liberalization soon after the February 1994 rulemaking.[71] The annual productivity factor adjustment was abandoned, and the FCC moved away from the February rules that new programming could only be added to systems at cost plus 7.5 percent. In other words, if a channel costing twenty-five cents per subscriber per month were added to a system's basic lineup, the monthly basic rate could be raised no more than twenty-seven cents. In November 1994, just two days after the congressional elections, the commission voted for "going-forward" rules that permitted rate increases of $1.50 (over two years) if as many as six channels were added to the basic package.

By July 1995 the Kagan cable operator stock price index had risen nearly 50 percent over its April 1994 low: "[April] was when investors were at the depths of their despair over FCC treatment of the industry."[72] By the time that the Telecommunications Act of 1996 paved the way for a second round of cable rate deregulation, the process was well underway at the FCC.[73]

---

69. Often price caps, as enacted by regulatory agencies, are less than "pure," meaning that some profit regulation remains in effect.

70. In February 1994 the FCC battened down other escape hatches, including a ruling that "cost of service" showings (whereby an individual cable system is given a waiver to charge above benchmark rates owing to high costs) would not be able to include any capital costs above book value. That presumably ruled out about two-thirds of acquisition costs for systems purchased within the past several years. One area of seeming liberalization in the new rules, however, was the regulation of small cable systems. Easing controls on those companies (defined as having fewer than 250,000 subscribers in total, no system with more than 10,000 subscribers, and having an average system size of under 1,000 subscribers) reportedly proved important in gaining two commissioners' support for the rate rollbacks. *Cable Execs, supra* note 67, at 5.

71. Vincente Pasdeloup, *An FCC Olive Branch?* CABLE WORLD, May 30, 1994, at 2.

72. CABLE TV INVESTOR, July 31, 1995, at 1.

73. Mark Robichaux, *FCC's "Social Contract" for Cable Companies Draws Ire,* WALL ST. J., Jan. 19, 1996, at B4. The article was subtitled *Double-Digit Rate Increases Prompt Angry Complaints Against the Agency.*

FEDERAL DEREGULATION REDUX, 1996

Continuing the cycle, Congress again elected to deregulate cable rates in the Telecommunications Act of 1996. That measure, passed only forty months after the 1992 Cable Television Consumer Protection and Competition Act, provided for the immediate deregulation of small cable systems, which serve about 20 percent of the estimated sixty-one million U.S. cable households; a three-year phaseout (concluding March 1, 1999) of rate controls imposed on larger system operators; and deregulation for any market experiencing head-to-head competition with a telephone company providing video services (the 1992 Cable Act already exempted systems pitted against nontelephone company rivals). The results of that (second) national deregulation, though not yet observable, will soon be available to compare with the conclusions drawn in this book.

5

The Economic Effects of Deregulation, 1987–1992

PERHAPS THE MOST OBVIOUS changes following cable television deregulation involved pricing, but others were equally important. Cable output trends, cable operator cash flows, tiering, and program quality were all in flux as dynamic forces buffeted the industry.

PRICE CHANGES

Price increases assuredly followed the cable television deregulation measures included in the 1984 Cable Act (which became fully effective December 29, 1986). Whether those were increases from trend and whether they presaged quality-adjusted rate increases must await further analysis. But it is apparent that the nominal price of cable television service rose in the post-1986 period. Increases are evident in all the series we examine, including the price data contained in three General Accounting Office surveys and summarized in table 5-1.[1] The fifty-two-month interval between November 30, 1986, and April 1, 1991, was accompanied by a nominal price increase of nearly 61 percent for basic cable. In real terms that amounted to a 36.5 percent price increase.[2]

---

1. GENERAL ACCOUNTING OFFICE (GAO), TELECOMMUNICATIONS: NATIONAL SURVEY OF CABLE TELEVISION RATES AND SERVICES, GAO/RCED-89-193 (Aug. 3, 1989); GAO, TELECOMMUNICATIONS: FOLLOW-UP NATIONAL SURVEY OF CABLE TELEVISION RATES AND SERVICES, GAO/RCED-90-199 (June 13, 1990); GAO, TELECOMMUNICATIONS: 1991 SURVEY OF CABLE TELEVISION RATES AND SERVICES, GAO/RCED-91-195 (July 17, 1991).

2. GAO, TELECOMMUNICATIONS: 1991, *supra* note 1, at 5. The GAO has not published standard deviations with its mean data, so tests of statistical differerences are ruled out.

Table 5-1
Price and Channel Data from GAO Cable Television Surveys, 1986–1991

Date	Mean Basic Cable Rate[a] ($)	Mean No. of Basic Channels[a]	Mean Price per Channel ($)	Revenue per Sub- scriber per Month ($)	Percentage of Systems Offering One Tier Only
Nov. 30, 1986	11.71	27.1	.44	21.78	74.3
Dec. 31, 1988	14.91	32.2	.47	25.00	NA
Dec. 31, 1989	16.33	33.6	.49	26.36	83.4
Apr. 1, 1991	18.84	35.3	.53	28.76	58.6
% Change					
1986–1988	27.3	18.8	6.8	14.8	NA
1986–1989	39.5	24.0	11.4	21.0	12.2
1986–1991	60.8	30.3	20.5	32.0	−21.1
Annualized % change					
1986–1991	11.6	6.3	4.4	6.6	

Note: NA = not available.

a. Most popular basic tier.

Source: General Accounting Office, *Telecommunications: 1991 Survey of Cable Television Rates and Services* (GAO/RCED-91-195) (July 17, 1991).

Only a small number of sources for cable industry data exist. The most frequent and reliable continuous series of rate data is that collected by the Bureau of Labor Statistics: a monthly price series on a package of cable services (representative of the typical consumer's) since January 1984. Paul Kagan Associates publishes annual data, going back to 1976, that track a number of different cable rates: the price of basic service, the price of expanded basic, revenue per subscriber, and rate-based revenue per subscriber. Those data are national averages. The GAO has done three surveys, which report price data (basic rates and revenue per subscriber) for a sample of cable systems from 1984 through 1991. (Those data are reported approximately annually, not monthly.) Finally, the FCC conducted a survey of cable rates in the fall of 1993 in an effort to discover the results of rate regulation that went into effect on September 1, 1993.

The CPI Cable Index

The Bureau of Labor Statistics monthly data provide interesting evidence on the impact of rate controls.[3] The cable component of the consumer price index attempts to track a typical cable subscriber's bill and is therefore analogous to what the cable industry describes as "rate-generated revenue-per-subscriber." That component leaves out such revenues as advertising or telecommunications bypass charges. It would, however, include pay cable, pay-per-view, installation, converter, and remote-control charges. It appears to be a better measure of cable rates than simple basic cable charges, with the caveat that as the mix of services included in the typical subscriber's cable "bundle" changes, the CPI cable index will tend to misstate changes in the effective quality-adjusted rate.[4]

The BLS publishes various price indexes but monitors cable rates separately in only two: the urban consumer price index and the urban worker consumer price index. Not surprisingly, the series are highly correlated. In figure 5-1, we present the urban consumer price index, deflated by the corresponding CPI series to produce real cable rate changes from January 1984 to December 1993. Note, again, that those rates are not adjusted for changes in the quality of programming or for the "size" of the cable television service package.

The vertical lines in figure 5-1 indicate major changes in regulatory regime, so that we may observe market pricing patterns by cable companies in response to the passage of the 1984 Cable Act (October 30, 1984); deregulation of systems serving 99 percent of U.S. cable subscribers (December 29, 1986); passage of the 1992 Cable Act over President Bush's veto (October 5, 1992); and FCC initiation of a rate freeze at levels prevailing September 30, 1992 (plus inflation), pursuant to that act (April 5, 1993).

---

3. The series has been referenced by the GAO, which found that its survey results indicated that revenue per cable subscriber had increased some 21 percent between November 1986 and December 1989 and that "[i]n comparison, for the same 37-month period of our survey, the Bureau of Labor Statistics' Urban Consumer Price Index (CPI) showed a 26-percent increase in the average consumer's monthly bill for cable television service." GAO, TELECOMMUNICATIONS: FOLLOW-UP, *supra* note 1, at 25. The FCC has also expressed the viewpoint, however, that the CPI cable index included an excessive number of services.

4. Of course, there is an even larger pitfall in solely analyzing basic rates as the basic cable package goes through tiering, detiering, and retiering. The charges paid by typical cable consumers should, presumably, constitute those that rate regulation is said to control. So the variable observed in the CPI cable series is of great interest.

Figure 5-1
Real Cable Rates under Deregulation, January 1984–April 1993

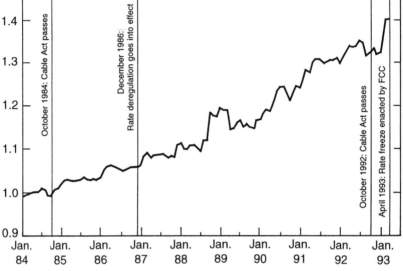

Source: Bureau of Labor Statistics; cable television component of consumer price index had exurban.

From a general examination of the BLS-charted price series, it is difficult to see where rate regulation had a significant impact. Prices for the overall cable package did not rise dramatically in the wake of deregulation. But the slope of the line—the rate of increase in real cable rates—appears to increase after deregulation. Three observations are appropriate.

First, the upward trend in cable rates is pronounced and virtually monotonic. As discussed below, the observation of *rising* prices over the several-year deregulation period is inconsistent with the null hypothesis, in that price increases resultant from relaxation of regulatory constraints should fly up to unconstrained profit-maximizing levels and, *ceteris paribus*, stay there. Here prices appear to be gradually rising throughout the decade (even before deregulation). The presence of rising real prices over time, as opposed to a break in trend, is evidence that demand or supply shifts were pushing the profit-maximizing price up throughout the period. The most likely driver is demand, insofar as penetration was also increasing (that is, price and quantity demanded were rising together). Demand, of course,

Table 5-2
Regression Results: Cable Rates over Time,
January 1984–December 1993

			Parameter			
	α	β_0	β_1	β_2	β_3	β_4
Estimated value	.95778	$.35782e^{-2}$	$.22706e^{-1}$	$-.19670e^{-1}$	$.51866e^{-1}$	$.11797e^{-1}$
t	203.5	52.49	.5266	$-.7874$	2.057^a	.7915
$R^2 = .9651.$						

a. significant at 95% level.

could be growing in response to perceived increases in cable service or program quality.

Second, no obvious trend breaks occur at points demarcating deregulation. To determine whether the data behave as they look, we extended the price series through December 1993[5] and estimated the following model:

$$RCR_i = \alpha + \beta_0 MONTH + \beta_1 DEREGLAW + \beta_2 DEREG + \beta_3 FREEZE + \beta_4 REREG + \varepsilon_i,$$

where

RCR_i	= real cable rate for month i,
$MONTH$	= 1 (for January 1984), 2 (February 1984), . . . ,
$DEREGLAW$	= 1 if $MONTH \geq 11$ (November 1984), 0 otherwise,
$DEREG$	= 1 if $MONTH \geq 37$ (January 1987), 0 otherwise,
$FREEZE$	= 1 if $MONTH \geq 112$ (April 1993), 0 otherwise, and
$REREG$	= 1 if $MONTH \geq 117$ (September 1993), 0 otherwise.

The results appear in table 5-2.

The only dummy coefficient that is statistically significant is the coefficient on the *FREEZE* variable, and it is significantly *positive*. That is, prices increase from trend about the time the FCC began implementing the reregulation mandated in the 1992 Cable Act. From examining those data it is clear that the fly-up in prices occurs in late 1992 or early 1993—before

5. In chapter 6 we extend the CPI rate series through May 1995 in figure 6-1.

Table 5-3
Chow Tests for Price Line (over Time) Slope Changes

First Period	Second Period	Chow Statistic	Critical Value at .05
1/84–12/86	1/87– 3/93	42.764	19.485
1/84–12/86	1/87– 9/93	51.313	19.486
1/84–12/86	1/87–12/93	49.513	19.486
1/84–12/86	1/87–12/92	41.598	19.485

official imposition of rate controls on April 5, 1993. As for the impact of deregulation, there is actually a negative (but insignificant) coefficient on the January 1987 deregulation date. In terms of the overall price of the cable package, deregulation does not appear to send prices flying up, nor does reregulation quickly push them down. (We discuss the latter issue in greater detail in chapter 6.)

Third, the slope of the price line appears to increase after rate deregulation. If we break the data at the starting point for deregulation—January 1987—and follow it up to the legislative advent of reregulation—April 1993—we can test for the hypothesis that the slope of the price-against-time line changes via a Chow test.

The Chow test divides the data set and considers whether the coefficients for the respective subsamples are, given some confidence interval, distinguishable. Running such a test on the CPI urban cable series regressed against time and truncated as indicated results in a highly significant Chow statistic (see table 5-3). That result is impervious to the precise date one designates as ending the deregulation period (December 1992, March 1993, September 1993, or December 1993) and implies a slope difference between the regulated and deregulated periods at the 95 percent confidence level. The evidence strongly suggests that the growth in cable rates increased after deregulation.

As is commonly understood, monopoly implies high prices, not rising prices. Price adjustments following deregulation would be expected to result in immediate (or relatively short-term) price increases, with general inflation-related price increases thereafter, all else (besides deregulation) remaining constant. Five years after the fact, however, substantial annual increases were still in evidence. That suggests that demand continued to shift outward, presumably owing to increases in program or service quality.

As prominently as the argument figured in the public debate over cable reregulation,[6] it is interesting that cable prices' steady rise (in real terms) throughout the deregulation period was itself evidence that something more complicated than a deregulation-induced fly-up in prices was at work. Some economists have suggested that firms might be timid about price increases where aggressive, profit-maximizing behavior might increase the probability of heightened regulation. Of course, such reregulation was introduced in the wake of rate increases over time. Yet, for the individual cable system owner, a rational strategy would have been to price very aggressively in anticipation of rate rollbacks—a pattern of behavior that does appear (in the CPI data) to have occurred following passage of the 1992 Cable Act— during the deregulated period.[7] Moreover, if systems were generally wary of reregulation following from local price increases, then presumably large systems (with greater visibility in Washington, D.C.) would be more timid. Small operators could raise rates to monopoly levels, free riding on the restraint shown by the "socially responsible" industry giants. Yet the GAO data break down price increases by system size and show no correlation,[8] while the FCC was to find in its cable rate regression analysis that *larger* systems charged higher prices.[9]

Also working against the "implicit regulation" view is the fact that the 1984 Cable Act had so successfully secured the operator's franchise rights that the threat of nonrenewal was rendered moot. Indeed, both the Federal Trade Commission and the Department of Justice filed comments with the Federal Communications Commission in 1990 that argued for a relaxation of the 1984 Cable Act on the grounds it ensured that "[a] decision not to renew a cable franchise may not be based on the prices charged by the

---

6. The standard proregulation argument was made by then-Senator Albert Gore (D-TN): "According to a 1991 GAO study, monthly rates for the lowest priced basic service increased by 56 percent from the beginning of deregulation in December 1986 to April 1991. . . . [M]onthly rates for the most popular basic cable service increased by 61 percent. . . . These rates of growth are three times that of inflation." CONG. REC. S662 (daily ed. Jan. 30, 1992).

7. In hindsight, that would have been the optimal strategy as rate rollbacks were mandated on the basis of prices being charged by systems as of September 30, 1992.

8. GAO, TELECOMMUNICATIONS: 1991, *supra* note 1, at 19.

9. FCC, In the Matter of Implementation of Sections of the Cable Television Consumer Protection and Competition Act—Rate Regulation, Report and Order and Further Notice of Proposed Rulemaking, MM Dkt. 92-266 (adopted Apr. 1, 1993; released May 3, 1993); FCC, In the Matter of Implementation of Sections of the Cable Television Consumer Protection and Competition Act—Rate Regulation, Buy-Through Prohibition, Third Report and Order, MM Dkt. Nos. 92-266 and 92-262 (adopted Feb. 22, 1994; released Mar. 30, 1994).

operator, nor on the mix, quality, or level of cable services or other services provided over the system."[10] Both agencies argued that gutting municipality discretion removed explicit or implicit incentives for cable operators to mitigate monopoly pricing.

The continuing price increases in the postderegulation environment then suggest that demand was shifting outward over time. The most straight-forward explanation of that is that new channels were added to basic cable packages while more desirable programming was being telecast on exist-ing channels. That can explain the annual price increases in excess of infla-tion beyond 1987 and 1988 and is consistent with the rapidly rising expenditures for programming inputs into cable service. Moreover, it is the only explanation consistent with the rising penetration rate.

The Pattern of Basic Rates and Revenue per Subscriber

The industry data describing cable rate changes over the 1976–1993 pe-riod[11] tell a story that is also at odds with the popular version of a 1987 price fly-up in the wake of deregulation. What is striking about those data, listed in table 5-4 and displayed graphically in figures 5-2 and 5-3, is that, while regulation and deregulation appear to have some impact on the rate charged for basic cable, the overall package price of cable service seems only modestly correlated—at best—with the regulatory regime. We assert that the most plausible connection between rate regulation and the overall quality-adjusted price of cable television is indirect. That is, the regulatory regime influences the level of business risk, which influences investments in program and infrastructure quality, and those, in turn, influence con-sumer demand for cable television service. Such a sequence implies that whatever regulatory constraints are imposed are mediated by the decisions of cable suppliers to invest or disinvest in network quality.

One can observe from the price data that while large increases in basic cable rates followed the December 29, 1986, deregulation, the largest an-nual increases in program costs for the typical cable customer came in the early 1980s, as new premium services were coming on line and being ag-gressively marketed by cable firms. The revenue-per-subscriber growth rates do increase slightly after deregulation but stay at about the 1987 level for

---

10. GAO, TELECOMMUNICATIONS: FOLLOW-UP, *supra* note 1, at 43.

11. Those data are collected by Paul Kagan Associates, an industry consulting firm that publishes various newsletters, trade journals, and databases. The data are reported to Kagan researchers voluntarily by the firms, although public SEC filings, FCC data, or other sources are used directly and indirectly. CPI data are collected by field agents of the Bureau of Labor Statistics, who make personal visits to cable sales offices to inquire about rates.

Table 5-4
Cable Television Subscription Rates, 1976–1994

Year	Basic Rate ($)	Change (%)	Rev./ Sub./Mo. ($)	Change (%)	Rate-Based Rev./ Sub./Mo. ($)	Change (%)
1976	6.45		7.06		6.94	
1977	6.86	6.4	8.20	16.1	7.70	11.0
1978	7.13	3.9	9.18	12.0	8.62	11.9
1979	7.40	3.8	10.42	13.5	9.77	13.3
1980	7.69	3.9	12.14	16.6	11.34	16.1
1981	7.99	3.9	14.17	16.7	13.17	16.1
1982	8.30	3.9	16.35	15.4	15.17	15.2
1983	8.61	3.7	18.15	11.0	16.85	11.1
1984	8.98	4.3	19.69	8.5	18.16	7.8
1985	9.73	8.4	20.98	6.5	19.18	5.6
1986	10.67	9.7	22.13	5.5	20.00	4.3
1987	12.18	14.2	23.83	7.7	21.27	6.4
1988	13.86	13.8	25.63	7.6	22.84	7.4
1989	15.21	9.7	27.50	7.3	24.27	6.3
1990	16.78	10.3	29.46	7.1	26.02	7.2
1991	18.10	7.9	30.86	4.8	27.06	4.0
1992	19.08	5.4	32.30	4.6	28.26	4.4
1993	19.39	1.6	33.74	4.5	29.35	3.9
1994	21.62	11.5	32.49	(3.7)	28.07	(4.4)

Notes: Rate-based revenue includes only basic, expanded basic, and pay or minipay services. Rev./sub./mo. = revenue per subscriber per month.

Sources: Paul Kagan Associates, *Cable TV Investor,* Mar. 31, 1994, p. 9, and June 30, 1995, p. 5.

four years. Only after 1990, the year that saw the U.S. Congress nearly pass cable reregulation legislation, did average price increases for the total package decline. That evidence is inconsistent with the view that price controls were constraining operators' pricing directly but clearly supports the hypothesis that deregulation encouraged firms to invest in new services and capacity, thus raising demand over time (as the new services became available).[12]

12. The evidence is not inconsistent with the depressing of demand that likely occurred because of the 1990–1991 recession.

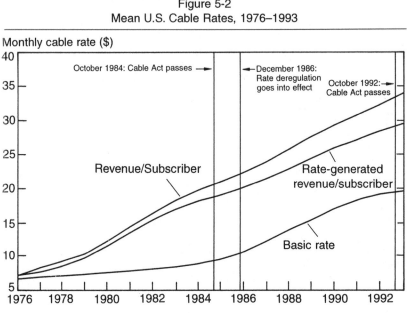

Figure 5-2
Mean U.S. Cable Rates, 1976–1993

Source: Paul Kagan Associates, *Cable TV Investor,* Mar. 31, 1994, p. 9.

Unregulated System Price Increases

The GAO's survey conveniently includes data from both newly deregulated systems (as of December 29, 1986) and already deregulated systems. The latter comprised some 24 percent of the systems surveyed.[13] Comparing the price increases of the deregulated systems with those of the systems that were already unregulated at the beginning of the test period provides an opportunity to use the latter subsample as a control group. Because those systems were not released from regulatory constraints, their pricing pattern does not include the direct effects of deregulation.

---

13. "Although the Cable Act restricted local rate regulation effective December 29, 1986, our survey showed that 24 percent of the cable systems reported that they were already not regulated on November 30, 1986, prior to the date the Cable Act took effect. Our survey also showed that only 3.5 percent remained regulated on December 31, 1989, a number too small for meaningful statistical analysis." GAO, TELECOMMUNICA-TIONS: FOLLOW-UP, *supra* note 1, at 21–22.

Figure 5-3
U.S. Cable Rate Growth, 1977–1993

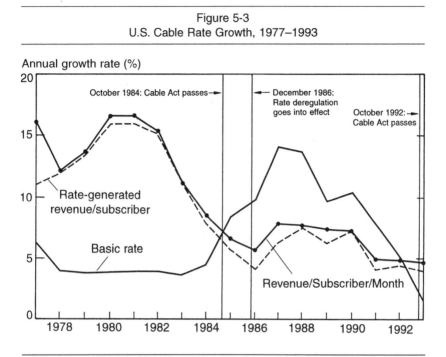

Source: Paul Kagan Associates, *Cable TV Investor,* Mar. 31, 1994, p. 9, and June 30, 1995, p. 5.

The comparison is highly informative (see figures 5-4 and 5-5 and table 5-5). Unregulated systems charged about 6.6 percent more for basic service at the end of the regulated period, although they received just 1.5 percent more in revenue per subscriber, a measure of price that includes all ancillary, unregulated services. Moreover, the latter differential seems to have shifted back and forth during the regulated period: in 1984 unregulated revenue per subscriber was slightly below the regulated system mean. During the first three years of deregulation, deregulated basic rates increased more: 42 percent compared with 32 percent.[14] That brings them roughly into parity with unregulated systems. Revenue per subscriber, however, stays close to parity.[15] The increase in basic charges seen in the regulated sys-

---

14. That is very close to the 10.22 percent higher prices we see in newly deregulated systems in California following the state's 1979 deregulation, when we use nonderegulated systems as a control. See chapter 4.

15. Revenue per subscriber is more reflective of the typical customer's bill than the

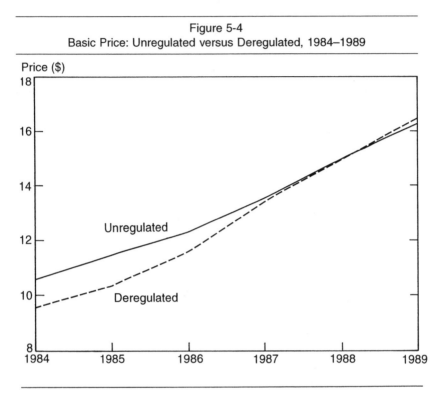

Figure 5-4
Basic Price: Unregulated versus Deregulated, 1984–1989

Source: GAO (1990), pp. 52, 58.

tems (relative to nonderegulated systems) does not result in higher overall charges to consumers. It appears that the price increases reported by the GAO are simply accounting artifacts, as other charges are decreased to offset them. What we observe are not increases in cable costs to subscribers but repricing: basic charges up, other charges down, tiers collapsed.

CABLE OUTPUT TRENDS

A key variable reflecting changes in the quality-adjusted price of cable television is the penetration rate (subscribers per homes passed) of regulated versus deregulated cable systems. If regulation works to lower the effective price of cable, one obvious indicator of that would be an expansion of cable output: penetration increases. If deregulation, conversely, allows cable op-

basic rate alone. Although it includes advertising, the third-party revenue streams were so small during the period in question as to be inconsequential.

Figure 5-5
Revenue/Subscriber/Month: Unregulated versus Deregulated, 1984–1989

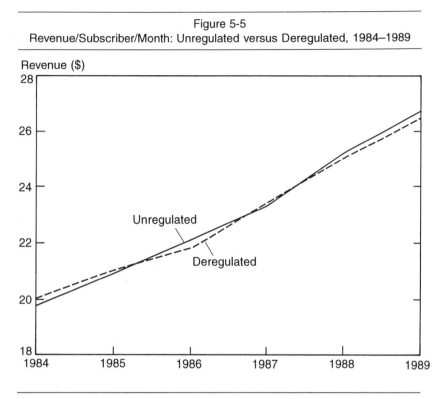

Source: GAO (1990), pp. 52, 58.

erators to increase price-cost margins and extract monopoly rents, then the cessation of rate regulation should result in output contraction: penetration decreases. In a time-series framework, such output changes should be observed as deviations from trend.

Observing penetration changes, as opposed to price differences, allows the revealed preferences of consumers to evaluate changes in the price-quality package. Absent that approach, one must inquire whether increased quality has accompanied higher rates (following deregulation) or lower rates (following reregulation), a question that is objectively difficult to answer. Further, if such quality enhancement or depreciation is plausible, one must weigh those package changes against the attendant price changes. The difficulties inherent in such a procedure have affected both the popular debate and the scholarly literature. The GAO surveys found, for instance, that while real basic cable rates had increased in the deregulation period, the mean number of channels provided on basic had increased commensurately, leav-

Table 5-5
Unregulated System Price Changes Following Deregulation

Date	Basic Price ($)		Revenue/Subscriber/ Month ($)	
	Unregulated	Deregulated	Unregulated	Deregulated
Dec. 31, 1984	10.58	9.62	19.70	19.98
Dec. 31, 1985	11.44	10.36	20.90	20.99
Nov. 30, 1986	12.31	11.55	22.11	21.78
Dec. 31, 1987	13.50	13.46	23.32	23.40
Dec. 31, 1988	14.94	14.93	25.24	25.04
Dec. 31, 1989	16.24	16.42	26.74	26.41
% Increase 1984–1989	53.4	70.7	35.7	32.2
% Increase 1986–1989	31.9	42.1	20.9	21.3

Source: General Accounting Office, *Telecommunications: Follow-up National Survey of Cable Television Rates and Services* (GAO/RCED-90-199) (June 13, 1990). Note that the 1991 GAO report does not include a comparison of those systems. Hence, the data only go through what appeared in the 1990 report.

ing the real price per channel virtually unchanged. In the absence of information on the value of such channels, there is no clear way to interpret either the cause or the consumer effect of the price changes. Moreover, quality changes on inframarginal channels are entirely unobserved. The public debate, which focused exclusively on price changes of the basic package, was ill-informed because no method was employed to account for the changing size and content of that package.

Robert Rubinovitz's 1991 finding[16] that virtually half the price increases following deregulation resulted from market power also fails to shed light on the essential comparative statics: were consumers worse off

16. Robert N. Rubinovitz, *Market Power and Price Increases for Basic Cable Service Since Deregulation,* 24 RAND J. ECON. 1 (1993); citations are to an earlier draft, ROBERT N. RUBINOVITZ, MARKET POWER AND PRICE INCREASES FOR BASIC CABLE SERVICE SINCE DEREGULATION (U.S. Dept. of Justice, Antitrust Division, Economic Analysis Group Discussion Paper No. 91-8, Aug. 6, 1991).

after such price increases? If market power enabled cable firms to raise prices in excess of marginal cost, and that market power were exercised only after deregulation, then consumers would presumably be worse off under deregulation. But the finding that market power is being exercised by price-searching firms in the wake of deregulation does not reveal that information. If firms respond to deregulation with higher prices and higher quality, the presence of market power (which may also have been exercised before deregulation) is insufficient information upon which to conclude that consumer welfare has been lowered at the (de)regulatory margin.

Under the assumption that linear demand curves shift parametrically, however, it is clear that penetration rate changes are perfectly correlated with consumer surplus changes. When price and quality rise (or fall) together, the net effect on consumers can be gleaned from whether penetration rises or falls. An increase in penetration indicates that consumers consider the price-quality package preferred in the instance where penetration is rising; the reverse is indicated when penetration declines. In a pragmatic, policymaking sense, we may say that if rate regulation of cable "works," at a minimum it ought to be able to expand the number of households that volunteer to pay for the regulated package above the number that would elect to subscribe to the unregulated package.[17]

The evidence examined here relates to aggregate U.S. data on mean penetration rates for cable systems serving the national market.[18] Those mask some important differences between systems, perhaps, but allow such idiosyncrasies to be smoothed out over large numbers of systems. Although the Kagan data on national penetration rates are available only annually, the trend of the U.S. mean penetration rate (figures 5-6 and 5-7) reveals an interesting pattern, given the regulatory regime switches of the past decade. In 1987, in the wake of deregulation, the U.S. penetration rate did not fall but increased.[19] It appears that the increase was relative to trend, as the growth rate also increased.

---

17. That abstracts from the costs of regulation and the long-run dynamics of regulated markets, factors that tend to lower the value of rate regulation. In other words, that is a necessary, if insufficient, condition to indicate the efficiency of controls.

18. Paul Kagan Associates supplied those data as contract research in March 1994. They are slightly different from what is reported elsewhere by Kagan. The differences in reported data are not important in the deregulation period, as all series exhibit the same trend. There is some disagreement during the data reported during the reregulation period, which we discuss in chapter 7.

19. Alternative sources appear to agree on the general trend. According to an FCC study, average basic cable penetration was 55 percent in 1980, 56.7 percent in 1985, and 61.4 percent in 1990. FLORENCE SETZER & JONATHAN LEVY, BROADCAST TELEVISION IN A

Figure 5-6
U.S. Cable Penetration Rates, 1982–1993

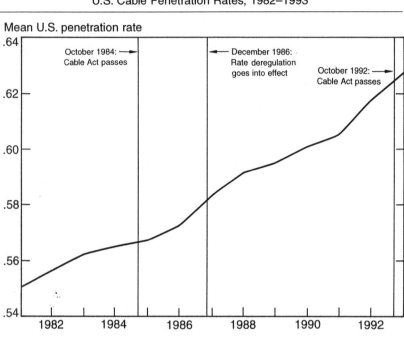

Source: Paul Kagan Associates, contract research (Mar. 1994).

To allow for macroeconomic influences and to test the hypothesis that rate regulation lowers effective prices to consumers, we estimate the following regression equation for the period 1981–1993:

$$\%\Delta PEN_t = \alpha + \beta_1 \%\Delta PERS_t + \beta_2 DEREG + \varepsilon_t,$$

where

$\%\Delta PEN_t$ = percentage change in basic cable penetration rate (= subscribers/homes passed) in year t (annual data from Paul Kagan Associates),

MULTICHANNEL MARKETPLACE (Federal Communications Commission OPP Working Paper No. 26, June 1991), at 68. The GAO finds cable penetration increasing from 55.5 percent as of December 1986 to 57.1 percent as of October 1988. GAO, TELECOMMUNICATIONS: NATIONAL, *supra* note 1.

Figure 5-7
U.S. Cable Penetration Growth, 1982–1993

Percentage change in mean U.S. penetration rates

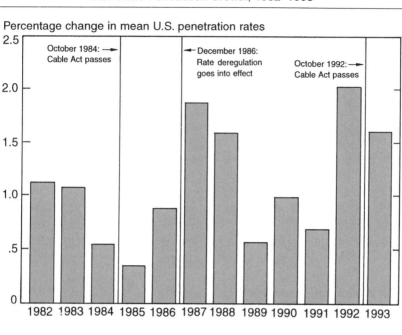

Source: Paul Kagan Associates, contract research (Mar. 1994).

$\%\Delta PERS_t$ = percentage change in real personal consumption during year t (data from the *Economic Report of the President, 1994*, at 286),

$DEREG$ = 1 if 1987, 0 otherwise (equation (1)), and

$DEREG$ = 1 if 1987 or 1988, 0 otherwise (equation (2)).

Using changes in personal consumption expenditures as a macroeconomic variable, that simple model seeks to test whether deregulation lowered the cable penetration growth rate. Because the variables are stated as percentage changes from the previous year's levels, no time trend is included (the constant should pick up a trend growth rate). And because the effect of reregulation may be spread over more than one year, we allow the deregulation dummy to equal one during just 1987 in equation (1), but to equal one during both 1987 and 1988 in equation (2). The estimated coefficients on the dummy should measure penetration changes temporally cor-

Table 5-6
Cable Penetration Regressions

Variable/ Statistic	Equation (1) (Deregulation = 1987)	Equation (2) (Deregulation = 1987–1988)
Constant	.60616 (2.865)[a]	.58725 (3.221)[b]
Personal consumption coefficient	.073279 (1.230)	.057528 (1.113)
Dereg. dummy coefficient	1.0165 (2.265)[a]	.93002 (3.232)[b]
Degrees of freedom	10	10
R^2	.4147	.5668

Note: *t*-statistics in parentheses.

a. Significant at .05.

b. Significant at .01.

related with deregulation and not accounted for by changes in personal consumption.

As summarized in table 5-6, the regression results imply that output restriction did not accompany price decontrol in the cable television market. In fact, that measure of output responds *positively* to deregulation at the 95 percent confidence level (when 1987 is set as the deregulation period) or 99 percent confidence level (when 1987–1988 is the relevant period). The deregulation of cable rates does not appear to result in a restriction of output; while cable rates clearly rose (see price data above), programming quality, service quality, or both rose sufficiently to more than offset such rate increases so households were more, not less, likely to subscribe.

Another way to examine the output of basic cable television service is to focus on the basic programming channels themselves. If output is being contracted because of the exercise of market power, the coverage (or subscribership) of the major cable program services carried on the basic tier should decline. Data are available for the subscribership of the top ten cable programming services[20] upon deregulation, and they strongly support the hypothesis that decontrol resulted in an expansion of output.

---

20. That refers to the number of households to which a given cable network, such as MTV or C-SPAN, is distributed.

Table 5-7
Subscribership Changes in Top Ten Basic Cable Networks, 1985–1987

Network	Began	Subscribers (millions)			Percentage Change	
		8/85	8/86	8/87	1985–1986	1986–1987
ESPN	9/79	36.50	37.60	43.40	3.0	15.4
WTBS	12/76	35.20	36.94	41.95	4.9	13.6
CNN	6/80	33.50	34.36	41.08	2.6	19.6
USA	4/80	31.00	32.00	39.00	3.2	21.9
CBN	4/77	29.70	30.92	36.71	4.1	18.7
MTV	8/81	28.10	30.70	35.80	9.3	16.6
TNN	3/83	23.80	26.80	34.60	12.6	29.1
Nick	4/79	25.90	29.00	34.20	12.0	17.9
Lifetime	1/84	26.20	24.90	33.25	(5.0)	33.5
C-SPAN1	3/79	21.50	22.25	31.50	3.5	41.6
Weather	5/82	19.20	20.60	28.15	7.3	36.7
CNN-HN	12/81	17.20	19.76	27.09	14.9	37.1
Average		27.32	28.82	35.56	5.5	23.4

Source: Paul Kagan Associates, *Cable TV Investor,* Sept. 28, 1987, p. 2.

Cable network subscriber growth appears to take off during the first year of deregulation, growing on average by 23.4 percent, as compared with growth of just 5.5 percent during the final year of rate regulation (see table 5-7). New cable construction was slowing over that period, and overall economic growth was fairly steady. Therefore, the cause of that spurt in cable network subscribership is not likely to be associated with macroeconomic changes or nonregulatory structural events within the cable industry. Because the increase in cable network growth far exceeds the increases in cable penetration, it appears that systems were aggressively adding new programming immediately after deregulation. The industry view of that phenomenon was bluntly stated by the article in *Cable TV Investor* headlined: "Surprise: Rate Dereg Could Mean *Higher* Penetration." The article succinctly summed up what seemed to be occurring: "The big fear at the start of the year was that deregulated rate increases might meet a consumer backlash. The real story may be that the public perceives the new marketing packages as more for their money, and is signing on."[21]

---

21. *Surprise: Rate Dereg Could Mean* Higher *Penetration*, CABLE TV INVESTOR, Sept. 28, 1987, at 2.

In addition to rate deregulation, there was a shift away from marginal broadcast signals toward more highly valued cable programming after the federal courts tossed out "must-carry" rules as unconstitutional in 1985. Looking at per-channel costs alone may thus hide the fact that program quality was rising on a per-channel basis.

CABLE OPERATOR CASH FLOWS

The purpose of rate regulation is to lower the monopoly markup, and successful controls therefore imply that price-cost margins are squeezed. Financially, that in turn means that operating ratios are substantially affected. In the case of cable television, with about 55 percent of cable revenues going to operating costs (exclusive of depreciation, amortization, taxes, or interest), the cash flow margin is about 45 percent. If deregulation leads to a price fly-up with no change in operating costs, price increases should lead to dramatic increases in cash flows per subscriber and (somewhat less dramatically) in cash flow margins. For instance, a 10 percent price increase resulting from deregulation would increase the cash flow per subscriber by 22.2 percent and would increase the cash flow margin by 11.1 percent.[22]

It should be noted that the squeezing of price-cost margins is a necessary but insufficient indicator for successful rate regulation. In that rate regulation may serve to enforce various transfer schemes, such controls may well raise costs, thereby reducing margins without lowering prices. Similarly, if system operators are deterred from investing in higher-quality networks or programming, even at lower prices and operating margins consumers may not benefit.

Table 5-8 and figures 5-8 and 5-9 show cash flow data for major cable operators, a group of firms serving about half of total U.S. cable subscribers.[23] During the 1984–1992 period, the cable industry experienced substantial growth both in cash flow and in the cash flow margin, which rose from about 33 percent to 46 percent. Obviously, revenues were rising faster than operating expenses over the period. Yet it is also true that variable

---

22. That assumes that operating costs per subscriber do not change. Hence, for every one dollar of revenue, a 10 percent price increase causes operating profits to increase from forty-five cents to fifty-five cents (22.2 percent) and the cash flow margin to increase from 45 percent to 50 percent (11.1 percent).

23. The number of firms included in the Kagan data varies from year to year but usually includes about fifteen MSOs (multiple system operators), all of which are publicly held.

Table 5-8
Selected Cable Data from Company Reports, 1984–1994

Year	N	Subscribers per Homes Passed	Revenue per Subscriber ($)	Cash Flow per Subscriber ($)	Cash Flow Percentage	Costs per Subscriber ($)
1984	.50	.558	242.47	80.15	33.1	162.32
1985	.53	.556	261.68	97.93	37.4	163.75
1986	.54	.570	254.41	98.73	38.8	155.68
1987	.48	.574	289.92	118.63	40.9	171.29
1988	.56	.589	297.13	127.13	42.8	170.00
1989	.56	.583	309.40	132.57	42.8	176.83
1990	.48	.597	356.19	144.98	40.7	211.21
1991	.48	.604	363.32	163.54	45.0	199.78
1992	.49	.582	371.75	171.29	46.1	200.46
1993	.50	.608	383.34	179.82	46.1	203.52
1994	.52	.602	377.02	170.86	45.5	206.16

Note: N = proportion of total U.S. subscribers served by MSOs in sample.

Source: Paul Kagan Associates, *Cable TV Financial Databook* (1985–1994).

costs were rising as well, an indication that quality enhancement was taking place.[24]

What is most striking about those data, perhaps, is that deregulation does not appear to have had anywhere near the effect on cash flow margins that the press and scholarly observers expected. Should real prices have increased 36.5 percent over four and a half years of deregulation, as the 1991 GAO survey was interpreted as showing, the implied increase in cash flow margins, 1986–1991, would have been about 42 percent.[25] Not only

---

24. Increased costs could also reflect higher rents for television actors or program owners, of course. Because there is free entry into that sector, and because cable systems face no capacity constraints similar to those imposed on broadcasting markets, that appears unlikely as an explanation of the entire increase in programming costs. Conversely, the rise in quality-related expenditures could be rising faster than variable costs in aggregate, as rate deregulation indirectly lowered operator cross-subsidies for non-remunerative services.

25. Take one dollar of revenue and add $.365 due to the deregulation price fly-up. If operating costs are constant at 1986 levels, then variable costs amount to $0.612. The

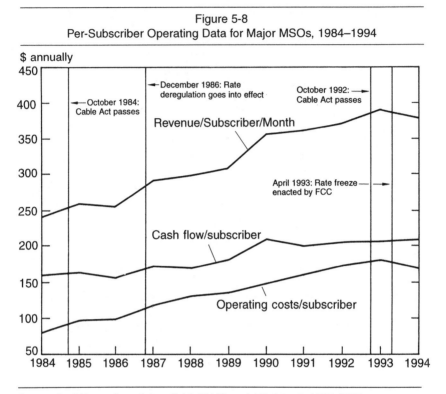

Figure 5-8
Per-Subscriber Operating Data for Major MSOs, 1984–1994

Source: Paul Kagan Associates, *Cable TV Financial Databook,* 1985–1995.

was the increase less than half as large (16 percent), but the rise clearly began before decontrol. Moreover, the cash flow margin itself would have jumped from 39 percent to 55 percent. Quite similar magnitudes of change are implied by Zupan's estimate of a 34 percent price decline attributable to rate regulation.[26] The corporate data do not suggest such dramatic rate effects, but do support the view that both prices and costs were generally increasing over time. That is consistent with the hypothesis that quality increased after deregulation and that we cannot determine the effect of deregulation on consumers solely by examining price data.

---

price increase then increases the cash flow margin from .388 to .552, for an increase of about 42 percent.

26. Mark A. Zupan, *The Efficacy of Franchise Bidding Schemes in the Case of Cable Television: Some Systematic Evidence,* 32 J.L. & Econ. 401 (1989).

Figure 5-9
Cash Flow Ratio, 1984–1994

Cash flow as percentage of cable revenues

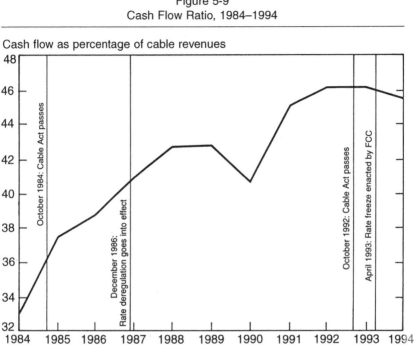

Source: Paul Kagan Associates, *Cable TV Financial Databook*, 1985–1995.

DETIERING

A predicted result of rate regulation is observed in the creation and elimination of tiering schemes. Under the price regulations imposed by local governments, firms were often able to shift desirable channels off the regulated package and into unregulated "expanded basic." When decontrol came, industry analysts instantly proclaimed a shift away from tiering.[27] "Expanded basic" subscribership reached a peak in 1986 with 6.6 million subscribers, declining to 3.5 million subscribers in 1989, and then rising rapidly with

---

27. Paul Kagan wrote: "Expanded basic, which was originally intended to circumvent basic rate restrictions, will be a casualty of deregulation." PAUL KAGAN ASSOCIATES, CABLE TV FINANCIAL DATABOOK, June 1987, at 10.

the threat of reregulation to 7.1 million in 1990 and 13.8 million in 1992 (before jumping, in the wake of reregulation, to 24.6 million in 1993).[28]

The same pattern emerges in the GAO data: tiering declines during deregulation, and seemingly rebounds in preparation for reregulation. In table 5-1 cable systems can be seen to eliminate expanded basic in the 1986–1989 period, during which the percentage of systems offering more than one tier falls from 25.7 percent to 16.6 percent. A turnabout occurs between 1989 and 1991, when the number of systems offering more than one tier climbs to 41.4 percent. The 1991 GAO analysis clearly ties that to an industry vamp up for reregulation:

> The results of our most recent survey indicate that there was a sizable decrease in the number of systems offering only one tier of service. . . .
>   Some of the legislative proposals introduced in 1990 would have generally restricted rate regulation to only the lowest priced basic service.[29]

It becomes clear that what constitutes the cable television package can be changed in multiple dimensions and that the package is elastic with respect to the regulatory regime. During the period in which Congress considered reregulation, tales of retiering strategies were legion. In his June 1990 summary, Paul Kagan spoke of "continued [basic] rate-increasing (to stay one step ahead of whatever bill might emerge) and a resurgence of tiering (for the same reason)."[30] The congressional debate over reregulation also contains repeated references to the problem of retiering. The Senate report on 1990 rate control legislation, for example, warned against allowing "cable operators to use monopolistic conditions triggering regulation to retier programming to avoid regulatory scrutiny."[31] Several members of the House and Senate raised the retiering issue in debate over the 1992 Cable Act, as well.

The cable trade press interpreted the adjustment to a deregulated environment in 1987 in terms that generally fit the theory. The cable industry, expanding its efforts along the newly deregulated margins, shifted its marketing practices dramatically. Paul Kagan summarizes:

> Rate deregulation's inauguration Jan. 1 [*sic*] has demonstrated just how undervalued basic cable service has been. Operators took the opportunity to

---

28. Those data are for the top fifty MSOs. PAUL KAGAN ASSOCIATES, CABLE TV INVESTOR, Feb. 12, 1993, at 5.

29. GAO, TELECOMMUNICATIONS: 1991, *supra* note 1, at 6.

30. PAUL KAGAN ASSOCIATES, CABLE TV FINANCIAL DATABOOK, June 1990, at 6.

31. SENATE COMMITTEE ON COMMERCE, SCIENCE, AND TRANSPORTATION, REPORT ON S. 1880, THE CABLE TELEVISION CONSUMER PROTECTION ACT OF 1990 (July 19, 1990), at 61.

repackage and remarket services by emphasizing basic's value and cutting pay prices. Despite double-digit basic price hikes in early 1987, the industry found little if any price resistance from subscribers. New services and original programming are easing the transition to higher rates and have attracted new subscribers.

Expanded basic, which was originally intended to circumvent basic rate restrictions, will be a casualty of deregulation. Already operators are shifting expanded basic into the basic package as price hikes are administered. The recent upturn in pay TV subscriptions indicates the pay TV business may have stabilized. Programmers have cut prices and differentiated product to attract new subscribers, but we have yet to see evidence that the industry can again market multi-pay [homes subscribing to more than one premium channel] successfully.

As a result, our new 10-year projections for the industry call for a large portion of pay TV revenue to be replaced by new basic revenue.[32]

When basic cable is deregulated, operators shift sales efforts to enlarged, higher-quality, higher-priced basic cable. That implies that under rate regulation, operators are more likely to earmark marketing expenditures for premium channels. Such a view is buttressed by the pattern in figure 5-10, which shows the proportion of cable operator revenues derived from three broad categories: basic, premium, and other.

When content controls were lifted on cable around 1980, operators scrambled for desirable programming to sell subscribers. The most easily tapped new product involved recently released feature films, which were quickly packaged by HBO (the first cable satellite network, launched in 1975) and other premium channels. In addition, basic cable packages were generally rate regulated by local governments, and charging for higher-quality basic programming incurred regulatory costs and risks. Pay revenue thus rose quickly relative to basic revenue in the early 1980s. With deregulation, cable systems found that basic cable was relatively more profitable, and they targeted their efforts accordingly. Basic revenue, just 46 percent of total revenue in 1984, rose to 57 percent by 1990. Pay cable dropped from 43 to 29 over the same period.

---

32. PAUL KAGAN ASSOCIATES, CABLE TV FINANCIAL DATABOOK, June 1987, at 10. In noting that basic penetration was increasing rather than declining under rate deregulation in 1987, *Cable TV Investor* commented that "[o]ne explanation [of the increase in penetration] could be the stepped-up marketing and promotion employed by operators in conjunction with this year's rate increases. Consumer friendliness toward basic-oriented, rather than pay-oriented, packaging could go a long way toward justifying some of the assumptions in recent system acquisitions." *Surprise: Rate Dereg, supra* note 21.

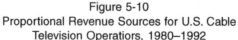

Figure 5-10
Proportional Revenue Sources for U.S. Cable
Television Operatiors, 1980–1992

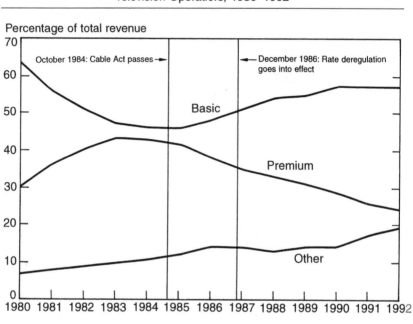

Source: NCTA, *Cable Television Developments* (Oct. 1993), p. 8-A.

An alternative explanation for those trends could be that as the de-regulated price flew up to monopoly levels, cable systems would naturally collect relatively more revenue from the monopoly services—the assumption being that premium channels are more competitive with videocassette rentals, movie theaters, and other entertainment media. Yet that explanation would imply that increasing price-cost margins for basic service was forcing a restriction in subscriber access to basic cable networks. Instead, the data indicate that more and more cable networks were being successfully launched. Indeed, cable penetration of the top ten basic networks increased dramatically following deregulation (see table 5-7). Pay subscribership, by contrast, was relatively stagnant throughout the deregulation period. Hence, it appears that demand shifts, likely driven by quality changes and redirected marketing efforts of cable operators, drove the changes in the revenue mix.

QUALITY CHANGES AFTER DEREGULATION

It is clear that the number of channels offered on the typical basic cable package rose significantly after deregulation. A 30 percent increase in the size of the package, as measured in channels, occurred between December 1986 and April 1991, the time frame of the final GAO report. The price-per-channel increase amounts to just 20.5 percent over the fifty-two-month interval: only slightly above the 17.8 percent inflation rate.[33] It is noteworthy that the number of satellite programming networks available to cable operators nearly doubled—from forty-three to seventy-eight—between 1983 and 1988 (see table 5-9), an impressive expansion of the video programming sector that appears to be driven by heightened demand after deregulation.

The pattern revealed in table 5-9 is informative. Two deregulations appear to boost cable network formation. The first, eliminating controls on programming in a late-1970s deregulation by the FCC,[34] leads to a boom in 1978–1981 (when national satellite video networks increased from eight to thirty-eight); the second, federal rate decontrol, promotes a boom in 1983–1988 (when basic networks, specifically, jumped from thirty-one to sixty-one). Although cable's growing acceptance and market share are not solely related to rate deregulation, the fact that (unregulated) premium services contracted from eleven to eight over the latter period suggests that rate deregulation is at least an important driver.

Further evidence suggests that quality improved after deregulation not just in numbers of channels but in the desirability of the programming on existing channels. Cable system expenditures for basic cable programming amounted (nationally) to $255 million annually ($8.12 per subscriber) before deregulation in 1983; by 1992 operators were spending nearly $2 billion (or $35.14 per subscriber) on those key inputs. (See table 5-10.) On a per-subscriber basis, that constituted a nominal increase in program costs of 333 percent and a real increase of about 209 percent.

Quality may be more definitively evaluated by examining viewing shares. That alternative measure of output takes into account inframarginal consumers who continue to subscribe to cable at higher prices. Viewing shares within cable households, in fact, largely abstract from changes in the

---

33. We use the same deflator used by the GAO in determining that a nominal 60.8 percent rate increase was equal to a 36.5 percent real increase.

34. In the 1960s the FCC had enacted anticable rules to protect television broadcasters from competition. Stanley M. Besen & Robert W. Crandall, *The Deregulation of Cable Television*, 44 LAW & CONTEMP. PROBS. 77 (1981).

Table 5-9
Cable Network Growth, 1976–1994

Year	Basic[a]	Premium	Pay-per-View	Other	Total Networks
1976	2	2	0	0	4
1977	3	2	0	0	5
1978	6	2	0	0	8
1979	14	5	0	0	19
1980	19	8	0	1	28
1981	29	9	0	0	38
1982	30	11	1	0	42
1983	31	11	1	0	43
1984	37	10	1	0	48
1985	41	9	4	2	56
1986	54	8	4	2	68
1987	59	9	5	1	76
1988	61	8	5	1	78
1989	60	5	4	3	76
1990	61	5	5	4	79
1991	61	7	4	4	82
1992	64	8	4	4	87
1993	80	9	7	5	101
1994	94	20	8	6	128

a. Includes superstations and networks distributed at no charge to cable operator.

Source: National Cable Television Association, *Cable Television Developments,* Spring 1995, p. 7.

size of the cable television subscriber universe. Those data (table 5-11) reveal that while the all-day average viewing share of basic cable networks was seventeen in 1983–1984, the last season before passage of the 1984 Cable Act, the share more than doubled, to thirty-five, by 1990–1991.[35] Whether that constituted an improvement from trend is difficult to discern; Paul Kagan Associates provides audience ratings for cable networks only back to 1983.

35. "Share" refers to that percentage of television households tuned to a particular type of programming. Because some homes tune in to multiple television sets simultaneously, shares generally sum to slightly more than 100.

Table 5-10
Cable Program Expenditures, 1980–1993

Year	Basic Program Spending ($ millions)	Percentage Change Year on-Year	Spending per Sub-scriber ($/yr.)	Percentage Change Year-on-Year
1980	234[a]	NA	NA	NA
1981	NA	NA	NA	NA
1982	NA	NA	NA	NA
1983	255	NA	8.12	NA
1984	325	27	9.50	6
1985	368	13	10.04	7
1986	496	35	12.50	28
1987	572	15	13.43	7
1988	739	29	16.17	20
1989	1,006	36	20.41	26
1990	1,410	40	27.27	34
1991	1,720	22	32.15	18
1992	1,940	13	35.14	9
1993	2,189	13	38.47	10

Note: NA = not available.

a. National Cable Television Association, "Growth of Cable Television," fact sheet distributed at June 1993 annual convention in San Francisco.

Source: Paul Kagan Associates, *Marketing New Media,* Mar. 15, 1993, p. 1, augmented and updated by research request to Kim Weill at Paul Kagan Associates (February 1994).

If viewing shares are seen as a direct measure of output, it may be more instructive to look at consumer choices within the universe of all U.S. (not just cable) television households (see table 5-12). Here, the increase from before deregulation to after is from a nine share to a twenty-four (1983–1984 to 1991–1992). Although the upward trend in homes passed would tend to increase cable viewership during that period even in the absence of rate deregulation, it is striking that despite higher nominal prices, basic cable nearly tripled its share of television viewing time in the wake of deregulation. Broadcast network affiliate viewing shares were in virtual free fall during that period, and it is easy to ascribe the declining popularity of broadcasting to the increasing attractiveness of cable. Indeed, broadcasting

Table 5-11
Broadcast and Cable Viewing Shares in U.S. Cable Television Households

Category	1983–1984	1984–1985	1985–1986	1986–1987	1990–1991	1991–1992
Broadcast network affiliates	58	56	56	53	46	47
Independent broadcast stations	17	17	17	17	17	16
Public stations	3	3	3	3	2	3
Basic cable networks	17	19	19	23	35	35
Pay services	11	11	10	10	9	8

Source: Nielsen ratings reported in National Cable Television Association, *Cable Television Developments,* June 1993, p. 5A.

interests have repeatedly done so.[36] That program substitution clearly suggests output expansion by cable, offering consumers alternatives more attractive than those previously enjoyed, and viewer ratings growth appears to be at least partly attributable to rate deregulation. Certainly, the reverse hypothesis, that rate deregulation made consumers worse off, enjoys no support from the viewing share numbers.

THE GAO'S OWN CAVEAT

The three GAO reports on cable[37] following federal decontrol clearly supplied the factual basis for the argument for reregulation in congressional debate and the popular press. The ironic aspect of those surveys is that, read analytically, their findings do not support the claim that rate regulation was effective (before deregulation) in suppressing quality-adjusted cable

36. KEN AULETTA, THREE BLIND MICE (Random House 1991).

37. GAO, TELECOMMUNICATIONS: NATIONAL, *supra* note 1; GAO, TELECOMMUNICATIONS: FOLLOW-UP, *supra* note 1; GAO, TELECOMMUNICATIONS: 1991, *supra* note 1.

Table 5-12
Broadcast and Cable Viewing Shares in All U.S. Television Households

Category	1983–1984	1984–1985	1985–1986	1986–1987	1990–1991	1991–1992
Broadcast network affiliates	69	66	66	64	61	54
Independent broadcast stations	19	18	18	20	20	20
Public stations	3	3	3	4	4	3
Basic cable networks	9	11	11	13	15	24
Pay services	5	6	5	4	7	6

Source: Nielsen ratings reported in National Cable Television Association, *Cable Television Developments,* June 1993, p. 5A.

rates. In fact, they imply the reverse and are entirely consistent with our description of cable rate regulation detailed above.

We have already seen that cable rates for deregulated systems rose at just about the same pace as rates for systems that were already unregulated in December 1986. The GAO surveys also dutifully reported the expansion of cable output even as prices rose under deregulation. In its 1989 report, for instance, the GAO found that the rates for the most popular basic cable tier rose 19 percent faster than inflation in the first twenty-three months of deregulation, while penetration was rising from 55.5 percent to 57.1 percent (see table 5-13). Price increases did not result in output restriction.

While the three GAO cable rate surveys were helping to fuel the drive for reregulation of the sector, the GAO analysts were themselves careful to observe that the nominal price increases reported for basic cable packages determined neither the existence of market power nor, given supracompetitive pricing, the correct public policy remedy. For instance, the 1990 report stated:

> GAO's survey showed, in the 3 years since deregulation, average increases
> of 39 and 43 percent, respectively for the most popular and the lowest priced

Table 5-13
1989 GAO Cable System Survey

	Dec. 1, 1986	Oct. 31, 1988	Percentage Change
Most popular tier price (all systems)	$11.70	$14.77	26
			19[a]
Price in newly deregulated systems	$11.58	$14.76	27.4
Price in systems already deregulated in 1986	$12.03	$14.90	23.8
Number of channels (all systems)	26.6	32.1	20.7
Price per channel (all systems)	$.44	$.46	−1.4[a]
HBO price	$10.46	$10.31	−7.0[a]
Price for a package of two premium channels	$18.64	$17.82	−9.8[a]
Revenue per subscriber	$21.58	$24.68	7.9[a]
Penetration	.56	.57	2.8
Percentage of systems offering just one tier	76.5	84.1	

a. Inflation-adjusted by the GNP implicit price deflator.

basic services, and a 21-percent increase in revenue per subscriber. During this period, cable subscriptions increased by 22 percent, and system penetration (total number of subscribers divided by the number of homes having access to cable) increased from 56 to 58 percent. The lack of close substitutes to which consumers can switch (which gives cable operators market power) is often cited as a reason that the subscriber base has not decreased despite substantial rate increases, although there are other potential explanations, such as improved cable programming.[38]

---

38. GAO, TELECOMMUNICATIONS: FOLLOW-UP, *supra* note 1, at 3. The report's poor analytics regarding monopoly pricing and "close substitutes" should be corrected: market power unleashed by decontrol will result in fewer unit sales, because the elasticity of demand is generally conceded to be above zero and, in fact, above unity (in absolute-value terms).

The GAO report puts the price increases in their proper context: what did they do to output? The picture that emerges from the GAO surveys is that cable operators responded to free-market pricing by consolidating packages, adding basic channels, upgrading basic program quality (spending more per channel), marketing basic service more aggressively, and dropping premium rates. The fact that output appears to rise during the deregulation period is evidence that the price increases were driven—and matched—by quality improvements. It is curious that only the GAO data on naked price increases made news, while the consumer welfare framework was excluded from the public debate.

6

The Economic Effects of Reregulation, 1993–1994

THE REREGULATION of the cable television industry has had a power-ful impact, in many ways comparable to that of deregulation. Since the Cable Television Consumer Protection and Competition Act was passed over President Bush's veto on October 5, 1992, the federal government and cable operators have been partners in a continuing regulatory dance. The economic effects are interesting but not obvious. Public debate, virtually ignoring the actual results of reregulation, has focused on regulatory pro-nouncements and the self-interested analyses of government regulators and the regulated industry.[1]

Yet the price and output effects of reregulation are now fairly well established. A substantial effort to regulate cable rates has been made, and both basic rates and revenue per subscriber appear to have been seriously constrained in 1993–1994. The most important questions revolve around how the rate controls affected consumers: Did quality suffer? Did subscribership and viewership increase? In short, how did customers re-spond to the price reductions imposed by the Cable Act of 1992?

---

1. According to a well-placed agency insider, the FCC has twice denied formal staff requests to conduct a study of the effects of reregulation on consumers. Interestingly, the public is skeptical that the aims of the 1992 Cable Act have been fulfilled. In a 1995 poll commissioned by *Cable World,* U.S. citizens answered this question: "Do you think the 1992 Cable Act in fact accomplished what it was supposed to?" The responses: yes, 18 percent; no, 62 percent. Thomas P. Southwick, *Is Cable Ready to Compete?* CABLE WORLD, May 18, 1995, at 120.

CABLE RATES UNDER REREGULATION

The False Start, 1993

After the FCC instituted what was billed as a 10 percent rate rollback on September 1, 1993, the press exploded with stories of cable systems that were not reducing, but raising, their rates. That led to a public outcry, and embarrassed legislators quickly reacted by calling the FCC on the carpet. A trade journal headline read: "Markey: Rate Increases Will Prompt Hearings," and key congressmen were reported to be "incensed by press reports that some cable rates would rise despite reregulation."[2]

At that point, both the FCC and the cable industry were being pressed to demonstrate that price controls were being instituted in good faith. The acting chairman of the commission, James Quello, sent a clear signal to the industry, saying: "I think an explanation is in order. Based on our own calculations, overall cable rates will go down. That's the story the cable industry has to get out."[3] The National Cable Television Association was ready to explain that its members had lowered prices and had been losing billions of dollars of revenue since the imposition of the rate regulations. That was a 180-degree reversal of the story the association had nationally advertised before passage of the Cable Act of 1992, when it warned that the measure would raise rates, but it was clear where the industry's interests now lay: unless cable operators appeared to have been hit and hit hard by reregulation, tougher rules would be likely.

It was in that context that the FCC decided to survey the twenty-five largest cable MSOs in an effort to determine how rates had changed between April 1993 (when the rules were announced) and the following September (when the rules were implemented). The results of the survey were confusing, however. Given operators' radical restructuring of basic packages along with substantial shifting of program services to à la carte status, eleven of the twenty-five MSOs responded in a manner that made it impossible for the FCC to determine what had happened to the price charged for a given package of services.[4] The FCC delayed the survey's release, originally scheduled for October 20, 1993, and issued further clarifications in an attempt to account for the changing nature of the basic package. The results were finally released on February 22, 1994 (see tables 6-1 and 6-2).

---

2. Vincente Pasdeloup, *Markey: Rate Increases Will Prompt Hearings,* CABLE WORLD, Sept. 6, 1993, at 1.

3. *Id.* at 36.

4. Vincente Pasdeloup, *Playing by the Numbers: FCC Holds Survey Results,* CABLE WORLD, Oct. 25, 1993, at 1.

Table 6-1
FCC Survey of Regulated Rate Changes, April–September 1993

	April 1993 ($)	September 1993 ($)	Per-centage Change
Non-Cable-Ready Television Households			
(a) Limited basic service + 1 converter + 1 remote	12.81	12.07	−5.8
(b) Expanded basic + 1 converter + 1 remote	25.92	22.93	−11.5
(c) Same as (b) but adjusted for à la carte charges	25.92	24.32	−6.2
(d) Same as (c) with HBO	37.45	36.22	−3.3
(e) Same as (c) but with 2 converters, 2 remotes, 1 A/O	33.14	25.72	−22.4
(f) Same as (e) with HBO	46.32	39.31	−15.1
Cable-Ready Television Households			
(a) Limited basic service + 1 converter + 1 remote	10.91	11.18	2.5
(b) Expanded basic + 1 converter + 1 remote	23.95	22.11	−6.9
(c) Same as (b) but adjusted for à la carte charges	23.75	23.62	−.5
(d) Same as (c) with HBO	36.60	35.94	−1.8
(e) Same as (c) but with 2 converters, 2 remotes, 1 A/O	28.80	24.32	−15.6
(f) Same as (e) with HBO	44.62	38.76	−13.1
Programming Charges			
Limited basic	10.71	10.92	2.0
Expanded basic	23.39	21.70	−7.2
Expanded basic adjusted for à la carte	23.39	23.05	−1.5
Expanded basic adjusted for à la carte and HBO	34.50	34.55	.1
Equipment Charges			
Nonaddressable converters	.66	.65	−1.5
Addressable converters	1.70	2.14	25.9
Remotes	2.08	.23	−88.9
Additional outlets	4.69	.14	−97.0
Prewired installations[a]	38.52	27.89	−27.6
Unwired installations[a]	46.08	42.00	-8.9

a. One-time charge. All other charges are monthly.

Source: FCC (1994, 6A).

Table 6-2
1993 FCC Survey Data: Average Price Declines for Regulated Services

Total U.S. Revenue ($ billion)	April Rate ($)	September Rate ($)	$ Change	% Change
Regulated rev./sub./mo.: systems without à la carte charges	25.33	23.62	−1.71	−6.8
Regulated rev./sub./mo.: systems with à la carte adjustments	26.32	25.34	−.98	−3.7
Mean across all systems	25.61	24.11	−1.50	−5.9

Source: FCC (1994, table 2).

Yet even before the public release date, a cable industry spokesperson was (triumphantly) declaring defeat: "The preliminary survey results show that the FCC's rate-regulation rules have achieved their goal. Regulated rates are lower and consumers are benefiting."[5]

Cable industry spin aside, serious problems were encountered in interpreting those data. First, rate schedules are complex, which is why the commission itself was stymied for months in its survey efforts. Many judgments must be made in deciphering rate changes when the underlying package of services is shifting; in that survey no account is made, for instance, for channels substituted into or out of the basic package.[6] Replacing C-SPAN1 or Discovery with a home shopping network, for example, would not be recorded as a pricing change.

Second, the time frame is extremely problematic. There were widespread reports that cable operators hurriedly raised prices soon after the enactment of the Cable Act in October 1992,[7] and the CPI for cable service suggests that prices did increase rapidly at about that time. Those price changes may have been in anticipation of rate controls, rather than prompted

---

5. *Id.* at 5.

6. Or, most obviously, for changes in quality on a given cable network.

7. "Just 10 weeks after Congress passed a law to grant cable subscribers relief from years of escalating rates, many systems are racing to impose a new round of increases, surcharges and pricing packages before the new law takes effect." Mark Robichaux, *Cable Concerns Are Scrambling to Raise Rates,* WALL ST. J., Dec. 14, 1992, at B1.

by changes in supply or demand. A cable firm that had raised its rates steeply at the end of 1992 might have lowered prices (or kept them constant) during the middle of 1993, even if the firm were unregulated. More generally, then, if prices flattened or even declined during the April to September 1993 period, attributing such changes to reregulation would still be questionable.

Abstracting from all such problems, the survey indicated that the average gain (that is, price reduction) per subscriber was somewhere between 1.8 percent for cable-ready television customers and 3.3 percent for those subscribers with non-cable-ready sets (each subscribing to expanded basic, one converter, one remote, and HBO, adjusted for à la carte network shifting). Still, the survey did not track additional charges for unregulated services, which may have offset even those modest savings. The FCC survey also indicated that whatever savings accrued were skewed toward those customers with multiple outlets—presumably upper-income households.

In any event, the entire survey was suspect for the same reason that public utility commissions do not simply ask a telephone company to map out its average cost curve. The cable firm answering the FCC's questionnaire was essentially responding to an IQ test. It experienced a huge incentive to shade its answers toward showing that its rates had been lowered in response to regulation.[8] One does not need to be particularly astute to figure out the right survey answers when Congressman Ed Markey explicitly threatens to "roll back rates further if cable bills rose Sept. 1."[9]

Given the room for discretion in interpreting rate schedules, firms were surely driven to report those customers' rates in each class that had shown the largest reductions and to avoid troubling data that could be ignored. Moreover, the FCC survey results are contradicted by other industry sources; Paul Kagan Associates' data, for instance, show revenue per subscriber and rate-generated revenue per subscriber increasing in 1993 at about the same rate as they did in 1991 and 1992. Perhaps the most cogent analysis of the operative forces at work was delivered by Nick Allard: "The dirty little secret is that both the FCC and cable operators have the same interest: to prove that the rules work and that rates don't go up."[10]

---

8. "*A regulated firm will use its private information in the way most advantageous to the firm*. . . . Why not simply ask the firm what its average cost curve is (or should be)? One reason is that the firm may lie to regulators." MICHAEL L. KATZ & HARVEY S. ROSEN, MICROECONOMICS 504 (Irwin 1991) (emphasis in original).

9. Pasdeloup, *supra* note 4, at 1, 5.

10. Allard, a partner in the law firm of Latham & Watkins, is a noted telecommunications expert. Vincente Pasdeloup, *Can the FCC Cope?* CABLE WORLD, May 23, 1994, at 172.

So anxious to show rate reductions was the FCC that it touted, on the basis of the operators survey released in February 1994, price cuts of 5.9 percent for the typical cable customer (table 6-2). Not only does that 1993 rate reduction not reveal itself in the annual data now available, but it has been abandoned by the FCC itself. Writing to fellow staff members in December 1994, the Cable Services Bureau conceded: "Rates did not decline in 1993 because operators raised rates in anticipation of regulation."[11] Yet rates clearly did decline after that false start in 1992–1993, as revealed by a variety of price data, to which we now turn.

Price Reductions under Rate Controls

Figure 6-1 shows the CPI–urban cable TV series, deflated by the overall CPI–urban consumer series and extended through May 1995. The shaded area denotes the period between the passage of the 1992 Cable Act and the "bottom" of the observed rate reductions. We noted in chapter 5 that that price series did not reveal any fly-up in rates around the time of cable deregulation, but it is apparent that subscriber charges were knocked below trend by reregulation as of mid-1994. Although a run up in rates does appear in the immediate postact period, presumably an adjustment by firms anticipating future rate rollbacks, the period following September 1993 is marked by a sharp downturn in real rates. Between the high-water mark for rates (April 1993) and the low point (October 1994), nominal cable rates (for the complete package of services received by the typical cable customer) fell by 4.07 percent while the general CPI–urban index was rising 3.82 percent, for a real reduction in rates of 7.60 percent.

Because rates were rising in real terms throughout the previous periods (both under local regulation until year-end 1986 and under federal preemption of rate controls between 1987 and 1992), the extent to which reregulation lowered rates from their long-term trend appears substantial. In the twenty-four months before the enactment of the 1992 Cable Act (September 1990 through September 1992), the typical subscriber bill rose 7.4 percent in real terms. In the two years following the act (October 1992 through October 1994), the average cable subscriber paid 2.1 percent less in real terms.[12] The overall cable bill at the moment rate regulation had its

---

11. FCC, 1 CABLE INDUSTRY TRENDS (Dec. 15, 1994), at 2.

12. From October 1994 through May 1995, real cable rates were once again increasing at about twice the rate of inflation; see the upward-sloping tail in figure 6-1.

Figure 6-1
Real Cable Service Rates under Reregulation, January 1984–May 1995

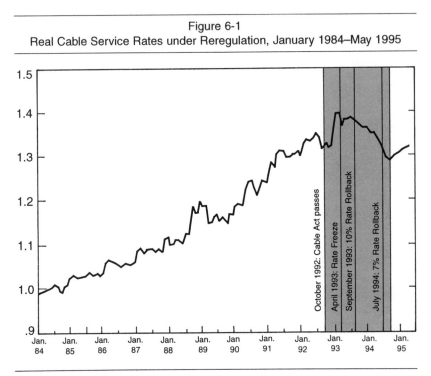

Source: Bureau of Labor Statistics; cable television component of consumer price index had exurban.

tightest constraint was thus about 9.7 percent lower than if the previous trend (established in the two years before Cable Act passage) had continued unabated.

The FCC has heavily publicized its estimates of the price effects ensuing from reregulation. The commission issued one such estimate the very day on which the second round of rate rollbacks was mandated (July 14, 1994).[13] The commission issued the results of a survey of cable operators in large markets, announcing that average basic rates had fallen by 16 percent in connection with the three rollbacks instituted.[14] Yet the commission

---

13. The actual effective date of the second rollback was May 15, 1994, but the commission allowed operators an extension until July 14 if necessary. Most operators apparently took the extension. Kate Maddox, *FCC: Cable Rate Rules Successful,* ELECTRONIC MEDIA, July 15, 1994, at 3.

14. *Id.* That includes the April 1993 "freeze," which rolled back rates to the level prevailing as of September 30, 1992, plus inflation.

has chosen to promote a different rate-rollback calculation since the beginning of 1995. That estimate of the gains ensuing from rate regulation forms the basis for claims that as of late 1994 and early 1995 subscriber benefits totaled about $2.8 billion.[15] That figure is derived from two monthly rate cuts identified by the commission: a $1.10 reduction in "the average rate charged for basic and extended basic services"[16] and "average equipment rates [that] declined from a pre-regulation monthly rate of $3.85 per subscriber to $2.41."[17] Because a gain of $2.54 per subscriber per month takes about nineteen months to total $2.8 billion with a U.S. cable subscriber base of fifty-seven million to fifty-nine million homes, the annualized savings are estimated at about $1.77 billion, and the reduction in the typical cable consumer's bill is about 8.7 percent from the 1993 average of $29.35.[18]

Both the FCC-estimated rate reductions and the CPI decrease from trend estimate given above are roughly comparable to what appears to be the decline in trend in the Kagan rate series. (See table 6-3.) If the annual increases in revenue per subscriber per month (RSM) over the 1990–1993 period (4.6 percent) had continued through 1994, the RSM would have risen to $35.29. Instead, the 1994 RSM figure stood at $32.49, implying a decrease of 7.9 percent from trend (Kagan 1).[19] If, alternatively, rate-based revenue per subscriber is used and the 1990–1993 trend extrapolated through 1994, the reduction from trend appears to be about 8.1 percent (Kagan 2).

As a whole, the plausible cable rate reduction estimates are grouped in the 8–10 percent range, an impressive performance on two grounds. First, there appears to be no net price reduction due to rate controls in 1993. Second, the rate reductions of 8–10 percent of the typical subscriber's bill were achieved via controls on basic cable and equipment charges constituting only about two-thirds of total charges. That suggests a fairly tight constraint on the regulated portion of revenues.

---

15. FCC, *supra* note 11, at 2. *See also* Testimony of Reed Hundt, Chairman, Federal Communications Commission, on FY 1996 Budget Estimates Before the Subcommittee on Commerce, Justice, and State, the Judiciary and Related Agencies, Committee on Appropriations. U.S. House of Representatives, Mar. 22, 1995.

16. FCC, *supra* note 11, at 2.

17. *Id.*

18. That is the Kagan estimate of "rate-based-revenue per subscriber," which is below the 1993 revenue-per-subscriber mean of $33.74. CABLE TV INVESTOR, June 30, 1995, at 5. The cable customer is typically paying only the rate-based portion of the bill; the residual accrues from advertising, telephone bypass charges, and so on. If the total revenue figure is used, the proportionate reduction, as calculated by the FCC's $2.54 price-cut estimate, is 7.5 percent.

19. See table 5-4.

Table 6-3
Estimated 1994 Rate Reductions under Regulation

Data Source	Method	Percentage Reduction
CPI	Extrapolate Oct. 1990–Oct. 1992 percentage rate increases to Oct. 1994	9.7
FCC 1	Survey of cable operators in large cities— basic only	16.0
FCC 2	Cable operator survey shows $2.54 monthly reduction in typical customer's bill	8.7
Kagan 1	Extrapolate 1990–1993 increases in rev./sub./ mo. to 1994	7.9
Kagan 2	Extrapolate 1990–1993 increases in rate-based rev./sub./mo. to 1994	8.1

Sources: Bureau of Labor Statistics, cable-urban consumer price index and overall consumer price index (urban); FCC, *Cable Industry Trends,* vol. 1, no. 1 (Dec. 15, 1994), p. 2; Paul Kagan Associates, *Cable TV Investor,* June 30, 1995, p. 5.

The evidence suggests that the first of the two criteria necessary for successful, proconsumer price controls—price ceilings that bind on market prices—was met. Our attention now turns to whether controls were sufficient to lower effective, quality-adjusted prices, prompting sales to rise. Did consumers respond to lower nominal prices by increasing purchases, or did quality depreciation offset the effect of lower prices?

SUBSCRIBERSHIP AND PENETRATION

One can evaluate the consumer response to the rate cuts produced by reregulation by examining penetration and subscribership data. Four major series are available from the two leading sources of market research in the sector, A. C. Nielsen and Paul Kagan Associates, each of which produces two different estimates of cable system subscriber growth rates over time. The Nielsen data sets are likely to be the more reliable of the two sources, for reasons explained below, and they have the added advantage of generally agreeing with each other. The Kagan series offer a more complicated picture. It may be clarified, however, by examining two other sources of industry information: a series recording the growth in basic cable networks[20] and a February 1994 FCC survey showing the extent of retiering under rate regulation. Because the Nielsen data present such a compelling portrait of the effects of reregulation, the question will be asked, Should the mixed Kagan results cause us to reevaluate what the Nielsen numbers tell us? We believe the answer is clearly no, in that the Kagan data, carefully considered, can best be seen as reinforcing the verdict rendered by the strong trends in both Nielsen series.

The A. C. Nielsen Data

Although there are differences between the two Nielsen series that track cable subscriber growth owing to the way in which the respective surveys are created, the trend they exhibit in the period of reregulation is symmetric. More important, perhaps, is the fact that the manner in which the rival series are created yields a robustness to the procedure, particularly given that one of the data sets is most fastidiously maintained by the data-gathering organization.

The first Nielsen series is the so-called official universe estimate, in which information is gathered from cable operators and supplemented by local surveys. Those data are tabulated for February, May, July, and November of each year. Figure 6-2 shows data for February 1985 through November 1994. The fact that the series runs from rate regulation into deregulation (December 1986) and back into reregulation (October 1992) allows us to divide penetration growth into five two-year periods (except for the first period, for which only seven "quarters"[21] are available). The regulation-era growth of 3.5 percent (annualized) rises to growth rates of 5.7 and 5.1 percent in the deregulation period. Growth then falls to 2.6 percent in the late-deregulation period, likely the result of recession, disincentives created by the threat of reregulation, or both, and continues to fall in the post–Cable Act period to an anemic 1.2 percent.

One could argue that the Nielsen numbers, which define penetration as the percentage of all television households subscribing to cable, are bi-

---

20. Cable network subscribership refers to the number of households that receive a particular programming service such as CNN or ESPN. In that sense, it is possible to talk about the subscribership of cable networks, even though the customer subscribes indirectly (that is, through a local cable television system or other multichannel video supplier).

21. The Nielsen reporting periods are not precise quarters, of course. Hence, the first period examined here goes from February 1985 to November 1986.

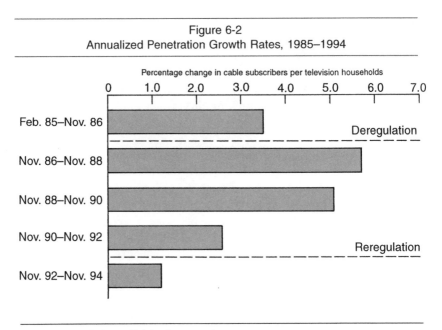

Figure 6-2
Annualized Penetration Growth Rates, 1985–1994

Source: A. C. Nielsen official universe estimates.

ased in failing to account for changes in homes passed. That is, when cable operators build less cable plant, growth in penetration (as defined by Nielsen) will automatically slow. It may be reasonable to believe that regulation is itself having an impact on investment in cable plant, with the threat of rate controls' lowering incentives to build out systems, but it is not unreasonable to believe that exogenous factors—for instance, the increasing cost of cable extensions as saturation approaches 100 percent or macroeconomic fluctuations—also have an impact on the annual change in homes passed. Fully adjusting for the change in homes passed (dividing the penetration growth rate by the same-year homes-passed growth rate), however, does not produce an increase in growth in the reregulation period (see figure 6-3).

The other Nielsen series, the A. C. Nielsen people meter, is collected from a panel of about 4,000 households whose television viewing patterns are monitored continuously by Nielsen computers. The series is, therefore, very clean,[22] although unfortunately it is not available before 1989 to demonstrate subscribership changes associated with deregulation.

---

22. Because there are over 11,000 U.S. cable systems, each with its own method of counting subscribers, cable operator subscriber data are sometimes difficult to interpret.

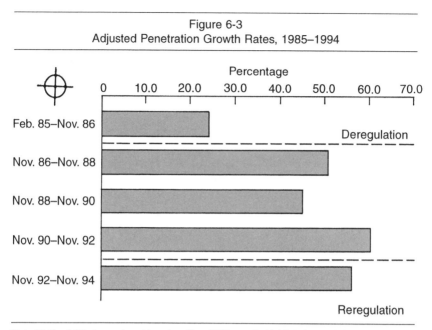

Figure 6-3
Adjusted Penetration Growth Rates, 1985–1994

Note: Ratio of: (% change in cable subscribers/TV households)/(% change in homes passed).
Source: A. C. Nielsen official universe estimates.

The performance of the people meter penetration index is stunning (see figure 6-4). Sharp growth in the pre–Cable Act period gives way to a two-year flat line. The November 1990 to November 1992 growth in penetration is 7.1 percent; the November 1992 to November 1994 growth in penetration is a *negative* 1.4 percent. Some of that 8.4 percent decline from trend can be explained by the drop in growth in homes passed. According to Kagan data, the 1990–1992 homes-passed growth of 4.3 percent fell to just 1.1 percent in the 1992–1994 period. Some of the diminution in that variable was likely to be causally related to the price controls scheme levied on cable investments; the saturation rate, which hit 93.7 percent in 1991, stalled thereafter (see table 6-4). But let us assume that the homes-passed slowdown was an exogenous factor accounted for wholly by industry maturation. The decline in cable penetration related to non-build-out is still 5

Issues that generate confusion include the question of when "churn" is reported (subscribers who disconnect); how to count bulk-rate subscribers who "sign up" via a landlord or homeowners' association contract; and differentiating between limited basic and full basic subscribers.

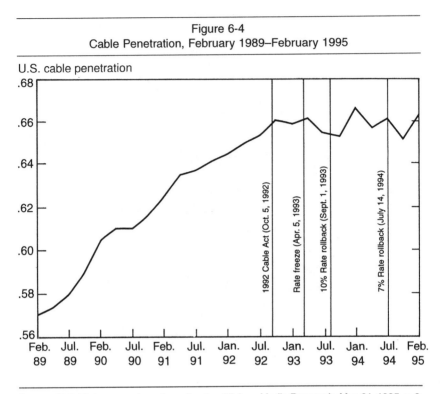

Figure 6-4
Cable Penetration, February 1989–February 1995

Source: A. C. Nielsen people meter estimates, Nielsen Media Research, Mar. 21, 1995, p. 3.

percent according to the people meter time series (the 8.5 percent decline from trend in cable subscribership minus the 3.2 percent drop in homes-passed growth). That finding strongly suggests that cable penetration declined from trend in the reregulation period.

The Kagan Data

The story told by the Kagan data is more complex. The most positive indication that rate regulation is favorable to consumers is found in Paul Kagan Associates subscriber and penetration data as adjusted in June 1995 (see table 6-4). Because the series differs materially from the same data set published earlier[23] and conflicts with alternative Kagan series published cur-

---

23. Obviously, the earlier data sets did not extend so far forward. The series conflict, however, with respect to overlapping periods.

Table 6-4
Cable Television Industry Growth, 1976–1994

Year	Basic Subscribers[a] (millions)	U.S. Households[a] (millions)	U.S. Households Subscribing (%)	National Saturation (homes passed per households) (%)	Homes Passed (millions)	Mean U.S. Penetration (subscribers per homes passed) (%)	Total U.S. Revenue ($ billions)
1976	11.8	72.9	16.2	31.2	23.1	51.1	0.932
1977	12.6	74.1	17.0	32.7	24.2	52.1	1.200
1978	14.2	76.0	18.7	35.3	26.8	53.0	1.476
1979	15.8	77.3	20.4	37.9	29.3	53.9	1.875
1980	19.2	80.8	23.8	43.2	34.9	55.0	2.549
1981	23.0	82.4	27.9	50.7	41.8	55.0	3.656
1982	27.5	83.5	32.9	59.3	49.5	55.6	4.984
1983	31.4	83.9	37.4	66.7	55.9	56.2	6.425
1984	34.2	85.3	40.1	70.9	60.5	56.5	7.774
1985	36.7	86.8	42.3	74.5	64.7	56.7	8.938
1986	39.7	88.5	44.9	78.4	69.4	57.2	10.144
1987	42.6	89.5	47.6	81.7	73.1	58.3	11.765
1988	45.7	91.1	50.2	84.7	77.2	59.2	13.595
1989	49.3	92.8	53.1	89.2	82.8	59.5	15.678
1990	51.7	93.3	55.4	92.2	86.0	60.1	17.855
1991	53.4	94.3	56.6	93.7	88.4	60.4	19.463

(Table continues)

115

Table 6-4 (cont.)

Year	Basic Subscribers[a] (millions)	U.S. Households[a] (millions)	U.S. Households Subscribing (%)	National Saturation (homes passed per households) (%)	Homes Passed (millions)	Mean U.S. Penetration (subscribers per homes passed) (%)	Total U.S. Revenue ($ billions)
1992	55.2	95.7	57.7	93.7	89.7	61.5	21.044
1993	57.4	96.4	59.3	93.9	90.6	63.1	22.755
1994	59.7	97.1	61.5	94.3	91.6	65.2	22.786

a. At year-end.

Sources: Paul Kagan Associates, *Cable TV Investor*, Mar. 31, 1994, p. 9, and June 30, 1995, p. 5. Source for U.S. households: December figures for each year from U.S. Department of Commerce, Bureau of the Census, series P-20, via DRI/McGraw-Hill.

rently, the numbers generate controversy. Yet the FCC has staked its argument supporting the social benefits of rate regulation on those data; therefore, they warrant close consideration.[24]

First, note that this empirical assertion was a reversal of the FCC's initial position that basic subscribership was down from trend in the reregulation period. Chairman Reed Hundt articulated that view in May 1994: "The industry is not in any way ruined. They're just going through a period of flatness."[25] At the 1994 annual convention of the National Cable Television Association, industry experts repeatedly claimed that cable subscriber growth was down. The *New York Times* reported the event in a front-page headline: "Cable TV Industry Shifts Approach as Growth Slows[;] 'Basic' Services on Wane[;] Instead, Operators Promote 'à La Carte' Programming—Rate Limits Cited."[26]

Figure 6-5 displays 1977–1994 subscriber data from *Cable TV Investor*. The pattern is one of rapid percentage gains in the early 1980s followed by generally declining growth rates. The decline is arrested, however, in the 1986 to 1989 period, during which annual percentage changes hover between 7.4 percent and 7.9 percent. There is, additionally, a modest increase in the 1993 and 1994 growth rates. The commission suggests that this indicates that rate regulation has partly reversed the long secular decline by lowering the real, quality-adjusted price of cable service. That a similar pattern was evidenced during the deregulation period makes that interpretation theoretically problematic, but we must examine the empirical evidence further to deduce the actual output response after reregulation.

Figure 6-6 shows penetration data from 1977 to 1994 from the same source.[27] They reveal a pattern of rapid growth both in the period following deregulation (1987 and 1988) and in the reregulation period (1993 and 1994), when even larger increases are recorded. The rise in the growth rate begins, however, in 1992, the last year of decontrolled cable rates. (The first rate freeze was not instituted until April 1993.) Again, the implication drawn by the FCC is that lower (regulated) prices led to higher penetration levels.

---

24. FCC, Annual Assessment of the Status of Competition in the Market for the Delivery of Video Programming, Second Report, CS Dkt. No. 95-61 (Dec. 11, 1995), at 9; *see also* Michael Katz, Cable Rate Regulation Is Good for Consumers (letter to the editor), WALL ST. J., Aug. 10, 1995.

25. Comments of Reed Hundt, *quoted in* Bill Carter, *Cable TV Industry Shifts Approach as Growth Slows,* N.Y. TIMES, May 23, 1994, at C9.

26. Carter, *supra* note 25, at A1.

27. Penetration is here (again) defined as subscribers/homes passed. Penetration represents the percentage of households that have access to cable television and actually subscribe.

Figure 6-5
Cable Television Subscribership, 1977–1994:
Basic Subscribers and Percentage Change

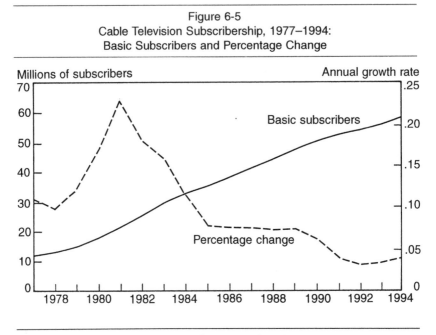

Source: Paul Kagan Associates, *Cable TV Investor,* June 30, 1995, p. 5.

The Kagan data are rather slippery. Although the above series shows a year-end 1994 penetration rate of 65.2 percent, other series published by Kagan indicate otherwise.[28] In table 6-5, for instance, we see that the Kagan measurement variance is large relative to the small changes from trend that are the focus of attention. In calculating year-end 1994 U.S. cable penetration, three different Kagan sources give estimates that differ by at least a full percentage point.

It is necessary to examine various Kagan series to see whether the pattern of penetration increase exhibited above is robust. We begin with the Kagan data set for the top 100 MSOs, a series that is reported intermittently

---

28. Even that particular Kagan data set has changed over time. In the same series, published in Paul Kagan Associates' *Cable TV Investor* on March 31, 1994, the 1992 penetration rate was 60.9 percent. In June 1995, the Kagan penetration figure listed for 1992 was 61.5 percent. Although subscribers stayed the same between the surveys, the 1992 homes-passed figure mysteriously diminished from 90.6 million to 89.7 million. (Similarly, 1993 homes passed fell from 92.9 million in the earlier data set to 90.6 million in the newer.)

Figure 6-6
U.S. Cable Television Penetration, 1977–1994

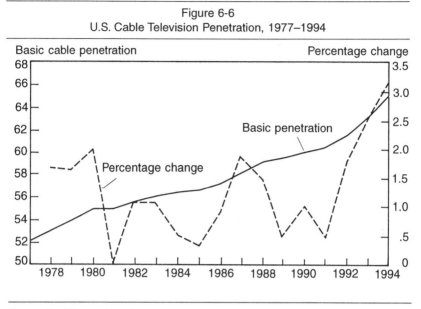

Source: Paul Kagan Associates, *Cable TV Investor,* June 30, 1995, p. 5.

(never more frequently than monthly) in *Cable TV Investor.* Because the proportion of U.S. subscribers who are accounted for by the top 100 opera- tors is in excess of 97 percent (see notes to table 6-5), the bias created by the omission of non–top 100 MSO subscribers should be trivial.

The top 100 MSO data (see figure 6-7) allow us to examine pre- and postregulation periods more precisely than the annual data permit. Owing to data availability, we chose a priori one time period: twenty-seven months. That permits us to compare penetration changes from July 1990 through October 1992 with changes occurring from October 1992 through January 1995. It appears that the trend line's slope does not increase; in fact, a small decline obtains.[29]

Table 6-6 sets out the cable market changes evident in the top 100 MSO data, along with concurrent changes in pricing and personal spend-

29. A top 100 MSO penetration rate of 63.3 percent was reported for September 30 1995; thus, the trend appears unaffected through that date. PAUL KAGAN ASSOCIATES, MARKETING NEW MEDIA, Dec. 11, 1995, at 3. (By September 1995, only ninety-eight MSOs were left in the industry, owing to mergers and consolidations.)

Table 6-5
Conflicting Kagan Penetration Data

Date	Universe	Penetration Rate	Source
Dec. 31, 1994	All U.S.	.642	*Marketing New Media* (Dec. 19, 1994)
Dec. 31, 1994	All U.S.	.652	*Cable TV Investor* (May 31, 1995)
Dec. 31, 1994	Top 100 MSOs	.629[a]	*Cable TV Financial Data-book* (June 1995)
Dec. 31, 1994	Top 100 MSOs	.631	*Marketing New Media* (Mar. 31, 1995)
Jan. 31, 1995	Top 100 MSOs	.626	*Cable TV Investor* (Mar. 24, 1995)
Mar. 31, 1995	Top 100 MSOs	.629[b]	*Marketing New Media* (June 19, 1995)

a. Top 100 MSOs account for 97.31 percent of U.S. cable subscribers, using December 31, 1994, data for both categories in Kagan's *Cable TV Financial Databook* (58.097 million top 100 MSO subscribers divided by 59.7 million U.S. subscribers). If the remaining non–top 100 MSO cable system subscribers exhibited a penetration of 100 percent, the U.S. penetration rate would be .639.

b. Top 100 MSOs account for 99.33 percent of cable subscribers, using January 31, 1995, *Cable TV Investor* (top 100 MSO subscriber count of 58,409,000) and December 31, 1994, *Marketing New Media* (total U.S. subscriber count of 58,800,000). If the remaining non–top 100 cable system subscribers exhibited a penetration of 100 percent, the U.S. penetration rate would be .631.

ing growth for the U.S. economy. Unsurprisingly, the period after the Cable Act (October 1992 through January 1995) demonstrated overall consumption growth of twice the inflation-adjusted level of the period before the act, which occurred largely during a recession. We also see that cable package prices were constrained to a little less than zero real growth during the postact period, contrasted with significant real price increases in the deregulated time frame. Presumably, both those factors would, were everything else held constant, substantially increase the growth rate of cable subscribership in the postact period. Yet the 3.21 percent growth rate in penetration in the twenty-seven months preceding rate regulation is greater

Figure 6-7
U.S. Cable Penetration for Top 100 MSOs, July 1990–January 1995

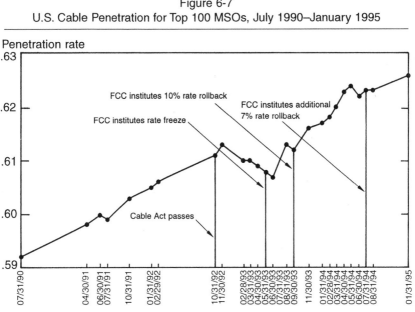

Source: Paul Kagan Associates, *Cable TV Investor,* various issues.

than the 2.45 percent growth in the twenty-seven months following. Hence, the Kagan data series, when viewed together, tend to cancel. Overall, those data reveal no change in the growth rate of cable subscribership.

The Kagan Basic Network Subscribership Data

To cross-check the Kagan penetration data further, we may examine the trend in the household subscribership of the most popular basic cable television channels. The trend in cable subscriber (or penetration) growth should be highly correlated with basic cable network growth, particularly if we limit our analysis to mature cable networks. (Young networks might add new subscribership by increasing their saturation of existing systems, whereas those channels that have already achieved full coverage within the cable household universe will grow only with new subscribership.) It would be anomalous—and important to investigate—if major cable networks were not adding subscribers at least as fast as cable systems were.

Table 6-6
Cable Penetration and Rate Changes:
Preregulation versus Postregulation

	27 Months Preregulation (July 1990– October 1992)	27 Months Postregulation (October 1992– January 1995)
Penetration rate (%), top 100 MSOs	59.2 → 61.1	61.1 → 62.6
% Change	3.21	2.45
% Change real personal spending	2.93	7.32
% Change in cable service bill (CPI-U)	15.76	4.75
% Change in overall CPI-U	8.74	6.00
% Change in real cable subscriber bill (CPI-U)	6.45	(1.17)
% Change (real) annualized	2.82	(.52)

Source: Paul Kagan Associates, *Cable TV Investor,* various issues; Bureau of Labor Statistics.

Table 6-7 provides subscribership data for the thirteen largest basic cable networks at the end of 1994. We chose the top thirteen because we were attempting to measure changes in fully saturated services, and the fourteenth-largest network, the Weather Channel, covered just 93.3 percent of the cable subscriber universe, whereas the thirteenth-rated service, MTV, appeared in 98.3 percent of cable households.[30] In column 1 we show the numbers of household subscribers for 1991 through 1994, at year-end, and in column 2 we show the degree to which each service has saturated the U.S. cable household universe. Note that some popular channels have over 100 percent penetration, having captured virtually every cable television household and penetrated a substantial number of households via other multichannel video delivery systems.[31]

---

30. The next largest service after the Weather Channel, Headline News, suffered large losses (about 12 percent) in household availability in 1994, and to include it would have resulted in a significant downward adjustment in the 1994 growth figure. It is curious that Headline News experienced such a unique decline in penetration, and it is excluded from the analysis here.

31. The cable television industry claims it has a 91 percent market share of the multi-

Table 6-7

Census of Basic Cable Television Services as of December 31, 1994

Channel	House-holds (millions), 1994	Percentage of 59.7 Million Cable House-holds, 1994	Percentage Change			
			1990– 1991	1991– 1992	1992– 1993	1993– 1994
A&E	58.8	98.5	6.4	7.8	4.3	.6
CNN	63.6	106.5	3.7	3.9	2.7	1.2
C-SPAN	61.7	103.4	5.5	5.6	2.6	2.8
Discovery	62.3	104.4	5.6	4.8	4.9	.7
ESPN	63.5	106.4	3.1	3.9	2.7	.7
Family Channel	59.5	99.7	4.3	5.8	4.1	.0
Lifetime	59.1	99.0	3.3	7.0	4.1	.1
MTV	58.7	98.3	3.2	4.8	2.9	−.4
Nickelodeon	60.9	102.0	4.3	3.8	5.3	.1
TBS	63.0	105.5	3.5	4.5	3.4	1.5
TNN	59.6	99.8	3.5	5.8	4.9	−.2
TNT	61.5	103.0	7.8	4.8	4.8	.6
USA	62.7	105.0	7.0	3.9	2.4	1.9
Average			4.7	5.1	3.8	.7

Source: Paul Kagan Associates, *Cable TV Financial Databook,* July 1995, p. 53.

Given that multiple-media approach to nationwide coverage, the sharp drop in basic cable network subscribership growth in 1994 is all the more startling. The 1991 and 1992 growth levels of 4.7 and 5.1 percent declined moderately in 1993 to 3.8 percent and then substantially in 1994 to just .7 percent (see figure 6-8). Among the thirteen top basic networks, not a single one witnessed an increase in 1993–1994 growth over 1991–1992, the last year of deregulation. Even if the top thirteen networks are culled down to the two with the widest penetration—CNN and ESPN—services whose coverage virtually defines the cable programming universe, we see the pattern just as starkly: growth slowed in 1993 and fell sharply in 1994 (figure 6-9).

channel video distribution market. Paul Kagan Associates, MARKETING NEW MEDIA, July 17, 1995, at 1. If so, the maximum (1995) saturation level for a basic cable network would be 109.9 percent (1/.91).

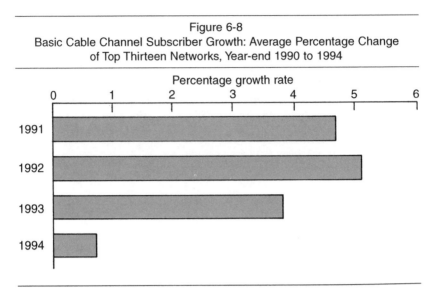

Figure 6-8
Basic Cable Channel Subscriber Growth: Average Percentage Change
of Top Thirteen Networks, Year-end 1990 to 1994

Source: Paul Kagan Associates, *Cable TV Financial Databook,* July 1995, p. 53.

The drop in basic cable network growth in 1994 is truly stunning when the rise in alternative (noncable) multichannel delivery systems is factored in. That same year, authorized backyard satellite dishes rose from 1.41 million units to 2.14 million, an increase of 730,000 households. Wireless cable subscribership rose from 401,000 to 582,000, a gain of 181,000 households.[32] The increase in wireless cable distribution for mainline cable networks such as CNN and ESPN thus amounted to something close to 911,000 units. That increase exceeds the total 1994 increase registered by CNN (800,000) or ESPN (400,000). (Indeed, it exceeds the 1994 subscriber increases of eleven of the thirteen largest basic cable networks.) Net growth for the major basic cable program services on cable TV systems, therefore, was most likely *negative* in 1994, a radical break from the growth trend of fifteen years.

Individually and collectively, those series offer a test of the hypothesis that cable subscriber growth increased in 1993–1994. Each of them, as well as the sample in aggregate, shows a marked pattern of slower growth under reregulation. If cable penetration were really rising quickly in 1994, as the first Kagan series examined suggests, we would need to explain why basic network coverage was virtually flat. But if cable growth stalled in 1994, the

32. PAUL KAGAN ASSOCIATES, MARKETING NEW MEDIA, Dec. 19, 1994, at 4.

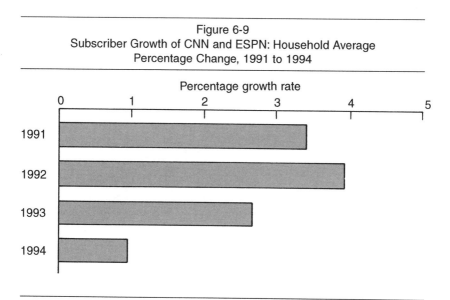

Figure 6-9
Subscriber Growth of CNN and ESPN: Household Average
Percentage Change, 1991 to 1994

Source: Paul Kagan Associates, *Cable TV Financial Databook*, July 1995, p. 53.

parallel stall in cable network coverage would be entirely expected; indeed, that compelling evidence casts a large shadow of doubt over any set of data indicating even so much as steady subscriber growth. The cable network coverage records strongly support the falling growth rate patterns that appear in both the Kagan top 100 MSO data and the A. C. Nielsen cable penetration data.

The FCC's February 1994 Tiering Survey

There may be a way to reconcile the Kagan data showing a 1993–1994 increase in penetration growth with at least the basic cable network pattern of decline. According to the FCC's survey data released in February 1994, massive shifts took place in the cable marketing structure in the adjustment process associated with reregulation. Among other changes, there was a large increase in the proportion of subscribers receiving "basic-only" programming, the lowest tier offered by the cable operator. That had traditionally been called "limited basic" service before the 1992 Cable Act and typically consisted of a "lifeline" service, restricted to retransmission of off-air broadcast signals, public access, local origination, and government channels.

The FCC survey report notes a pronounced shift in 1993 toward limited basic service. The nearly 300 percent rise in the proportion of total

Table 6-8
1993 Tiering Changes for Basic Programming

	Limited Basic Subscribers (%)	Mean Channels		
		Limited Basic	Expanded Basic	Per Subscriber
Apr. 1993	3.4	17.5	41.7	40.29
Sept. 1993	13.4	20.5	40.1	34.68

Source: FCC (1994).

cable customers taking only the lowest basic tier was tied to the collapsing of expanded tiers into limited basic by the FCC.[33] That explanation hides the fact that a wholesale restructuring was taking place within the industry, as limited basic continued (even after the collapsing of some larger packages into basic-only) to feature far fewer channels. In fact, after the first rollback in September 1993, the FCC found that the lowest basic tier had only about half as many channels on average as the typical expanded basic package (see table 6-8).

On net, then, the mean number of channels offered customers dropped by about 13.9 percent between April and September 1993. The retiering efforts were clearly having a profound impact on the cable "package." Such activity could well explain the devastating effects of reregulation on basic cable network (and viewing share) growth, even as some measures of cable subscribership do not account for customer switching between limited and expanded basic. Specifically, the Kagan penetration data showing 1993 and 1994 growth from trend could be accurately reflecting the expansion of limited basic, while masking the collapse of basic cable program services.

PREDICTED OUTPUT INCREASES FROM RATE REDUCTIONS

That the grounds of debate concern whether cable penetration growth under reregulation increased 2 percent or fell 5 percent demonstrates an important outcome: no one argues that the rate regulation scheme has had anywhere near the impact on quality-adjusted cable rates that the nominal

---

33. "In September basic-only subscribers had climbed to 13.4% as the result of the collapsing of tiers into basic." FCC, CABLE SERVICES BUREAU, FCC CABLE REGULATION IMPACT SURVEY, CHANGES IN CABLE TELEVISION RATES BETWEEN APRIL 5, 1993–SEPTEMBER 1, 1993: REPORT AND SUMMARY (Feb. 22, 1994), at 14.

rate cuts suggest. Under any plausible scenario, the evidence indicates that consumers did not respond to rate regulation in a way consistent with substantial price discounting, *ceteris paribus*.

We can best see that by considering the magnitude of penetration increases that would have accompanied substantial (quality-adjusted) rate rollbacks. The FCC's elasticity estimates are in line with those discussed earlier in chapter 3, hovering around an own-price demand elasticity of an absolute value of two. The FCC relies on the econometric estimation of Robert Crandall, which was based on a large sample of TCI cable systems: "To the extent that TCI cable systems are broadly representative of cable systems more generally, estimated own-price elasticities for basic cable service in the vicinity of 2.0 are probably consistent with profit-maximizing prices for basic cable service."[34] That is what the Lerner index, relying on price-cost margins of between 1.67 and 2.0, would predict, and where the five econometric estimations of demand elasticity cited in the commission's report set it. (The five reported studies predict a mean value of 2.03,[35] and their estimates range from 1.31 to 3.38.)

Those demand elasticities appear to be for basic cable service.[36] That implies that a reduction of 16 percent in basic cable service rates, as announced by the FCC July 1994, should have increased subscribership (or penetration; both measures are used in the estimates listed) by about 32 percent.[37] To be conservative, one might also consider the regulation-

---

34. FCC, Annual Assessment of the Status of Competition in the Market for the Delivery of Video Programming, First Report, CS Dkt. No. 94-48, 9 F.C.C. Rcd. 7442 (Sept. 28, 1994), at H-13.

35. There is a sixth elasticity estimate, by George Ford, which is for duopoly cable systems. Since those are not regulated by the FCC under the 1992 Cable Act and are not the focus of the question concerning how output should rise for a given rate reduction as per reregulation, we exclude that estimate. It is, in fact, 2.62.

36. The passage just quoted on Crandall's elasticity measurement is explicit on that; the other elasticities are reported more vaguely.

37. That, of course, implies a constant (or, at least, arc) elasticity of demand of two (in absolute-value terms) over the incremental range. No discussion of the change in elasticity was included in the FCC's estimates, but it is reasonable to think that competitive markets that exhibit competitive entry achieve something close to that. In Montgomery, Alabama, an overbuilder began offering service in 1990 and has garnered 9,200 subscribers, 3,700 of whom are reported to have left the incumbent. Debbie Narrod, *Overbuilds '95,* CABLE WORLD, May 1, 1995, at 49. Because initial penetration by the monopoly incumbent was about 65 percent, the competitive entry increased aggregate market penetration by about 36.8 percent. If the FCC is correct in its calculation that quality-adjusted price is 17 percent less in a duopoly market than the monopoly alternative and if the effect of competition in Montgomery is typical, an arc elasticity of 2.16 is implied.

Table 6-9
Output Responses Implied by FCC Elasticity Estimates
versus 1.5 Percent Growth

FCC Elasticity Estimates	Assumed Rate Cut Estimates (%)	Implied Output Increase (%)	Output Gap (%)
Mean = 2.03	16	32.5	95.4
Mean = 2.03	9	18.3	91.8
Lowest = 1.31	16	21.0	92.9
Lowest = 1.31	9	11.8	87.3
Highest = 3.38	16	54.1	97.2
Highest = 3.38	9	30.4	95.0

induced rate reduction for the full cable package, about 9 percent (see table 6-3). Yet, according to the FCC's assessment, subscriber growth rose about 1.5 percent above trend after reregulation.[38] Even assuming away the voluminous output trend data to the contrary and crediting all such growth to cable rate cuts (and not macroeconomic factors nor underlying technology or marketing trends), it is clear from examining table 6-9 that the vast proportion of the implied output gains failed to materialize—presumably because of offsetting declines in product quality.

BASIC CABLE VIEWER RATINGS

Viewer ratings serve both as corroboration of the penetration data and as a direct measure of basic cable program quality. There is likely to be a strong correlation between the penetration growth of cable and the growth of cable viewership, particularly when the relevant market is designated as all U.S. television households. As more households subscribe to cable, we would expect that more households would view basic cable channels. Conversely, if cable channels are becoming less interesting to consumers, it would be

---

38. Penetration growth for 1994 in the Kagan series shown in figure 6-6 was 3.22 percent, or 1.43 percent above the 1992 growth rate of 1.79 percent. Because rate reductions did not begin until well into 1993, using 1992 as a base year should not be controversial.

Figure 6-10
Basic Cable Television Viewing Share, 1983–1994:
Twenty-four Hour, All U.S. Television Households
(shares based on total viewing = 100%)

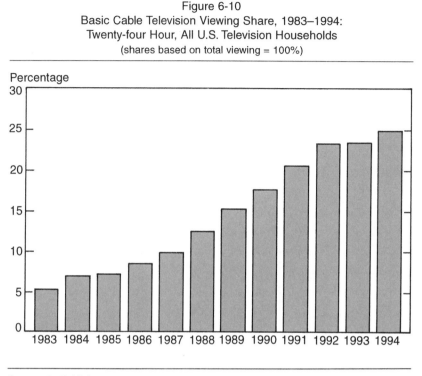

Source: A. C. Nielsen.

curious if cable subscriptions rose. A priori, total U.S. basic cable viewership growth should be highly correlated with cable penetration growth.

The trend in basic cable audience gains before and after the 1992 Cable Act is dramatic. A. C. Nielsen annual data for twenty-four-hour viewing share among all U.S. television households show a sharp break from trend in the 1993–1994 period.[39] Double-digit gains were exhibited throughout the deregulation years (see figures 6-10 and 6-11), with a geometric mean of 18.5 percent annual growth (from an 8.4 twenty-four-hour share in 1986 to a 23.3 twenty-four-hour share in 1992). The ratings growth abruptly halted in the first year of reregulation, with a minuscule gain of 0.4 percent (to 23.4). Growth resumed haltingly in 1994, with a 6.4 percent rise (to 24.9).

---

39. Those data are standardized such that viewing shares sum to 100 percent. Raw share data typically sum to over 100 percent because of the use of multiple television sets within households.

Figure 6-11
Annual Change in Television Share by Basic Cable Networks, 1984–1994:
Twenty-four Hour, All U.S. Television Households
(shares based on total viewing = 100%)

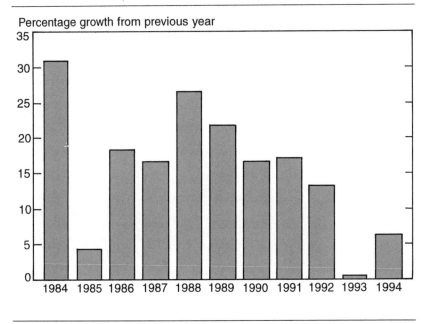

Percentage growth from previous year

Source: A. C. Nielsen.

If the 18.5 percent gains before reregulation had continued through 1993–1994, basic cable viewership would have been 31.5 percent higher in U.S. television households in 1994.

We can more directly appraise the quality of basic cable television programming by focusing on the A. C. Nielsen ratings of viewing time strictly within cable television households. Excluding noncable television viewers keeps the data set "clean" by eliminating the effects of a changing cable penetration margin. At any moment, therefore, one can discern how those households on the inframargin—already subscribing households—believe the various television viewing alternatives (broadcast network affiliates, broadcast independents, basic cable, premium cable, public stations) measure up. Because the consumer (viewer) is allocating his time so as to maximize utility, one can infer that ratings measure the value, or quality, associated with various programming choices in the eyes of consumers.

Figure 6-12
Basic Cable Television Viewing Share, 1983–1994:
Twenty-four Hour, U.S. Cable Households
(shares based on total viewing = 100%)

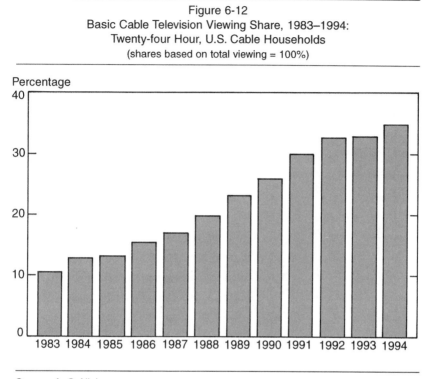

Source: A. C. Nielsen.

The basic ratings presented in figures 6-12 and 6-13 are for the package of basic cable channels (as are those reported in figures 6-10 and 6-11). The large gains in the period preceding reregulation mirror the pattern for all U.S. television households. The geometric mean of the gains exhibited throughout the deregulation years is 13.3 percent, annualized (from a 15.4 twenty-four-hour share in 1986 to a 32.6 twenty-four-hour share in 1992). Like other measures, the ratings growth among cable households also came to a halt in the first year of reregulation, gaining just .3 percent in 1993 (from 32.6 to 32.7). Growth in 1994 resumed, if at a paltry pace by historical standards, at 5.8 percent (to 34.6). If the 13.3 percent annual gains before reregulation had continued through 1993–1994, basic cable viewership would have been 21.0 percent higher in U.S. television households in 1994.

The industry saw the derailment of the growth trend as part of the operators' transition away from the basic (rate-regulated) package. "Niche Networks Hot as Basic Fare Goes Flat" was the subtitle on one trade peri-

Figure 6-13
Annual Change in Television Viewing Share by Basic Cable Networks,
1984–94: Twenty-four Hour, U.S. Cable Households
(shares based on total viewing = 100%)

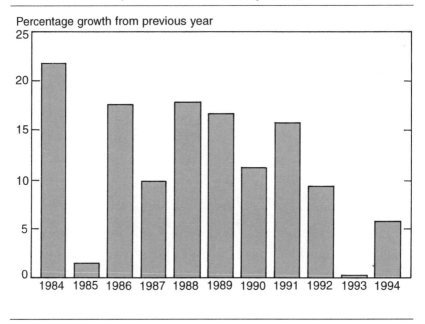

Percentage growth from previous year

Source: A. C. Nielsen.

odical story in June 1994. It noted that "[w]ith basic cable failing to continue its streak of ratings gains last season," cable networks would strain to
justify the ad rate increases that they had grown accustomed to imposing
annually. "Because of lack of growth," the article continued, an industry
expert "doesn't expect ad budgets for cable to show the percentage gains
they've had in the past."[40]

Cable viewer ratings were victims of the adjustment costs of
reregulation. As cable systems retiered in response to rate controls, cable
networks were moved up and down the dial (broadcasting stations were
protected from the shuffle by terms of the 1992 Cable Act). That process
created a major marketing disturbance, which industry insiders blamed for
the sharp fall in viewership: "Most of the established cable networks have

40. Junu Bryan Kim, *Cable Creating Another Niche,* ELECTRONIC MEDIA, June 13,
1994, at S-14.

been buffeted by channel switches stemming from last year's cable reregulation, resulting in viewer confusion and flat ratings."[41]

Beginning in 1995, large viewing increases were once again posted for basic cable channels. Not only did those come when real cable rates were again rising, but the trade press largely attributed the ratings success to the O. J. Simpson murder trial. Of the hundred top-rated shows on cable television in the first quarter of 1995, ninety-nine were related to that event.[42] Still, the rebound within the cable industry may also be causally related to the relaxation of rate controls. The spring 1995 projections offered in Kagan's *Cable TV Financial Databook* (June 1995) forecast basic rate increases of 6.7 and 6.5 percent in 1995 and 1996, with revenue per subscriber increases of 10.5 and 10.0 percent, respectively. Excitement over such price growth, two to four times projected consumer price index increases, stimulated marketing efforts by both cable operators and programmers. Paul Kagan noted:

> Cable operators' regulatory woes continued into 1994. The FCC followed up on its 10% basic rate rollback that took effect September 1993 with an additional rollback of 7% March 31. This became a 14% net reduction below September 1992 prices after allowing for a 3% inflation adjustment. But that was the final blow. In May, the FCC became far more conciliatory, realizing that it had perhaps gone too far in plaguing cable operators with revenue cuts and paperwork burdens. . . . While the FCC could spring new surprises at any moment, cable operators in May 1995 are beginning to sense that the regulatory restraints are lifting and cash flow is growing.[43]

CABLE OPERATOR CASH FLOW RATIOS

If reregulation cut customer rates while leaving customer service intact, one would expect that cash flow margins would be dramatically con-

---

41. Steve McClellan, *Programming Overhaul in Works at CNN*, BROADCASTING & CABLE, June 13, 1994, at 16. The article continues: "CNN has taken a harder hit than most. In the first quarter of this year, for example, the network's prime time ratings were down 15 percent from last year. . . . 'The impact of cable reregulation is a major factor in the audience declines,' [CNN vice president Tom] Johnson says. 'In the last 15 months more than 50 percent of our viewers find us on different channels.'"

42. Alan Breznick, *A 1stQ Ratings Boom*, CABLE WORLD, Apr. 3, 1995, at 2. "Basic cable's prime-time ratings climbed a surprising 18 percent in 1995's first three months." *See also* Lawrie Mifflin, *Cable Ratings at High, Aided by Simpson Trial*, N.Y. TIMES, Mar. 27, 1995, at C6.

43. PAUL KAGAN ASSOCIATES, CABLE TV FINANCIAL DATABOOK, June 1995, at 6.

strained.[44] The key assumption is that cable operators, as rational firms, minimize costs for any given level of service quality.[45] Because U.S. cable television operators were realizing cash flow ratios of approximately 45 percent before reregulation,[46] even an 8 percent rate rollback would have the effect of lowering the ratio substantially, to about 40 percent.[47]

The evidence now available does not indicate that anything close to that magnitude has been inflicted on the cash flow ratios of cable operators (see figure 5-9). Although the gradual upward growth in the ratio flattened in the 1992–1994 period, the 1994 ratio, at 45.5 percent, was still about where it was previous to rate regulation. When that ratio is juxtaposed with the average revenue per subscriber trend, it appears that the drop in revenue growth has been cushioned by (real) declines in input spending (see figure 6-13). Hence, lower costs of operation have helped to offset revenues lost under rate regulation.

The profile of operating costs and operating profits in figure 5-8 is instructive. It shows, as seen in the revenue and price data already examined, that rate controls began to seriously constrain cable rates in 1994: revenue per subscriber increases in 1993 but declines in 1994 by $6.24 (1.6 percent) in nominal terms. Operating costs per subscriber, while nominally increasing $2.64 (1.3 percent), decline in real terms. Over the 1984–1992 period, operating costs per subscriber rose 2.7 percent annually; over the 1992–1994 period, they rose at 1.4 percent. What makes that small change from trend impressive is the bias that it hides: because reregulation imposed substantial direct (operating) costs on cable systems, including those associated with must-carry and other requirements in the 1992 Cable Act,[48] it is likely that, for a given level of spending per customer, funds were shifted away from quality-enhancing activities. When the direct and indirect costs of regulation are included,[49] it seems reasonable to conclude that

---

44. Cash flow margin = (revenues − operating costs)/revenues. That excludes capital expenses such as depreciation, interest, and amortization.

45. In reality, a much weaker assumption is needed: that rate regulation does not make firms more efficient. That is uncontroversial. A profit-maximizing firm does not wait for price controls to behave in a rational economic fashion.

46. That implies that 55 percent of revenues are devoted to operating costs.

47. At revenue per subscriber 8 percent less under rate regulation, the calculation would be: $(.92 − .55)/.92 = .402$.

48. For instance, cable operators were assessed nearly $30 million annually in user fees under reregulation to help defray FCC regulatory costs. Kenneth Robinson, 11 TELECOMM. POL'Y REV. (Jan. 22, 1995), at 7.

49. Indirect costs would include the expense associated with reducing the impact of regulation—retiering, changing marketing strategies, and so on.

the 1.3 percent visible decline may well understate the tendency of firms to withdraw inputs in response to cable rate controls.

SHORT RUN, LONG RUN

It is clear that, in the eyes of the viewing public, cable quality suffered enormously in the two years following passage of the Cable Act of 1992. What is most startling is the immediacy with which ratings growth was curtailed, particularly considering that the long-run elasticities of supply and of program quality are so much higher than the short-run elasticities. Programming decisions are long-range. Years are required to create networks, develop shows, sign multiyear sports deals, buy studios, arrange joint ventures with software suppliers, and so forth. Cable plant—the co-axial hardware—is even more durable and usually takes longer to design and install. The instant dive in the polls for basic cable channels reveals the surprising extent to which the short-term margins of cable operator behavior changed following reregulation.

Even before the FCC proposed and officially implemented the new rules, cable systems began furiously tinkering with product offerings and pricing menus. In an effort to maximize earnings under regulatory constraints, system managers were pressed to find new channel line-ups, untapped (and, presumably, unregulated) charges, marketing tactics, and tiering arrangements that would defeat the imposed regulations. The initiation of must-carry rules in the 1992 Cable Act, requiring that some marginal broadcast stations be added in lieu of some marginal cable networks, added to the retiering momentum. Cable firms began shifting channel assignments, adding and subtracting tiers, repricing old services, and charging for new items. The net result confused and alienated many viewers.

Robert Alter, vice-chairman and acting president of the Cabletelevision Advertising Bureau and a cable industry insider, explained the derailing of basic cable ratings gains in 1993 and the resumption of modest growth in 1994 this way: "Cable's expanding viewership is consistent with a decade-long growth trend that was briefly interrupted earlier this year by two aberrant factors: the winter Olympics and consumer confusion caused by the channel position changes dictated by re-regulation and its retransmission-consent/must-carry provisions."[50]

---

50. *Quoted in* Rich Brown, *Cable Boasts Record Average Rating,* CABLE WORLD, July 11, 1994, at 17. Note that, while the winter Olympics may well have made broadcast television more competitive with cable channels in the winter of 1994, two sets of Olympic games (summer and winter) were included in the six-year annualized deregulation pe-

But all that involved tinkering at the margins of the cable television package. The long-run reactions to rate regulation would have been far grander if regulation had continued to bind heavily beyond 1994–1995. Substituting input expenditures into the unregulated, à la carte side of the service menu was already a key strategy by 1993. Marketing efforts were clearly shifting as well (see table 6-10). Beginning even before 1992, the year the Cable Act was passed, the proportion of marketing expenses devoted to regulated services began to plunge. The ratio of expenditures selling basic service to expenditures committed to premium sales was over 2 to 1 in 1990 and 1991; it was estimated to have fallen to 1 to 1 by 1995. Basic cable was getting less effort and premium services were receiving more. Only the relaxation of rate controls in late 1994 prevented that transition from going farther. Over time, investment in technology would surely have shifted, as TCI CEO John Malone predicted in his famous July 1994 interview,[51] to further circumvent regulatory constraint:

Question: What effect has the rollback of cable rates had?

Malone: I think the cable industry is only temporarily injured by the FCC. But for the last three or four years we've been shifting a lot of our attention into the international arena. I mean if you really look at TCI today, two-thirds of our market value is based on nondomestic business.

And we'll also continue moving into programming, which the government has a very hard time regulating because of First Amendment issues. These noxious FCC rules are not going to be able to constrain the economics of entertainment for very long. What's gonna happen is there'll be a shift from basic to à la carte services. If our programming is strong, then we'll see a quick recovery of the cable industry growth rate in entertainment and in interactive video and so on.

We'll continue to diversify away from the regulated government-attacked core. And meanwhile, we'll continue to slug it out in the trenches in the

---

riod growth of 13.3 percent (cable households) and 18.5 percent (all TV households). The article went on to note that the rebound in cable ratings growth was pictured as "welcome news for [ad-supported basic cable] networks, which have experienced some well-publicized ratings setbacks during the past year." *Id.*

51. It became famous largely because of the stir one particular answer made in Washington. Responding to a question about how TCI intended to build the Information Superhighway, Malone offered the following advice on national policy to the vice president, Al Gore: "I'll make a commitment to [the vice president], OK? Listen Al, I know you haven't asked for it, but we'll make a commitment to complete the job by the end of '96. All we need is a little help. . . . You know, shoot Hundt! Don't let him do any more damage, know what I'm saying?" David Cline, *Infobahn Warrior*, WIRED, July 1994, at 131.

Table 6-10
Marketing Expenditures: Regulated versus Unregulated Services, 1989–1995

Year	Percentage Spent on Basic	Percentage Spent on Pay	Percentage Spent on Pay-per-View
1989	58	30	7
1990	66	30	4
1991	63	30	7
1992	54	38	8
1993	54	36	10
1994	48	41	11
1995 (est.)	43	43	14

Source: Paul Kagan Associates, *Marketing New Media,* Mar. 20, 1995, p. 1.

domestic cable business, recognizing that the government's got to kill a lot of smaller cable operators before they can really hurt us much.[52]

That, certainly, was the conventional wisdom within the cable television industry. A July 1994 trade journal headline proclaimed, "Unregulated services latest target of MSOs," and reported that "[a]s cable operators look to the future, they see a much greater percentage of their revenues coming from unregulated sources such as pay-per-view, premium services and interactive TV."[53] Although the sector was enthusiastic over the decline in regulatory constraints heralded by the going-forward rules in November 1994 and the emergence of a Republican Congress, an industry analyst expressed the general expectation in early 1995: "Cable system operators will make up for any future shortcomings in subscription revenue by focusing on local advertising, pay per view and other unregulated revenue streams, [Arthur] Gruen says. Local advertising at cable systems grew by 16% in 1994, but continues to be a 'barely tapped' source of revenue, Gruen says."[54]

More dramatic changes in response to rate regulation could be economically instituted over the longer run. Because cable operators and pro-

---

52. *Id.* at 90. The interview was conducted just two weeks after the FCC's rulemaking (announced February 22, 1994) raised the rate-rollback standard from 10 to 17 percent.

53. Kate Maddox, *Unregulated Services Latest Target of MSOs,* ELECTRONIC MEDIA, July 25, 1994, at 4, 37.

54. Rich Brown, *Cable Rebound Forecast for '95,* CABLE WORLD, Jan. 2, 1995, at 8.

grammers retain wide discretion to determine what video content they deliver subscribers—infomercials or original dramas, home shopping or expensive documentaries—that freedom can be used to alter fundamentally the "package" regulators seek to control. It is revealing that in projecting the ten-year future of the cable television industry, forecasters believe that traditional cable services (both pay and basic), which today account for 93 percent of revenues, will make up only 54 percent of total receipts in 2004. Advertising, digital video, information services, and telephony are forecast to substantially displace the "regulated government-attacked core."[55]

REINVENTING THE CABLE TELEVISION INDUSTRY, 1993

Retiering is one low-cost method by which to avoid cable television rate controls. Policymakers were aware of that escape route as they put together the 1992 Cable Act, however, and they included legislative provisions that were designed to deal with it. In giving the FCC authority to regulate *all* tiers of basic programming,[56] Congress specifically targeted a loophole in earlier legislation. That provision increased the distance that cable companies had to traverse to liberate their programming from rate regulation. In 1993 the stipulation led to two forms of retiering: reallocating networks between limited basic and expanded basic tiers, which largely concerned operators preparing for the April 5, 1993, "freeze"; and shifting high-quality cable networks off basic altogether (either dropping channels or moving them to premium status).

In the first approach, limited basic service prices increased in most markets, while higher tier rates were lowered. Often the net result for the typical customer (who subscribes to both) was naught. (That is a distributional irony, however, in that basic tiers were traditionally created by local regulators as low-cost "lifeline" services.) Cable television subscribers in Los Angeles, California, for example, found the restructuring worked as shown in table 6-11.

That shift was prompted by concerns that regulations going into effect in April 1993 would freeze basic cable rates at artificially low levels. More complicated restructuring also took place. Generally, charges for additional outlets and remote controls fell, while other nonprogramming charges increased. For instance, some cable companies attached "cost-based" installation charges; what had been a free hook-up for Albertville, Alabama,

---

55. PAUL KAGAN ASSOCIATES, CABLE TV INVESTOR, May 31, 1995, at 7.

56. That did not include à la carte or pay-per-view, as already noted, but did include all "expanded basic" tiers.

Table 6-11
Retiering by a Los Angeles Cable Operator

	Current Price ($)	New Price ($)
Basic broadcast service	2.10	9.85
Standard service	19.90	13.50
Remote	2.10	.75
Basic broadcast service plus standard service and remote control package	24.10	24.10
Additional outlet with remote control package	7.88	7.88
Additional outlet	5.78	7.13
Additional outlet with remote control	2.10	.75

Source: Letter to Continental Cablevision subscribers in Hollywood/Wilshire franchise, announcing April 1, 1993, rate schedule.

subscribers rose to $10.05. Toledo, Ohio, cable customers had received converters and home service calls at no additional charge; after regulation, converter boxes and home wiring were billed at "cost"—$2.54 and $.31 per month, respectively.

In the second form of retiering, systems experimented with various combinations in an effort to make the newly regulated package "revenue-neutral" by shifting basic programming services to unregulated status. The strategy entails either raising premium channel prices (unregulated) and marketing them more intensely, or putting newer, cheaper, less-watched channels on basic tiers and shifting popular networks to à la carte status. A system in San Antonio, for instance, moved TBS and WGN from basic to per-channel status, charging $1 and $.50, respectively, or $1.25 a month for both. E! (part-time), VH-1, and the Comedy Channel were added back into basic. The net result: rates dropped seventeen cents per month.

Many systems actually increased prices for basic cable service in 1993. "In Paragon Cable's Manhattan system, the overall basic-plus-standard rates will rise from $22.95 to $23.65, which includes a $3.32 converter fee and a 20-cent charge for a remote."[57] Rates also rose, from $22.95 to $23.58, in

---

57. Matt Stump, *The Big Apple Rereg Picture,* CABLE WORLD, Aug. 30, 1993, at 12.

Time Warner's New York City system. In the Staten Island Paragon system, six channels (Madison Square Garden Network, MSG2, TBS, Discovery, AMC, and the Cartoon Network) were severed from the basic package and put on an à la carte basis. Costing from $.50 to $2.00 per channel, the package was priced at $3. Even including the tier of "à la carte" channels, however, the basic package dropped $1.60 per month.[58]

The degree to which nominal prices rose or fell following the September 1993 implementation of rate regulation is not well understood. Industry leader Tele-Communications, Inc., was chagrined when a memo written by one of its vice presidents and sent to over 500 system managers was leaked to the *Washington Post* in November 1993. The memo outlined how the company could raise prices for "downgrades, upgrades, service calls and VCR hook-ups," which were unregulated under the new rules. "We cannot be dissuaded from the charges simply because customers object," wrote the TCI executive. "It will take a while, but they'll get used to it." His conclusion was explosive: "The best news of all is we can blame it on reregulation and the government now. Let's take advantage of it!"[59]

Another response to reregulation is the substitution of cheaper or lower-quality programming for existing cable networks. C-SPAN, a public affairs network, suffered losses amounting to a million subscribers (either dropped entirely or reduced to part-time carriage) on "Sept. 1 [1993] as systems retiered rates and channel line-ups."[60] By June 1994, C-SPAN had been dropped entirely or reduced to part-time status in 4.2 million U.S. cable homes.[61] Although C-SPAN is not one of the more expensive networks, it is commercial-free, thereby denying the local operator any share of "local avails."[62] Independent UHF broadcast stations were added to basic packages to comply with "must-carry" rules contained in the 1992 act,

58. See Mark Robichaux, *How Cable-TV Firms Raised Rates in Wake of Law to Curb Them,* WALL ST. J., Sept. 28, 1993, at A1, A12.

59. Vincente Pasdeloup, *More Trouble on Rereg Front: FCC, AGs Investigate MSOs' New Cable Rates,* CABLE WORLD, Nov. 22, 1993, at 1, 65.

60. *In Rereg's Wake, C-SPAN's Losses Continue to Mount,* CABLE WORLD, Sept. 13, 1993, at 10. The network had lost 500,000 subscriber households during the summer to make room for marginal broadcast stations picked up as a result of "must-carry" regulations.

61. Richard Zoglin, *Cable's Big Squeeze,* TIME, June 27, 1994, at 66–67. *See also* James Lardner, *The Anti-Network,* NEW YORKER, Mar. 14, 1994, at 49–55. Those losses are not contradicted or rendered moot by overall gains registered by C-SPAN in 1993–1994 (table 6-7). Rather, they indicate distribution losses on the relevant policy margin.

62. Basic cable networks routinely allow cable systems some percentage of local advertising sales.

typically without any charge to the cable operator, and had the spillover effect of reducing the operator's per-channel rate. Home shopping networks became more advantageous to cablecast under rate caps in the sense that they also lower the per-channel basic rate (satisfying the price cap) even as they pay local cable operators for carriage (by splitting sales commissions). Indeed, satellite-delivered home shopping networks were thriving in the wake of the 1992 Cable Act, and several new shopping channels were launched.[63]

We cannot theoretically rule out that incentives to blunt the impact of per-channel rate rollbacks may also produce some positive impacts on basic cable quality by prompting operators to add channels, thereby giving some upstart networks additional audience coverage.[64] There is evidence that cable operators did increase their total basic channels offered by about 4.4 percent during 1993.[65] In addition, the FCC rate regulations may have led systems to lower charges for additional outlets, which may in turn have increased audience share of basic cable networks.[66] With enhanced advertising revenue streams, the quality of those channels could rise over time. Ultimately, however, channels that are added simply to alleviate binding price constraints may themselves be replaced by programming that is cheaper still.[67] Moreover, the overall impact on the quality of cable network pro-

---

63. K. C. Neel, *Home Shopping: Wall Street's Darling,* CABLE WORLD, Sept. 27, 1993, at 1, 79. Two cable shopping network stocks, QVC and Value Vision, were cited as outstanding performers, gaining 62 percent and 586 percent, respectively, from the start of 1993. New video shopping services include one launched by Macy's (*id.*), Fingerhut Company's "S" channel (*Marketer to Launch Service for Cable Home-Shopping,* WALL ST. J., Mar. 23, 1994, at B6), and Time Warner/Spiegel's "Catalog 1" (Stephanie Strom, *Mail Order Shifts Its Pitch to Cable,* N.Y. TIMES, Mar. 21, 1994, at C1, C5). The fact that the home shopping hoopla of 1993–1994 realized disappointing sales only reinforces the regulatory causation: cable operators evidently overinvested in home-shopping "shelf space." Gregory Patterson, *Spiegel and Time Warner to Scale Back Cable Shopping Venture, Use Internet,* WALL ST. J., Jan. 30, 1995, at B7.

64. "Operators facing basic rate regulation Sept. 1 continue adding small, less expensive basic cable networks to system lineups. The latest beneficiary: Court TV, which says it will add 3.5 million new homes by the end of the year." Toula Vlahou, *Regulation Bonus,* CABLE WORLD, Aug. 30, 1993, at 46.

65. FCC, *supra* note 33, at 20. The average subscriber appeared to receive fewer of those channels, however, as seen earlier in this chapter.

66. Rod Granger, *Will Re-regulation Give a Boost to Cable Ratings?* MULTICHANNEL NEWS, Oct. 25, 1993, at 14.

67. The conflicting nature of the incentives facing cable system managers was described by one programming executive: "Re-regulation is like a bullet ricocheting through a room; you never know what it's going to hit." *Id.*

gramming does not appear to be positive. According to the FCC's 1994 survey, the average number of channels delivered to cable subscribers declined from over forty to a little under thirty-five in the retiering scramble of 1993 (see table 6-8). That evidence, combined with the strong opposition to rate regulation expressed by cable television programmers (see chapter 7), makes it difficult to conclude that such ad hoc mechanisms to water down per-channel rates led to an increase in program quality.

It is also theoretically possible that reregulation promotes incentives that speed technological change. Over the medium to long term, rate-capped systems face greater incentives to change the (regulated) marketing margins altogether by upgrading cable plant to, for example, a 500-channel environment. Combined with addressable electronic controls, that would circumvent the regulatory regime almost entirely by shifting to virtual video-on-demand delivery and by entering whole new markets via integrated broadband services (that is, video, data, and voice over the same network infrastructure). Regulation could be rendered moot either by adding vast numbers of "fishbowl channels"[68] or by taking the entire cable package à la carte.[69] That was apparently the strategy selected by Cablevision Systems, the fifth-largest MSO and an industry leader in aggressive marketing strategies in years past.[70] In the short run that quality-enhancing response simply takes the form of bigger bundles:

> According to the [Cablevision] plan, subscribers may choose one of the three OptimumTV packages ranging from $29.95 to $64.95. They'll include access to premium service and four pay-per-view channels. . . . Under the old system, an equivalent entry-level "family" package is $22.90.
> Under the more controversial, a-la-carte OptimumTV offering, subscrib-

---

68. The term is industry jargon for worthless channels added simply to evade rate controls by diluting per-channel charges. It alludes to a network that simply televises a fishbowl. Of course, channels featuring continuous infomercials or homeshopping are "cheaper" yet to the cable operator, who is compensated for carriage.

69. That is the ultimate in price control evasion: exit the regulated market so as to simultaneously enter a deregulated market serving the same characteristic demand function. There are, of course, offsetting incentives that tend to discourage investment in the newly regulated sector, and the net impact on investment is ambiguous. Rate controls may create a discontinuous capital supply function, where small increments of capital are discouraged, but large expenditures (which jump the supplier to a new technology altogether) are encouraged.

70. For instance, Cablevision chairman Charles Dolan developed Home Box Office, the first satellite-distributed cable program service. He is widely regarded to be an industry visionary.

ers can combine their favorite networks into a distinct household package and change them anytime.[71]

Cablevision's response appears to have paid off, as it actually increased its cash flow margin in 1994 and "defended its profits most successfully among the MSOs, taking the full-rate rollback required by the FCC, then using creative new program packages to recoup lost revenue."[72] In the same vein, rate controls have prompted cable operators to shift efforts away from (regulated) video service toward other synergistic revenue sources such as providing competitive access in local telephony markets or deploying personal communications services. That is the margin that the president of the National Cable Television Association obviously had in mind in early 1993:

> But the point I really want to make is that these three trends: the dramatic transformation of cable technology; the fading of the RBOC's [regional Bell operating company's] one-wire vision; and the timely emergence of plausible business scenarios, suggest a wide open door through which our industry can move as we draw near the 21st century.
>
> Re-regulation means pain—it will bite—but it doesn't need to mean stagnation, and God and the Government willing, re-regulation of part of our traditional business may be the stimulus we need to push us through that door.[73]

THE REVIVAL OF PAY TELEVISION

The cable industry has made good on the prediction that repackaging would be a logical response to rate controls. Soon after reregulation, trade publications were filled with advertisements for premium programming services that highlighted the fact that operators could escape rate regulation by diverting channel space in their favor. Several à la carte services began multiplexing their offerings (transmitting the same programs on different schedules) or simply expanding their service across multiple channels (which the cable system subscribes to as a package). That is particularly true of so-called minipay services such as Flix or Encore, networks that are much cheaper than HBO or Showtime and more easily substituted for basic programming. That trend expands the opportunity to shift basic cable custom-

---

71. Rachel Thompson, *Cablevision System Rolls Out a la Carte in Yonkers, N.Y.,* CABLE WORLD, July 4, 1994, at 17.

72. PAUL KAGAN ASSOCIATES, CABLE TV INVESTOR, Apr. 30, 1995, at 5.

73. Remarks of James P. Mooney, President & Chief Executive Officer, National Cable Television Association, before the Metropolitan Cable Club, Feb. 17, 1993, Washington, D.C., at 10.

ers into premium and thus escape rate regulation. In 1994 issues of *Cable World*, no fewer than four cable programming services prominently featured the unregulated nature of their product in their sales pitches to cable operators.[74] Typical was the two-page ad spread for Encore, which introduced its six-channel minipay lineup:

> **The #1 source of unregulated cash flow.**
> Introducing channels and channels of unregulated cash flow. Encore Thematic Multiplex: six of your subscribers' favorite themes [Love Stories, Westerns, Mystery, Action, True Stories & Drama, and Tweens], each with its own channel. So your subscribers can always find what they're in the mood to watch. And Encore Multiplex delivers unregulated cash flow without the hassles of à la carte.[75]

The forms of the evasive maneuver—both multiplexing minipays and à la carte—were clearly responses to the efforts of Congress to seal off retiering as an avenue of escape from basic rate regulation. In earlier versions of the 1992 Cable Act, only limited basic service would have been subject to rate control, and retiering would have been the obvious escape route. In blocking that exit, the law steered cable operators toward the next safe (unregulated) harbor.

While the average price of a premium channel fell sharply from $10.17 in 1992 to just $9.11 in 1993 and $8.37 in 1994 (see table 6-12), changes in the product account entirely for that drop. With cable systems adding minipay tiers to get more programming on an unregulated basis, the pay category has been fundamentally redefined and is, on average, of lower quality. That is, HBO prices have apparently *increased* under reregulation. In the FCC's rate survey, HBO's monthly fee is reported to have gone from $11.11 in April 1993 to $11.50 in September 1993.[76] That indicates that those channels that have been traditionally defined as "premium" began increasing in price after reregulation—for the first time (in real terms) *ever*.

That increases in demand drive rate increases for HBO, the leading pay network, is suggested by the large gains in subscribership, absolutely and relative to trend. According to *Newsweek*: "HBO has recovered from

---

74. Those include Encore ("Unregulated Cash Flow for You") in CABLE WORLD, May 30, 1994, at 6–7; Showtime ("introducing five exciting new value added channels designed to give you unregulated streams of revenue"), *id.* at 18–19; The Box ("Great News! Unregulated Revenue!"), *id.* at 71; and Flix, which is part of Showtime Networks ("Here Are the Hard Facts: Flix is your best source of unregulated revenue today") in CABLE WORLD, June 6, 1994, at 30–31.

75. CABLE WORLD, May 30, 1994, at 6–7 (boldface in original).

76. FCC, *supra* note 33, at 6A.

Table 6-12
Average Monthly Prices for Premium Cable Channels

Year	Price ($)	Percentage Increase	Year	Price ($)	Percentage Increase
1976	7.71	NA	1986	10.31	.6
1977	7.92	2.7	1987	10.23	−.7
1978	8.01	1.1	1988	10.17	−.6
1979	8.27	3.2	1989	10.20	.3
1980	8.62	4.2	1990	10.30	1.0
1981	8.92	3.5	1991	10.27	−.3
1982	9.30	4.3	1992	10.17	−1.0
1983	9.70	4.3	1993	9.11	−10.4
1984	9.96	2.9	1994	8.37	−8.1
1985	10.25	2.9			

Sources: Paul Kagan Associates, *Marketing New Media,* June 20, 1994, p. 4; *Cable TV Investor,* June 30, 1995, p. 5.

its late-'80s doldrums to be a major cash cow for Time Warner. . . . With aggressive marketing, subscribers jumped by 3.5 percent last year [1993] after a long dry spell."[77] That implies that rate regulation does, as predicted by theory, lead suppliers to switch marginal investments (in salesmanship as well as in infrastructure) toward ancillary markets not covered by the regulatory scheme in question.[78] That, in turn, shifts the demand for such services outward, and tends to raise the profit-maximizing price charged by price-searching firms.

Typical of the industry's reaction to the growing importance of pay television networks was the report from *Marketing New Media* on March 20, 1995: "Cable operators, stung by FCC-mandated basic rate rollbacks, turned to pay TV in 1994 as an immediate source of incremental, unregulated revenue. The re-emphasis on premium-channel marketing paid divi-

---

77. Jolie Soloman, *What Michael Fuchs Wants You to Know,* NEWSWEEK, May 30, 1994, at 60–61.

78. In other words, the ancillary markets could be regulated under some other regime. At the margin, they would tend to become more attractive for sales effort, even if such regulation had previously shifted marketing efforts the other way. Hence, regulated foreign markets become relatively attractive for U.S. cable supplier investment, as noted earlier by TCI chief John Malone, even if regulation abroad has created investment disincentives of its own.

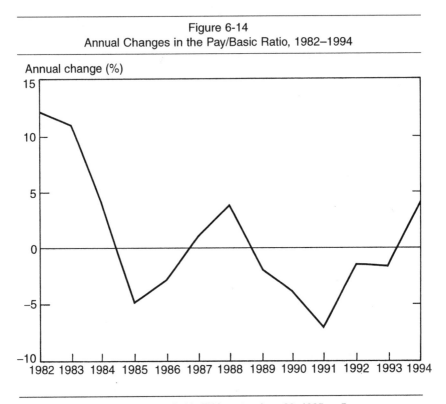

Figure 6-14
Annual Changes in the Pay/Basic Ratio, 1982–1994

Source: Paul Kagan Associates, *Cable TV Investor,* June 30, 1995, p. 5.

dends. The 100 largest MSOs netted more new pay subs (3.6 mil.) than basic subs (3.5 mil.)—a feat they hadn't come close to achieving since the 1980s."[79] Not only was the percentage change in the ratio of full- (as opposed to mini-) pay subscribers to basic subscribers positive for the first time since 1988, it was at its highest level since 1984, the year cable deregulation was enacted (see figure 6-14).

In a slightly different data series published by Paul Kagan Associates, the ratio of net new pay subscribers to net new basic subscribers in 1994 is sharply up from trend. Although the numbers are only suggestive owing to the availability of just two previous years of data, the 1994 change is impressive (see figure 6-15).

Regulation was explicitly tied to the industry's change in packaging

---

79. *1994: A Very Good Year for Pay TV,* MARKETING NEW MEDIA, Mar. 20, 1995, at 1.

Figure 6-15
Ratio of Net New Pay Subscribers to Net New Basic Subscribers, 1992–1994

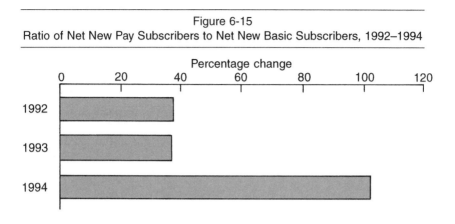

Source: Paul Kagan Associates, *Marketing New Media,* Mar. 20, 1995, p. 1.

strategy. *Cable World* led its January 23, 1995, issue with the headline, "In '94, Pay TV Category Posted Strongest Growth in Five Years" and explained the numbers as follows: "Thanks to its exemption from federal rate regulation, premium television growth surged in 1994, when it notched its biggest gains since 1989."[80] Growth of the top four premium services (HBO, Showtime, TMC, and Cinemax) was higher in 1994 than in any of the past six years (including 1989), both relatively and absolutely, as we can see in table 6-13.

Regulation continued to provoke tactical reactions by cable MSOs: "Industry watchers said premiums gained ground last year because they let cable operators replace revenues and cash flows lost to the 1992 Cable Act's impact. Along those lines, cable also became more adept at repackaging and pricing the category." The strategy in response to rate regulation was expected to continue to evolve: "[S]everal operators said they plan to focus more on new product tiers, another unregulated source of income, than on pay TV in 1995."[81]

---

80. Kim Mitchell, *In '94, Pay TV Category Posted Strongest Growth in Five Years,* CABLE WORLD, Jan. 23, 1995, at 1. Why the growth in pay services jumped in 1994 rather than in 1993, the first year of rate controls, can be explained as an adjustment lag. Because cable rates were not effectively constrained until late 1993, and basic retiering (as well as FCC rulemakings) occupied the industry up through early 1994, it could well have taken a year or more to intensify pay cable marketing efforts.

81. *Id.*

Table 6-13
Growth in Premium Subscribers, 1989–1994
(HBO, Showtime, TMC, Cinemax)

Year	Combined Pay Subscribers (millions)	Net Annual Change (%)
1989	33.7	1.4
1990	33.9	.2
1991	33.4	(.5)
1992	33.5	.1
1993	34.0	.5
1994	35.6 (est.)	1.5

Source: Paul Kagan Associates, as reprinted in *Cable World,* Jan. 23, 1995, p. 1.

A fascinating regulatory episode illustrating the importance of the premium channel loophole involved one minipay channel's efforts to classify its multiplexed offerings as à la carte services, thereby qualifying for unregulated status under the FCC's rate control rules. Encore, the TCI-owned channel featuring movies from the sixties, seventies, and eighties, expanded its offerings fivefold via multiplexing (as described in the advertisement quoted above). Yet Encore found that it was "stymied in its plans to expand distribution beyond TCI, in part due to industry uncertainty about whether its services are regulated," as *Cable World* wrote in 1995.[82]

Driving the uncertainty was a legal challenge to Encore's unregulated status by a movie channel competitor, Showtime, a subsidiary of Viacom. Showtime alleged that the regulatory exemption should not apply because the six channels aired different movies; Showtime, like HBO (owned by Time Warner), used multiplexing for time-shifting purposes, with each transmitted channel broadcasting the same programming on altered schedules. The FCC in May 1995 rejected the argument and bestowed unregulated status on Encore's six-channel multiplex. Encore immediately launched plans for a twelve-channel pay service, combining Encore's offerings with a multiplexed package of Starz!, another minipay service launched in early 1994. The service was promoted as "twelve channels for $12."[83]

82. Alan Breznick, *Encore's Multiplex Wins an FCC Boost,* CABLE WORLD, May 15, 1995, at 4.

83. *Id.* That is a quote from Encore's president, John Sie.

The elasticity of the cable programming package is vividly evident, as is the extent to which regulatory decisions affect business decision making. The fact that deregulated status was an important issue—so much so that one rival would lobby and litigate to exclude another from achieving it— implies that rate controls were at least partially binding. At the same time, however, it demonstrates that binding price controls are not the end of the issue for consumers: program packaging and its method of transport can change dramatically in response to such controls. That a rival firm would not like to see its competitor's prices rise via deregulation indicates something fundamental about the inability of rate controls to lower prices in quality-adjusted terms.

The evidence is exactly as predicted: regulation of some cable services gives operators an incentive to focus on alternatives not so constrained. The pattern holds across several different series, including those examined above (in the analysis of deregulation) showing the proportion of revenue obtained from the various service categories by cable television systems (see figure 5-10). In general, the evidence suggests that a pronounced shift in marketing effort in favor of deregulated basic occurred in the aftermath of the 1984 Cable Act and that a reverse shift occurred following reregulation imposed by the 1992 Cable Act.

THE GOING-FORWARD RULES

The going-forward rules resulted in addition by subtraction:

> The FCC giveth and the FCC taketh away. Having ordered cable television companies in February to cut their rates by 17 percent, the Federal Communications Commission today offset that action by giving the companies the right to raise prices when they add new channels. . . .
>
> For weeks, senior agency officials have struggled to reconcile two somewhat incompatible goals. They wanted to preserve the billion-dollar rate reductions they imposed earlier this year. But they also sought to encourage new programming services and investment in more sophisticated networks by cable operators.[84]

The period of declining cable TV rates (unadjusted for quality) pursuant to the 1992 Cable Act is calibrated by the monthly consumer price index data. From April 1993 to October 1994, the average cable customer's bill declined in real terms. The data then show a reversal, with rate increases about twice the rate of inflation occurring between October 1994

---

84. Edmund L. Andrews, *F.C.C. Approves New Rate Rises for Cable TV,* N.Y. TIMES, Nov. 11, 1994, at C1.

and May 1995. That change demarcates the period we call "dereregulation," in that it is associated with a conscious decision by the FCC to allow cable operators to increase prices.

That policy has encompassed various aspects of rate regulation, the most visible being the so-called going-forward rules. Perhaps as important were commission decisions to quietly drop some of the more severe aspects of the rate regulation scheme adopted in February 1994—for example, the annual productivity factor rollback, which would have further reduced regulated benchmarks by 2 or 3 percent (in real terms) annually to adjust for advances in efficiency.[85] The mood of cable industry investors began to change in April 1994, when cable operator stocks bottomed out. Whereas the Kagan MSO stock index fell 43 percent between October 14, 1993— the day after the announced merger between TCI and Bell Atlantic—and April 20, 1994,[86] there then began what industry analysts termed the "Reed Hundt rally," resulting in nearly a 50 percent rise in the index from that point through July 1995.[87]

A number of factors contributed to the stock market rebound, including the election of a Republican Congress and the subsequent round of procable telecommunications measures passed by both houses of Congress in 1995, but industry analysts never fail to include the fundamental impact of dereregulation. Predictions for subscription rate increases in 1995 and

---

85. The almost instant reversal of the FCC, after provoking such a sharp marketplace reaction to the reregulation rules February 22, 1994, was noted with glee by the cable industry: "The irony of the story is that, ever since February 22, 1994, the FCC has been trying to figure out how to ameliorate the effects of its regulations." Publisher's Letter, PAUL KAGAN ASSOCIATES, CABLE TV FINANCIAL DATABOOK, July 1995, at 4.

86. *The Public Market,* CABLE TV FINANCIAL DATABOOK, July 1995, at 54.

87. PAUL KAGAN ASSOCIATES, CABLE TV INVESTOR, July 31, 1995, at 1. A landmark event occurred when the FCC chairman, Reed Hundt, spoke to cable executives in May 1994 at their annual trade show in New Orleans and expressed the view that regulations should be loosened. At that point the commission abandoned the annual productivity factor adjustment and gave assurances that à la carte scrutiny would not be tight. Cable operator stocks rose by 6 percent following Hundt's speech. Kim MacAvoy, *Hundt Has Encouraging Words for Cable,* BROADCASTING & CABLE, May 30, 1994, at 14; Harry A. Jessell, *Agency Staff Urges Revamping of Programming Incentives,* BROADCASTING & CABLE, May 30, 1994, at 45; K. C. Neel, *NCTA Show Buoys Spirits,* CABLE WORLD, May 30, 1994, at 1, 65; Vincente Pasdeloup, *An FCC Olive Branch?* CABLE WORLD, May 30, 1994, at 2; Thomas P. Southwick, *Class Bully: Hundt Promises Not to Do It Again,* CABLE WORLD, May 30, 1994, at 10; Vincente Pasdeloup, *Stressing the Positive,* CABLE WORLD, May 30, 1994, at 20; *Washington: Policy Pow-Wow,* BROADCASTING & CABLE, June 6, 1994, at 73.

beyond were pegged at 7 percent, more than twice inflation.[88] Indeed, the one-year catch-up in 1995 was depicted as closer to a 10 percent increase in revenue per subscriber, or about $3 per month.[89] Regulated basic rates were themselves anticipated to rise in excess of 6 percent annually.[90] Even the FCC chairman's chief of staff was led to challenge cable operators griping about rate regulation in May 1995: "'Let's be candid. If you look at the $1.50 for going forward, inflation and external pass-throughs, you're not far from the maximum of where you want to be,' said [Blair] Levin."[91]

The "going-forward" rules were the centerpiece of the FCC's deregulation strategy. Though haunted by the political fallout that could be expected from caving in to cable industry demands for higher-priced programming charges, the commission successfully pushed formal consideration of the going-forward rules back until two days after the November 1994 elections. That was exactly the timing the trade press anticipated.[92]

---

88. PAUL KAGAN ASSOCIATES, CABLE TV INVESTOR, June 30, 1995, at 4.

89. PAUL KAGAN ASSOCIATES, CABLE TV INVESTOR, Mar. 24, 1995, at 3. That calculation included cost-of-living allowances, about $1/subscriber/month in program cost pass-throughs, and an unregulated "new product tier" with (just) 10 percent penetration.

90. PAUL KAGAN ASSOCIATES, CABLE TV INVESTOR, May 31, 1995, at 7.

91. PAUL KAGAN ASSOCIATES, CABLE TV REGULATION, May 23, 1995, at 5.

92. For instance, as early as August 1994, an article in *Cable World* reported, "The rumor circulating in Washington, D.C., last week: Democrats in Congress have asked FCC chairman Reed Hundt to make sure cable rates don't rise until the November election to keep the party from losing some seats." Vincente Pasdeloup, *The "Going-Forward" Debate,* CABLE WORLD, Aug. 8, 1994, at 2. Later in the month came this report: "The whispering grew louder in Washington, D.C. that the commission may not release the so-called 'going-forward' rules until after November's elections—several weeks beyond the Oct. 13 deadline that many cable operators had been hoping the FCC would meet." *Cable World* Staff, *FCC Taking a Hard Look at a la Carte Regs,* CABLE WORLD, Aug. 29, 1994, at 1. Finally, in late October 1994 *Cable World* reported: "It's unclear whether the FCC will release the rules before or after the Nov. 8 general elections, and whether they'll be voted on at a public meeting or in private circulation. As the election draws closer, there's increased speculation in Washington, D.C. that the FCC will avoid making a decision until after Nov. 8 to avoid a political backlash against Democratic candidates." Vincente Pasdeloup, *Going Forward Rules Still Going Nowhere,* CABLE WORLD, Oct. 31, 1994, at 1, 44. Sure enough, the rules were released on November 10, 1994. That so little was made of the political timing of the deregulatory move is a product of the "dirty little secret," noted by Nicholas Allard, that it is in the interests of both the FCC and the cable industry (the parties with inside information regarding the underlying regulatory dynamics) to behave publicly as though rate regulation is working splendidly. The Clinton FCC had no interest in bucking Democratic members of Congress, and cable industry lobbyists had no interest in bucking the FCC, particularly as they were then the recipients of its regulatory largesse.

The going-forward rules were crafted to give cable operators an incentive to improve basic cable television programming by allowing rate increases for new channels added (going forward) to basic cable packages.[93] The rules set a new four-year horizon for price hikes but instantly (as of January 1, 1995) permitted monthly basic rates to rise by $1.50. (Basic rates would then be capped through years 1 and 2, allowed to rise another twenty cents in year 3, and be capped again in year 4.) The rate increases applied to expanded basic tiers, and to fully qualify for such rate increases the cable operator would have to add six channels (a seventh in year 3)— the allowable increase being $.20 per channel per month plus an additional $.30 (in year 1) to recover license fees for the new channels. The latter provision was to "[ensure] that they won't simply add six no-cost shopping channels."[94] Many systems had reacted to controls imposed in 1993 by substituting low-cost programming for high-cost, which severely embarrassed the FCC. Because home shopping channels pay cable systems for carriage, the FCC's rate controls, established on a price-per-channel cap, encouraged operators to reduce costs by terminating programming requiring license fees and generating additional cash flow via shopping networks.[95] The going-forward rules were crafted so as to mitigate that incentive.

The very logic of going forward demonstrates the underlying dynamics of cable television rate regulation. The rules replaced regulations established only eight months earlier in the February 22, 1994, FCC rulemaking. Those regulations provided for a 7.5 percent marketing markup for new program channels. In other words, if a new service cost the operator fifteen cents per subscriber per month, the cable system could add the channel to a regulated tier and increase rates by sixteen cents a month (7.5 percent of fifteen cents equals 1.125 cents). (In contrast, the going-forward rules allow a price increase of up to thirty-five cents for adding that (one) new service.) The FCC's motivation for enacting the first set of rules was straightforward: new programming was not to be used as a gimmick to end the constraint of rate control. The premise of regulation was that price-cost margins should be slashed to competitive levels, and the commission sought to apply a tight constraint. For an industry accustomed to 45 percent cash flows, a 7.5 percent markup over direct costs was a good-faith effort to squeeze out the monopoly increment in cable pricing.

---

93. Jube Shiver, *FCC Moves to Spur New Cable Channels*, L.A. TIMES, Nov. 11, 1994, at D1, D2.

94. John M. Higgins, *Wall Street Welcomes Going-Forward Rules,* MULTICHANNEL NEWS, Dec. 5, 1994, at 94.

95. Thomas W. Hazlett, *How Home Shopping Became King of Cable,* WALL ST. J., July 14, 1994, at A14.

That effort failed—as revealed by the FCC's quick reversal. The agency could not help but respond to the severe reaction of the industry against the February 1994 rules. First, while new program services had been very sluggish under the uncertainty ensuing from the 1992 Cable Act, there was a strong reinforcement of the informal programming freeze supplied by the February 1994 rulemaking. Operators argued that they had virtually no incentive to make marketing investments on 7.5 percent margins. That was more than industry talk: basic cable became neglected, with operators' devoting their marketing efforts elsewhere. By mid-1994 it was clear that basic subscriber growth was falling and that the industry was in a retrenchment mode. With tight controls in place, the trade press was dominated by stories with headlines such as: "Rate Rules Put Squeeze on Upgrades."[96]

Even more important than the operators' reaction to the 7.5 percent price margin cap was that emanating from cable programmers. Programmers would have welcomed a price control scheme that lowered retail margins and increased the quantity of programming demanded by cable consumers. Yet theirs were the shrillest voices demanding price liberalization at the FCC. When the going-forward rules overturned the tight caps of the February 1994 rulemaking, cable programmers were generally relieved, complaining only that the deregulation did not go far enough.

ESPN's senior vice president for marketing, George Bodenheimer, praised the going-forward rules as "much more conducive to adding networks" when compared with the previous 7.5 percent markup. "That looks a lot better to anybody in this industry looking for broad carry. It'd be a breath of fresh air."[97] The fact that the rules did not allow even greater operator rate increases drew criticism from fX (the Fox cable network) executives: "In the most harsh terms, it's government creation of programming monopolies," said Peggy Binzel, Fox Inc.'s vice president for government relations. "It's an entrenchment of existing services and anti-competitive."[98] The president of the Travel Channel saw continuing risks posed by potential FCC reversals: "The bad news is that the new pro-

---

96. Russell Shaw, *Rate Rules Put Squeeze on Upgrades,* ELECTRONIC MEDIA, May 30, 1994, at 18, 29. The article went on to note: "With the latest round of rate rollbacks, cable systems are pruning their wish list of desired technical upgrades. Wendell Bailey, the National Cable Television Association's vice president of science and technology, says that operators have been 'performing triage' on their equipment purchases and upgrade goals."

97. *Quoted in* Vincente Pasdeloup, *FCC Issues "Crawling Forward" Rules,* CABLE WORLD, Nov. 14, 1994, at 1, 8.

98. *Id.*

gram tiers are not definitely unregulated. They [the FCC] reserve the right to come back and reregulate if the prices get out of line."[99]

The rules soon turned out to be liberal enough, however, to prove a boon to new basic networks. By mid-1995, the trade press was commonly ascribing the apparent revival in cable programming growth to dereregulation. *Cable World* commented in May: "Almost six months after the FCC issued its so-called 'going forward' rules, the big winners continue to be the mid-sized programming services that had waited several years for shelf space to open up."[100] A few months later, it again noted:

> New and mid-sized networks continue to swim in new subscribers since the FCC issued its so-called "going-forward" rules late last year. The head of the pack for June [1995]: Country Music Television, the Sci Fi Channel and the Cartoon Network.[101]

It is also informative that the going-forward rules are not, for the most part, cost based. Of the $1.50 per month rate increase allowable immediately (and for the first two years), $1.20 is independent of the cost of programming. One industry securities analyst noted jubilantly, "[V]irtually all of the $1.20 fee would drop straight into an operator's cash flow, except for about six cents in added franchise fees to cities."[102] Thus, the FCC had in fact abandoned the cost-based rules adopted in February 1994 and had conceded that financial incentives, even at high-level profit margins suggestive of market power, were appropriate. The ability of operators to control programming decisions had apparently left the commission with little alternative.

The dynamics of rate regulation are further illustrated by the way that the bargaining terms between cable operators and cable programmers have shifted. In the deregulated environment, cable systems were unconstrained in what they could pay for programming and in what they could charge customers. The optimizing decision, then, was to maximize profit over both input costs and output revenues.

With rate regulation, revenues are constrained; hence, input costs are under increasing pressure. While the going-forward rules at least partially

---

99. Comments of Roger Williams, *quoted in Cable Disappointed as FCC Goes Forward*, CABLE REGULATION DIGEST, Nov. 14, 1994 (on-line address: gopher.vortex..../cable-reg/crd.94-11-14).

100. Alan Breznick, *More Going Forward Gains,* CABLE WORLD, May 15, 1995, at 52.

101. Will Workman, *Going-Forward Is Still a Boost for Some Nets,* CABLE WORLD, July 10, 1995, at 25.

102. Higgins, *supra* note 94.

succeeded in getting the operators to add new channels, cable programmers, seeking carriage for new services, are offering operators "'launch
support payments' as high as $2 or more per customer, as well as temporary
license-fee deferrals, license-fee rebates, temporary or long-term free carriage, price freezes, and plenty of marketing help."[103] In essence, where the
cable operator previously paid programmers license fees, under rate regulation new service suppliers pay operators for carriage (at least initially).
Because the going-forward rules essentially put six new channels onto basic tiers, any programmer desiring to get established in the marketplace is
forced to compete for one of those limited slots. With incentives for further
capacity upgrades constrained by the overall rate regulation regime, the
competition has become furious. In April 1995 one observer explained the
changing terms of trade in the industry:

> [I]n the constant wrangling between cable operators and programmers over
> carriage contracts, the balance has clearly shifted in favor of operators in the
> last few months. With up to six channels to fill on regulated service tiers and
> scores of networks from which to choose, systems are finding that most
> networks are very open to cutting deals after two years of industry stagnation.
>   . . . Cable operators and networks say that even programmers long notori-
> ous for driving hard distribution bargains are showing considerably more
> flexibility since the going-forward rules were issued late last year.
>   One prime example is Turner Broadcasting System Inc., which has been
> handing out generous launch support payments for Cartoon Network and
> reworking license fees for one-year-old Turner Classic Movies.
>   The usually hard-nosed Turner organization also has been giving away
> CNN International in many cases since that service launched in January.
> The bottom line for operators: Turner executives are generally stressing a
> willingness to be flexible.[104]

The author goes on to describe the experience of a newly launched
network, the History Channel (THC, owned by A&E Television Networks),
and a midsized network, the Learning Channel (TLC, owned by Discovery
Networks, Inc.). THC, which began operation January 1, 1995, originally
attempted to market on an "inflexible" rate card, at fourteen to twenty-five
cents per subscriber per month. To succeed in the regulated era, however,
the network had to abandon that strategy and gained carriage deals by agreeing to waive license fees for up to two years. Similarly, TLC adopted standard two-year no-charge deals for new carriage agreements.

---

    103. Alan Breznick, *Operators Gain Upper Hand,* CABLE WORLD, Apr. 24, 1995, at
62.
    104. *Id.*

Other programmers have paid substantial sums to cable systems upfront: "Not surprisingly, the networks reportedly writing the biggest checks—Court TV, E! and Cartoon Network—have ranked among those enjoying the largest subscriber gains in the going-forward sweepstakes thus far. . . . Conversely, the few networks that haven't handed out marketing incentives or tinkered with their license fees haven't fared as well."[105]

The clear implication is that the rate regulation scheme has lowered the returns to programming from what they would be in the absence of rate regulation. That may lead to diminished investment in software creation over the long run and result in quality losses for consumers down the road. That is, when constraining prices charged by cable operators results in lower input prices, one may reasonably expect a decline in the effort devoted to competing in the programming market. How effectively the FCC's deregulation and the 1996 Telecommunications Act will counter that uncertainty is difficult to say.

CABLE SATELLITE NETWORKS

As we saw in table 5-9, the number of cable satellite networks markedly increased during the reregulation period. Is that increase due to the expansion of cable audiences and the bolstering of network revenue streams under rate regulation or is it due to exogenous factors? The FCC has specifically noted that spurt in network formation and surmised that it is attributable to the latter: "Expanded channel capacity and the emergence of new distribution outlets for programming (DBS, VDT) are chiefly responsible for the [network formation] revival."[106] Lest there be any doubt that expanded channel capacity is unrelated (or negatively related) to rate regulation, the commission goes on to credit the price increases allowed under liberalized rules issued in late 1994 as pushing new network formation: "In the wake of the going forward rules and the freshly minted New Product Tier [totally deregulated tiers comprising new networks], it is likely that growth in the number of cable networks will reach new highs in 1995."[107]

There is little doubt that long-run competitive pressures, including the cable industry's strategy to expand service offerings in the face of direct rivalry from telephone and wireless video delivery systems, have led to industry expansion and a programming boom. The plummeting costs of

---

105. *Id.*

106. FCC, *supra* note 11, at 6. The cable competitors referred to are direct broadcast satellite (DBS) and video dialtone (VDT) systems.

107. *Id.*

broadband capacity upgrades were exciting industry planners with the possibility of "virtual video-on-demand" and other marvels of the 500-channel system before the 1992 Cable Act. Moreover, strong evidence suggests that the rate controls seriously suppressed demand for new programming. That evidence includes viewer ratings and FCC tiering data, buttressed by the position taken by programmers and—in pushing rate decontrol via going-forward rules explicitly designed to bring new networks to cable subscribers—by the FCC itself.

Another piece of supporting evidence is gleaned from an examination of cable network data (see table 5-9). The total number of networks, having only increased from 78 to 87 between 1988 and 1992, jumps to 101 in 1993 and to 128 in 1994. Although basic cable channels are a substantial part of the growth, their rise—which began in 1992—is far smaller than the 1992–1994 proportional increase in premium channels, which leap from eight to twenty, and pay-per-view networks, which go from four to eight. While the previous satellite network surge after the 1984 deregulation was led by basic network formation, with pay channels declining from eleven to five between 1983 and 1990, pay channels proportionally expand much more than basic networks in the most recent surge.

Indeed, the consensus view within the industry was that the post–Cable Act bubble in new program development was a product of the expectation (formed in recent years, with rapid technical advancements frequently announced) that future cable systems would demand greater quantities of cable channels.[108] Thomas Southwick, publisher of *Cable World,* noted the "seemingly paradoxical situation in which cable operators are pressed for channel space while dozens of new programming networks are launching, announcing or gearing up to do both."[109] His argument for new networks accepted the fact that rate regulation seriously diminished demand (at least in the short run) for cable channels: "The FCC's latest wave of rate regulations will put a big dent in system cash flows, forcing cutbacks in plans to expand channel capacity."

---

108. Alan Breznick reported the countervailing forces: "Despite a channel-capacity crunch and the FCC's decision to force basic cable rates down another 17 percent, would-be basic cable networks keep crowding onto the programming launch pad. But few, if any, cable operators intend to push the ignition button any time soon. In fact, many operators and existing programmers think the FCC's March 30 rate rules essentially sounded the death knell for basic channels not backed by retransmission consent deals." Alan Breznick, *Network Wannabes Press on Despite Dour Launch Outlook,* CABLE WORLD, Apr. 11, 1994, at 1.

109. Thomas P. Southwick, *Launches,* CABLE WORLD, Apr. 18, 1994, at 12.

At the same time, Southwick anticipated that the Supreme Court would overturn the "must-carry" rules on constitutional grounds, thus freeing up channel space, that new competition from direct broadcast satellites and telephone companies would push up video program demand, and that cable system upgrades that survived rate regulation would do the same—especially for unregulated services. Among the "[p]articularly attractive" services he listed were home shopping, "still unregulated premium services," pay-per-view, computer services, and networks that successfully target enthusiastic niche markets, such as the TV Food Network and the History Channel. Only the last two services are subject to rate regulation, and both firms marketing those have said that rate regulation has seriously hurt their efforts.

Network launches that were reportedly spurred by the advent of digital compression and the emerging 500-channel infrastructure received disappointing market response in the wake of the FCC's 1994 tightening of rate regulation.[110] While noting that a large number of planned networks were currently in their development stages, *Cable World* commented in April of that year: "Yet, with operators overwhelmed by the FCC's new rules and seeing few economic rewards for adding any regulated services, most prospective basic networks have run into trouble securing firm, specific carriage commitments. As a result, they're mum about launch distribution figures, fudging once-solid launch dates or only discussing household distribution targets months or years into the future."[111]

THE FINANCIAL IMPACT OF CABLE REREGULATION

Investments in a traditionally regulated public utility market are considered less risky than those in comparably capital-intensive industries because of the rate-of-return price-control mechanism. In that public utility commissions are charged with maintaining a given rate of return for investment in the utility, variances in returns are held below what would otherwise obtain. A high-profit year will predictably result in regulatory adjustments' imposing lower rates and, hence, returns, while just the opposite is anticipated following periods when returns are abnormally low. The rate control

---

110. Tim W. Ferguson, *Viewers Hurt as Cable Gets a Double Dose,* WALL ST. J., June 14, 1994, at A15. "More than 100 new networks loom on cable's horizon, spawned by pending 'digital compression' and other means of increasing channel capacity. Now that prospect has been clouded by the inability of cable systems to purchase as many offerings [under rate regulations imposed by the FCC]."

111. Breznick, *supra* note 108, at 50.

authority, were it to perform flawlessly and with omniscience, in fact, would eliminate all volatility and produce a risk-free asset in the public utility's stock.

Cable rate regulation is institutionally distinct. The rate of return realized by a cable operator is not a factor in setting rates.[112] Under the controls typically instituted before the 1984 Cable Act by local governments and in the regulatory scheme mandated in the 1992 Cable Act, rate caps have been set on the basis of criteria not directly related to the costs specific operators have incurred. That scheme, largely a product of administrative convenience, avoids the huge accounting burdens imposed by cost allocation, demand forecasting, and rate base analysis. Yet it also yields efficiency effects in avoiding the misalignment of incentives imposed via rate-of-return regulation. Under price caps, operators who engage in high-cost operations are penalized directly, via lost profits. Under traditional regulation, such wasteful costs are passed on to ratepayers.

For better and for worse, then, the rate-cap environment returns riskiness to the regulated entity. The issue is a central one. If rate regulation raises the risk premiums associated with investments in the cable television supply infrastructure, even short-run cost savings for consumers may be offset by long-run quality depreciation. That is, if the cost of investing in a given hardware configuration is driven up for reasons related to financial concerns and unrelated to technological or consumer acceptance uncertainties, the quality of the service available to consumers in future periods will decline, *ceteris paribus*. For a given price, consumers will be sold fewer outputs, some of which will be crowded out by the additional financial inputs required in the production process.

The Market Reaction to Re-reregulation, February 1994

The reaction of both the cable industry and the financial markets to the tighter constraints embodied in the FCC's February 1994 rulemaking was loud and virtually instantaneous. The huge Bell Atlantic–TCI merger was

---

112. The operator can select the cost-of-service rate regulation route under the FCC's reregulation rules, but the commission was slow issuing these rules and few cable systems initially attempted to take advantage of them. The imposition of rate rules on previously unregulated assets on a cost basis is extremely problematic when assets have traded freely in the marketplace at prices much above the replacement cost of tangible capital (as seen in the evidence showing q ratios above 3). What is the rate base when assets are purchased for prices that reflect expectations of monopoly profits? The commission has taken the position that only book values are permissible, which, while theoretically defensible, launches the agency into bookkeeping battles royale.

called off the day following the FCC's action, and both parties blamed rate regulation.[113] Although some press accounts emphasized other problems with the transaction,[114] there is little question that the credit markets re-evaluated the prospects for cable system acquisitions and cable infrastructure upgrades following the FCC's action. TCI, on its own again, announced that it would suspend half its own $1.1 billion capital budget pending clarification of the FCC's rate regulations—news that was sufficiently credible to send the stock prices of major cable equipment manufacturers plummeting.[115] The optimistic slant was that the investment disincentives created by re-reregulation would cause only temporary delay in capital expenditures by multiple system operators. *Newsweek* reported: "The collapse of the deal between Bell Atlantic and TCI won't bring construction of the Information Superhighway to a halt. Even the FCC's new cable price controls will only slow it down. Now the race to find detours begins."[116]

Other signs of cost reduction[117] in response to re-reregulation were evident across the industry. The second-largest cable system operator, Time Warner, announced a $100 million downsizing of its 1994 capital budget, a little more than one-fourth the amount of its 1993 budget. It also instituted a hiring freeze to cut staff expense via employee attrition.[118] Cablevision Systems, the fifth-largest MSO, with 2.134 million subscribers,[119] provided public information on what adjustments it would make in response to the July 14, 1994, rate rollbacks.[120] Cablevision announced that it would lower its basic rates from $21.89 to $21.00 for 360,000 subscribers in its Long

---

113. John Greenwald, *Disconnected,* TIME, March 7, 1994, at 60–61; K. C. Neel, *Rereg Double-Whammy,* CABLE WORLD, Feb. 28, 1994, at 1, 41. "The deal fell apart because [TCI president John] Malone wanted more shares of Bell Atlantic as compensation for the falling stock price; [Bell Atlantic chairman Ray] Smith wanted to pay less for TCI's cable properties because the new FCC rules meant they wouldn't bring in as much cash." Nancy Hass, *Full Speed Ahead—Maybe,* NEWSWEEK, Mar. 7, 1994, at 45.

114. Sandra Sugawara & Paul Farhi, *Bell Atlantic, TCI Call Off Merger,* WASH. POST, Feb. 24, 1994, at A1, A11.

115. Mark Robichaux, *The FCC's Rate Cuts Will Slow Traffic on Information Super-highway,* WALL ST. J., Feb. 25, 1994, at B1. *See also* Carl Weinschenk, *As TCI Reviews Cap-Ex Budgets, Manufacturers Sitting Tight,* CABLE WORLD, Feb. 28, 1994, at 5.

116. Hass, *supra* note 113, at 44.

117. Delaying capital investment is a cost reduction in the sense that current infrastructure is being depreciated longer.

118. Geraldine Fabrikant, *Time Cable Displeased, Cuts Outlays,* N.Y. TIMES, May 5, 1994, at C3.

119. NATIONAL CABLE TELEVISION ASSOCIATION, CABLE TELEVISION DEVELOPMENTS, April 1994, at 14-A.

120. The incremental rollback was targeted at 7 percent.

Island system and that 71 percent of its customers would see rate decreases. Just 1 percent would receive rate increases. The firm estimated that the price cuts would reduce cash flow by 5 percent. At the same time, the firm announced a $15 million cut in expenses, including a layoff involving 160 workers, or about 3 percent of its work force.[121]

Perhaps the clearest signal of industry retrenchment was the withdrawal of a public offering by Falcon Cable, a Los Angeles–based system operator serving 1.1 million subscribers, immediately after the FCC's February meeting. In the offering $125 million of new equity had been sought to provide fiber-optic backbone to replace over 2,300 miles of coaxial copper, easily doubling channel capacity.[122] The firm's chairman drew an analogy: "The uncertainty caused by the FCC is like an apartment owner suddenly having rent control imposed. It's not just the first rate cut of 10 percent; it's the second cut of 7 percent on top of that."[123]

That reaction—higher discounting of future returns under conditions of regulatory uncertainty—was widespread.[124] The response was not universal, however, as a few firms found that the escape route offered by upgraded technology was the preferred course to follow. The trade press reported: "Comcast Corp. and Cablevision Systems are among a handful of MSOs that say they won't let the impact of FCC-ordered rate roll-backs deflate aggressive construction plans this year."[125] The logic given was that the "strategy to push unregulated revenues over regulated revenues such as basic and extended basic service will require an exhaustive upgrade and rebuild schedule."[126] Yet expansion remained an exception to the consensus view that the re-reregulation had significantly delayed network upgrades and the "information superhighway."[127]

---

121. Vincente Pasdeloup, *Operators Begin to Announce Rate Changes,* CABLE WORLD, June 13, 1994, at 2; K. C. Neel, *Cablevision Dodges a Cap-Ex Bullet with 160 Job Cuts,* CABLE WORLD, May 16, 1994, at 1, 112.

122. John Greenwald, *Disconnected,* TIME, Mar. 7, 1994, at 61.

123. *Id. See also* MERRILL LYNCH & CO., PROSPECTUS: 8,641,000 SHARES FALCON CABLE TV CLASS A COMMON STOCK (preliminary prospectus) (Jan. 19, 1994).

124. The uncertainty was not primarily over how the extant rules would be applied. Although strong reactions were registered even before the details defining the commission's new rate regulations were released, the uncertainty concerned the long-run stability of investment. If the commission could toss out 500 pages of April 1993 rate regulations after just ten months and ambitiously expand out regulatory domain into areas explicitly exempted under the 1992 act (for example, à la carte channels), future cash flow forecasts evidently had a larger variance than previously.

125. K. C. Neel, *Building Expectations,* CABLE WORLD, Mar. 28, 1994, at 50.

126. *Id.*

127. Kenneth N. Gilpin, *Market Place: A One-Two Combination Staggers the Cable*

The working premise of the FCC was that regulating supracompetitive profits would have no impact on investments undertaken to provide services to consumers in the future. In the sense that monopoly rents are just that—rents—that logic is literally definitional. But the complication caused by real markets in an uncertain world is that current cash flows provide important information to financial markets. Future cash flows, particularly when they are attached to new technologies, are inherently problematic to evaluate. The cable industry was adamant that the blow delivered by rate regulation on current services was crucial in limiting access to capital markets for technical upgrades. Typical were the comments of Falcon CEO Marc Nathanson:

> Nathanson said he could not understand why the White House was calling upon cable operators to build the electronic superhighway while at the same time the FCC was designing rate regulations that hurt their ability to invest in the new technology.
>
> "This is such a schizophrenic policy," said Nathanson. "What the telecommunications gurus need to do is take some Prozac. We have to get rid of the highs and lows in telecommunications policy and get on a steady course."[128]

Not only are current cash flows linked to future cash flows because of the high cost of information about future returns, but the regulatory risks exhibit serial correlation. If rate regulations can be crafted so heavily as to influence current cash flows, it is more likely that future periods will be subject to similar constraints. That greatly reduces the attractiveness of financing opportunities within the sector. In short, nowhere do firms or credit markets divide cash flows into "competitive" and "economic rent" designations. Any regulatory action that puts cash flows at risk in the current period lowers the ability of suppliers to repay future obligations and raises the probability that future period cash flows will also be subject to regulatory risks of their own. That is the apparent explanation for the immediate withdrawal of capital from cable television investments upon price reduc-

---

Television Industry and Puts It on the Defensive, N.Y. TIMES, Mar. 7, 1994, at C4. "'The only reason to be investing in the cable business at this juncture is as a takeover play,' said Christopher P. Dixon, a cable analyst for Paine Webber Group. 'No one knows what the cash flow prospects will be over the next two to three years. In a week, we have gone from a seller's to a buyer's market.'. . . 'The industry will have trouble generating enough cash flow to find the necessary funds to build the superhighway,' Mr. Moran [a vice president of Salomon Brothers] said. 'That will delay its construction, perhaps as much as five years.'"

128. Rich Brown, *Rate Regs Could Impede Cable Investment,* BROADCASTING & CABLE, Feb. 28, 1994, at 12.

tions that still left firms with ample ability to repay existing indebtedness and achieve normal (or above-normal) long-run returns.

That dramatic response by capital markets in defunding technical upgrades was an immediate product of reregulation, yet its effect on consumer welfare is difficult to register. Infrastructure investment is a long-run phenomenon, and in this case the regulatory regime was relaxed fairly quickly—within months of the re-reregulation rulemaking. Still, the uncertainty generated by the process of regulation may raise the cost of capital for the industry over a substantial period of time.

The Risk Premium on Cable Investments

The evidence from financial markets is most informative: the risk premium on cable operator bonds rose about the time of both reregulation and re-reregulation.

The Paul Kagan Associates newsletter *Cable TV Investor* sporadically charts the yield spreads between a portfolio of long-term cable operator bonds (the Kagan Cable High-Yield Media Bond fund) and portfolios of general debt securities. The two control portfolios used are the Merrill Lynch High-Yield fund and the Lehman Long-Term Bond fund. The data are published in various issues of the newsletter and are reported here as completely as possible (see table 6-14). Unfortunately, there are only two data points before passage of the Cable Act of 1992, just one of which was registered before the legislative process to enact the measure was in full swing (with Senate passage in late January 1992). Moreover, the Kagan bond fund is redefined in October 1994, and the break in series makes further analysis difficult. Nevertheless, the series can be used to calibrate the effect on cable bond risk premiums up to that time by looking at the changing rate differentials.

First, note in table 6-14 that the period from January 1992 to October 1994 is one of declining rates for the Merrill Lynch High-Yield fund, which recedes from a yield of 12.20 percent to 10.82 percent, but one of steady rates overall for the Lehman Long-Term Bond fund, which begins at 7.84 percent and ends at 7.95 percent. (That masks declines initially offset by increases from February 1994.) The Kagan cable fund, however, increases from 13.05 percent to 14.48 percent. That increase is doubly impressive when we note that cable yields actually declined from January 1992 until July 1993, and then—after a brief move upward—resumed a sharp decline in the aftermath of the announcement that Bell Atlantic and TCI would merge (October 13, 1993).

The differential in yields, subtracting either control index's rate of re-

Table 6-14
Kagan Cable High-Yield Media Bond Performance
January 31, 1992–September 30, 1994

Yield Date	Cable High Yield (%)	Merrill Lynch High-Yield (%)	Difference (%)	Lehman Long-Term Yield (%)	Difference (%)
1/31/92	13.05	12.20	.85	7.84	5.21
6/30/92	12.84				
9/30/92	12.51				
12/31/92	12.71				
1/31/93	12.48	10.87	1.61	7.19	5.29
3/31/93	12.17				
4/15/93	12.30	10.45	1.85	6.74	5.56
5/15/93	12.33	10.29	2.04	6.93	5.40
6/15/93	12.26	10.10	2.16	6.78	5.48
6/30/93	12.28				
7/15/93	12.28	9.80	2.48	6.39	5.89
7/30/93	12.35				
7/30/93	12.35	9.83	2.52	6.41	5.94
8/15/93	12.40	9.80	2.60	6.27	6.13
8/15/93	12.40	9.80	2.60	6.27	6.13
8/31/93	12.49	9.79	2.70	6.09	6.40
9/15/93	12.61	9.80	2.81	6.03	6.58
9/30/93	12.63	9.82	2.81	6.09	6.54
10/13/93	12.52	9.75	2.77	5.85	6.67
10/15/93	12.17	9.75	2.42	5.85	6.32
10/31/93	12.01	9.75	2.26	6.09	5.92
11/15/93	11.93	9.75	2.18	6.29	5.64
11/30/93	12.06	9.75	2.31	6.42	5.64
12/15/93	11.88	9.67	2.21	6.40	5.48
12/31/93	11.84	9.62	2.22	6.42	5.42
12/31/93	11.84	9.62	2.22	6.42	5.42
12/31/94	11.84	9.62	2.22	6.42	5.42
1/15/94	11.81	9.49	2.32	6.34	5.47
2/15/94	11.89	9.32	2.57	6.47	5.42
3/31/94	13.59	10.07	3.52	7.18	6.41
3/31/94	13.59	10.07	3.52	7.18	6.41

(Table continues)

		Merrill		Lehman	
	Cable	Lynch		Long-	
	High	High-		Term	
Yield	Yield	Yield	Difference	Yield	Difference
Date	(%)	(%)	(%)	(%)	(%)
3/31/94	13.59	10.07	3.52	7.18	6.41
4/15/94	13.95	10.39	3.56	7.38	6.57
4/30/94	14.12	10.48	3.64	7.39	6.73
4/30/94	14.12	10.50	3.62	7.40	6.72
5/15/94	14.34	10.64	3.70	7.58	6.76
5/15/94	14.34	10.60	3.74	7.60	6.74
5/31/94	14.31	10.70	3.61	7.50	6.81
6/15/94	13.64	10.38	3.26	7.47	6.17
6/30/94	14.33	10.63	3.70	7.68	6.65
6/30/94	14.33	10.63	3.70	7.68	6.65
6/30/94	14.33	10.63	3.70	7.68	6.65
7/15/94	14.49	10.70	3.79	7.60	6.89
8/15/94	14.51	10.72	3.79	7.65	6.86
9/30/94	14.48	10.82	3.66	7.95	6.53

Table 6-14 (cont.)

Sources: Paul Kagan Associates, *Cable TV Investor,* Feb. 12, 1993–Mar. 24, 1995.

turn from the Kagan bond fund yield on the same date, gives us a reasonable estimate of the risk premium specific to investing in cable television markets. The change in that differential around the time of reregulation events would appear to be strong evidence that such regulatory changes are shifting that premium. As seen in figure 6-16, the difference in cable television operator yields against the two control series rises over time and demonstrates the following pattern: a modest increase around the time of Cable Act enactment in one series, gradual increases after the first round of FCC rulemaking (announcing the 10 percent rate rollbacks in April 1993) in both series, a sharp drop following the Bell Atlantic–TCI merger announcement in both series, and an even sharper hike about the time of re-reregulation at the FCC (February 22, 1994) in both series. From start to finish, the difference between the cable fund and the Lehman Long-Term Bond portfolio rises 132 basis points (or 25.3 percent of the starting level); the difference in the Merrill Lynch High-Yield series rises 281 basis points (306 percent). The evidence suggests that the risk associated with cable operator bonds rose substantially in the reregulation environment.

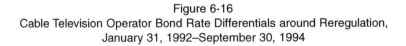

Figure 6-16
Cable Television Operator Bond Rate Differentials around Reregulation,
January 31, 1992–September 30, 1994

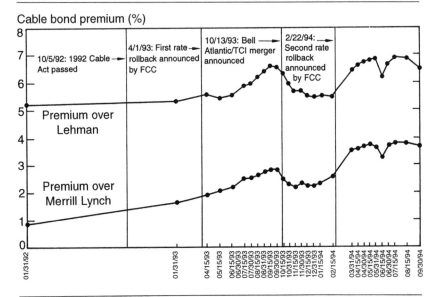

Source: Paul Kagan Associates, *Cable TV Investor,* Feb. 12, 1993–Mar. 24, 1995.

The Collapse of Cable's Public Debt Market, 1994

The enhanced riskiness associated with cable industry debt instruments predictably drove cable operators seeking capital back to private capital markets, whence they had finally emerged after years of attempting to gain access to public markets. The pattern of public debt and equity issues in figure 6-17 shows a striking abandonment of public debt markets in 1994. Fortunately, that came just as banks and other private credit sources were being allowed back into cable lending; the regulatory crunch in banking, including the ban on highly leveraged transactions in October 1989, had effectively eliminated banks as providers of cable credit in the early 1990s (see table 6-15).

The FCC has interpreted that change in financial sources as a result of interest rate hikes attributable to monetary policy of the Federal Reserve Board and has determined that it is of little importance in that private debt replaced public debt: "Early in 1994 the Fed began raising interest rates prompting a decline in the public debt market. . . . Despite this decline,

Figure 6-17
New Stock and Bond Issues: U.S. Cable Operators, 1988–1994

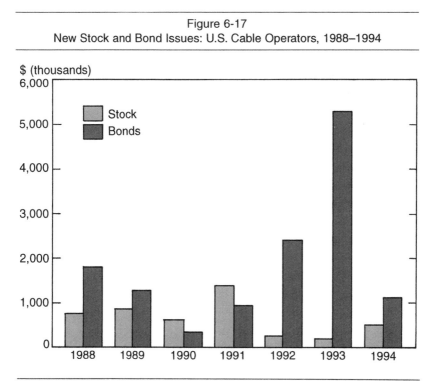

Source: Paul Kagan Associates, *Cable TV Financial Databook,* June 1992, p. 95; June 1995, p. 92.

however, the revival in cable financing activity continued in the form of private debt."[129]

That is faulty economic analysis. First, in that private debt is as sensitive to rate hikes (provoked by Fed policy or otherwise) as public debt, the proffered explanation does not explain the observed switch between financial instruments. Second, substituting private for public debt is not a cost-free solution for borrowers. Private debt is typically more expensive, and it is generally advantageous to gain access to public markets to obtain the lowest interest rate. For that reason, the cable industry, like any maturing sector, expends great time and public relations effort to gain acceptance on Wall Street.

After decades of frustration, cable operators began gaining access to public debt and equity markets in the late 1970s, and then only sparingly. It is true that the industry was able to feed its capital appetite from various

---

129. FCC, 1 CABLE INDUSTRY TRENDS, no. 2 (Mar. 15, 1995), at 8.

Table 6-15
Debt and Equity Flows in U.S. Cable Television Markets,
1988–1994 ($ millions)

Year	Banks, Insurance Companies, Other Borrowings	Total New Debt	Total New Equity
1988	5,078	6,867	746
1989	6,494	7,334	834
1990	3,900	4,390	597
1991	689	1,601	2,640
1992	−1,762	638	1,930
1993	−3,583	1,697	227
1994	4,772	5,861	870

Sources: Paul Kagan Associates, *Cable TV Financial Databook,* 1992, 1993, 1995.

sources before, during, and after reregulation. But exiting from public markets is costly; it adds to industry financing expense (because the lowest and most competitively priced capital is not available to cable borrowers), which will constrain firms' efforts to improve the quality of physical capital over the long run.

That experience in the bond market was assuredly a product of reregulation, particularly as reinforced in the February 1994 rulemaking. We can confirm that causality by examining the unregulated multichannel video investments that were increasing their creditworthiness during just the period that cable's riskiness was rising. In a study of the capital market effects of rate controls, William M. Emmons III, Adam B. Jaffe, and Jonathan B. Taylor wrote:

> While the bond market was tightening for domestic cable companies, overseas cable ventures and cable's competitors (direct broadcast satellites and wireless) experienced an increase in the receptiveness in the bond market, suggesting that bond investors were not troubled by video distribution *per se* but by distribution in the domestic *cable* market. Rogers Cable, a Canadian cable provider, raised $335 million in May of 1994. American Telecasting, a wireless [cable] company, raised $100 million in June. Collectively, Videotron Holdings, Bell Cablemedia and Diamond Cable Communications issued $625 million in debt securities for overseas cable investments, largely

in the United Kingdom. These unregulated cable television endeavors were well received, raising $1.3 billion in the bond market—more than six times the amount raised by domestic cable companies during the same period.[130]

By the end of 1994, however, the various credit markets were returning to normalcy in the eyes of cable investors. That switch was directly attributed to the easing of rate regulation: "One key factor behind bigger cable loans: the closing of the FCC's rate-freeze/rate-reduction window. Banks whose committees were afraid to make a cable loan while the FCC was at the wheel now look ahead to quarter-to-quarter cash flow gains and, eventually, double-digit annual increases."[131] Recovery came to financial markets as rate regulation faded.

CONFUSION, UNCERTAINTY, AND TRANSACTIONS COSTS

The task of regulating cable television rates under the mandate of the 1992 Cable Act has been an enormous burden on the agency charged with responsibility. The FCC has carried out dozens of rulemakings, received hundreds if not thousands of official comments, written innumerable notices of inquiry, notices of proposed rulemakings, reconsiderations, and reports and orders. The agency itself has not kept any formal record detailing the overall regulatory function it has performed under the act, but a 1995 document released by the commission bore the title: "Sixth Report and Order and 11th Order on Reconsideration."[132] A law review article described just one of the countless rulemaking iterations—rate regulations announced in April 1993:

> The scope of the rate regulation rulemaking in itself is daunting. After issuing the *Notice of Proposed Rule Making* in December 1992, running over one hundred typewritten pages and twenty pages in the Federal Register, the FCC received extensive comments from 176 parties, and reply comments from 121 parties. The April 1993 *Rate Order* and its accompanying materials were 521 typewritten pages and over one hundred pages in the Federal Register.[133]

---

130. WILLIAM M. EMMONS III, ADAM B. JAFFE & JONATHAN B. TAYLOR, THE INVESTMENT CONSEQUENCES OF THE RE-REGULATION OF CABLE TELEVISION (Economics Resource Group, Inc., Dec. 20, 1994), at 15 (emphasis in original).

131. *The Money Market,* CABLE TV FINANCIAL DATABOOK, July 1995, at 88.

132. FCC, In the Matter of Implementation of Sections of the Cable Television Consumer Protection and Competition Act of 1992: Rate Regulation, MM Dkt. No. 92-266, MM Docket No. 93-215 (June 5, 1995).

133. Nicholas W. Allard, *Reinventing Rate Regulation,* 46 FED. COMM. L.J. 63, 97–98 (December 1993) (footnote omitted). The author of the law review article did not claim

The FCC informed Congress in 1993 that it could not execute its mandated reregulation duties without additional funding. Congress stalled for some months, but then obliged: between fiscal year 1993 and fiscal year 1996, FCC staffing levels rose from 1,753 full-time employees to 2,267.[134] Moreover, a specific request to hire 240 people to staff the new Cable Services Bureau was rewarded with an emergency appropriation of $11.5 million in the summer of 1993.[135] That division, however, was to be plagued by staff turnover and management difficulties. By 1995 the Cable Services Bureau was already being "reorganized," and disgruntled administrators were speaking to the press. *Cable World* reported: "The bureau, which has been hindered by management problems and an exodus of cable experts, will be reorganized early this year. A new rate division with some 70 employees will be created. 'When we had 10 percent of the people we have today, we were more productive,' one bureau employee said."[136]

Management problems were probably inevitable, for the job assigned those new hires was immense: to rein in the profit-maximizing behavior of 11,000 cable systems, each with its own managerial staff—all with far greater knowledge of the cable television industry than all but a handful of FCC employees. From the beginning that was an overwhelming mission. Given that the commission elected to do battle, to actually fulfill the spirit of the 1992 reregulation law so seriously as to constrain cable operator revenues, brutal complications were unavoidable. Edmund Andrews wrote in the *New York Times,* reporting on the first batch of cable rate regulations (the 10 percent rollback) on May 3, 1993: "The numbing array of instructions, worksheets, charts, grids, definitions and exclusions defies easy answers."[137]

The complexity of regulation led the FCC to make frequent bureaucratic blunders. The dialectical manner by which it established a 10 percent rate rollback in April 1993, reconsidered the decision but let it stand in August 1993, then reversed itself and ordered an additional 7 percent roll-

---

to comprehend fully what he had read: "The Author freely concedes that, notwithstanding considerable effort, his understanding of the relevant regulatory passages might be flawed." *Id.* at 75.

134. Paul Farhi, *Closing the Cable Rate Loopholes,* WASH. POST, Aug. 5, 1994, at B1. The overall FCC budget mushroomed from $133 million in fiscal 1993 to $196 million in fiscal 1995. BUDGET OF THE UNITED STATES, 1996, app., at 975–76.

135. Kenneth Robinson, *How Much Wood Would a Woodchuck Chuck, If a Woodchuck Could Chuck Wood? The FCC, the New Congress, and Regulatory Spending,* 11 TELECOMM. POL'Y REV. 2 (Feb. 26, 1995).

136. Vincente Pasdeloup, *Hundt: FCC May Not Offer More Upgrade Incentives,* CABLE WORLD, Jan. 2, 1995, at 1, 25.

137. *Quoted in* PAUL KAGAN ASSOCIATES, CABLE TV INVESTOR, May 24, 1994, at 5.

back in February 1994, only to reverse itself yet again with the going-forward rules announced in November 1994, was indicative of the entire process. The commission shuffled and reshuffled rate rollback dates: the first (10 percent) rollback was to go into effect June 21, 1993, then October 1, 1993; finally September 1, 1993.[138] Similarly, the 7 percent rollback was scheduled for May 15, 1994, but cable operators were then given to July 14, 1994.[139] Errors were rife in the procedural aspects of regulation: a spreadsheet issued by the commission in February 1994 so that cable operators could figure out their "benchmark" regulated rates was done incorrectly, and a recall was issued.[140] Such mistakes were to become commonplace at the FCC. Ken Robinson, author of the weekly *Telecommunications Policy Review,* reprinted an agency press release, headed "Cable Services Bureau Revises FCC Form 1210," explaining one such foul-up:

> The Cable Services Bureau today issued an errata [*sic*] to the FCC Form 1210. Form 1210 ("Updating Maximum Permitted Rates for Regulated Cable Services") must be filed by cable operators who seek to justify rate changes to regulated services on account of changes in external costs, the addition or deletion of channels from regulated tiers, or inflation. This newly revised version of the form addresses three errors contained in the version of the form that was released on March 7, 1995 [forty-four days earlier].
>
> First, the revision makes a change to Line A2 on page 9 of the form. The March 1995 version of the Form 1210 stated that "[i]f you have previously filed a Form 1210, enter the updated permitted charge from line F3 from your most recently filed Form 1210 if that was the May version of the Form. If your most recent filing of the Form 1210 was the March 1995 version, enter this information from line I8." Line A2 on page 9 of the newly revised form states that "[i]f you have previously filed a Form 1210, enter the updated permitted charge from line F6 of your most recently filed Form 1210 if that was the May 1994 version of the Form. If your most recent filing of the Form 1210 was the March 1995 version, enter this information from line J8."
>
> Second, the revised Form 1210 deletes what was line D9 in the March 1995 version of the Form. Line D9 in the March 1995 version of the form asked for the "Cost of Programming Added Using Caps Method Being Claimed as an External Cost." This line has been deleted because Lines F6 and F11 ask for the same information.
>
> Finally, the formula contained in Line G7 of the spreadsheet for the March 1995 version of the Form 1210 has been eliminated. This formula has been

138. Allard, *supra* note 133, at 73.

139. Kate Maddox, *FCC: Cable Rate Rules Successful,* ELECTRONIC MEDIA, July 15, 1994, at 3.

140. Kim MacAvoy, *Hundt Has Encouraging Words for Cable,* BROADCASTING & CABLE, May 30, 1994, at 14.

removed from line G7 because the formula uses the mark-up methodology pursuant to the Commission's initial going forward rules. This causes a problem when in the same filing an operator adds channels to both (1) cable programming service tiers using the caps methodology pursuant to the new going forward rules and (2) the basic service tier using the mark-up methodology pursuant to the initial going forward rules. Under these circumstances, the formula incorrectly adds increases made pursuant to the mark-up methodology to increases made to the caps approach in module F of the form. The revised spreadsheet for Form 1210 no longer contains this formula. Operators using the spreadsheet are now required to make their own calculations for line G6 to fit their particular circumstances.

Operators who have filed incorrect information with either the Commission or a franchising authorities [*sic*] as a result of the problems contained in the March 1995 version of the Form 1210 must amend their filings with the correct information.[141]

Robinson makes his own translation of the bureaucratese: "We made a mistake and issued a 'Form 1210' that was messed up. We're sorry, but you will have to get a new 'Form 1210' and fill it out again."[142]

The iterations caused by commission mistakes and reconsiderations became profound. On January 19, 1996, the FCC issued the following rule correcting the Thirteenth Order on Reconsideration, regarding a single rate regulation form:

1. On September 22, 1995, the Commission released a Thirteenth Order on Reconsideration in MM Docket No. 92-266 ("Thirteenth Reconsideration"), FCC 95-397, 60 FR 52106 (October 5, 1995), establishing a new optional rate adjustment methodology. On December 15, 1996, the Office of Management and Budget approved the Commission's new FCC Form 1240 (Annual Updating of Maximum Permitted Rates for Regulated Cable Services), which implements that methodology. See Public Notice, OMB Approves FCC Form 1240 (Annual Updating of Maximum Permitted Rates for Regulated Cable Services), DA 96-7 (January 11, 1996). An error was found in the Instructions to the initially released paper copy of the December 1995 version of the Form. The Form has been corrected and a Public Notice has been released describing the error and how to obtain copies of the corrected January 1996 version of Form 1240. See Public Notice, Cable Services Bureau Corrects FCC Form 1240, DA 96-40 (January 19, 1996).

2. Operators are required to use the corrected January 1996 version of Form 1240. We are concerned, however, that operators may have already filed the December 1995 version of Form 1240 with their local franchising authority or with the Commission, or that they have made plans to do so in

---

141. Kenneth Robinson, *Things Worth Remembering,* 11 TELECOMM. POL'Y REV. 13–14 (May 7, 1995).

142. *Id.*

the immediate future. We do not intend the requirement to file a corrected Form 1240 to affect the review period of the filing. Therefore, operators that have already filed FCC Form 1240 with their local franchising authority or the Commission should submit a corrected Form 1240 by February 20, 1996. Operators who plan to file with their local franchising authority or the Commission by January 26, 1996 are permitted to file a December 1995 Form 1240, but must file a corrected Form 1240 by February 20, 1996. If a corrected filing is made after that date, the franchising authority will have the authority to extend the review period by as many days as the filing is late.[143]

Not just the form but the substance of regulation has been plagued by administrative error. The entire process of rulemaking has undergone a roller-coaster cycle, most often shifting course in response to political criteria. Democratic congressional leaders, embarrassed about negative press accounts of the first round of rate rollbacks in September 1993, pressed hard on the newly appointed Reed Hundt (who had not been on the FCC when the first rules were crafted) to push through a second and tougher series of rate controls. In responding to that pressure with the round of regulations announced February 22, 1994, the commission ignited a maelstrom of political opposition—not only from cable operators, but from cable programmers and financial institutions—because the rules were seen as devastating to new program services and to capital values, most immediately and notably in pushing the market-propelling Bell Atlantic–TCI deal past the point of no return. Just three months later, however, the commission was in obvious retreat, backing away from many of the more ambitious rules just formulated.

The uncertainty that the changing regulatory regime imposed on cable investors was substantial. In an article entitled "Rate Relief from the FCC?" industry analyst John Mansell gave his view of the situation in early 1995, as the FCC attempted—in the wake of Republican victories in Congress—to mollify cable operators' fears of overregulation:

> Meanwhile, the FCC appears to be floating another trial balloon suggesting a willingness to stave off Congress by granting regulatory waivers.
>
> In a speech by chmn. Reed Hundt last month and in a recent rate ruling, the FCC said there may be circumstances where a cable system, although not subject to effective competition, may be charging rates that are constrained by the presence of one or more multichannel competitors.

---

143. FCC, In the Matter of Sections of the Cable Television Consumer Protection and Competition Act of 1992—Rate Regulation, Thirteenth Order on Reconsideration, FCC Form 1240, MM Dkt. No. 92-266 (adopted Jan. 12, 1996; released Jan. 19, 1996), at 1–2 (footnote omitted).

"In such instances, the public interest may be served by relying on the market forces instead of our rate rules to ensure that the operator's rates are not unreasonable." In the Matter of TEL-COM, Inc. (Jan. 20, 1995).

The analyst reviewed FCC regulations as "two years of mistakes":

Given the FCC's frequent flip flops and ineffective ad hoc approach to regulation, most skeptics have grown cynical and simply don't believe the Commission has any intention of granting waivers.

If the FCC were serious, it would openly and clearly establish criteria for waivers instead of adding vague dicta to obscure rulings.

Unfortunately, this Commission has a serious credibility problem. Over the past two years, it has established rule after rule, only to later reverse and contradict itself.

The first set of benchmarks was completely abandoned and deeper rollbacks ordered. À la carte tiers were seemingly allowed, struck down, then deemed to be legitimate new-program tiers—but only if a limited number of channels was involved.

State negative-option rules were preempted to permit retiering. Then, the FCC said there was a role for states, a decision that has led to at least a half-dozen lawsuits by states against cable operators.

When cable operators complained that a skimpy 7.5%/ch. rate pass-through for adding new services wasn't an incentive for carriage, the FCC came out with "going forward" rules. But firms like Cox Cable and Continental, which hadn't migrated services to à la carte tiers were, in effect, penalized.

Even when attempting to right a wrong, there have been missteps. In November, the FCC purported to provide relief to small operators by permitting certain equipment costs of adding new channels to be passed through to subs.

The FCC's actual ruling, however, was an either/or decision. Small-system owners could either take the new going forward rule like everyone else, or take the equipment cost pass-through.

One month later, on its own motion, the Commission reversed itself and finally made the proper decision: small operators are entitled to both.[144]

The cable industry has clearly had to surmount a large degree of regulation-induced uncertainty at the same time that it prepares to do battle with newly emerging competitors in telecommunications. As late as mid-1995, even cable MSOs brimming with lobbyists, lawyers, and access to the best information money could buy could not tell their shareholders what, precisely, the regulatory story was. Adelphia, a publicly held cable operator serving about 1.6 million subscribers, stated in its 1995 annual report:

---

144. John Mansell, *Rate Relief from the FCC?* CABLE TV REGULATION, Jan. 27, 1995, at 2.

The FCC has adopted regulations implementing virtually all of the requirements of the 1992 Cable Act. As noted above, amendments to the rate regulations were recently announced and the FCC is also likely to continue to modify, clarify or refine the rate regulations. In addition, litigation has been instituted challenging various portions of the 1992 Cable Act and the rulemaking proceedings including the rate regulations. The Company cannot predict the effect or outcome of future rulemaking proceedings, changes to the rate regulations, or litigation. Further, because the FCC has only issued its interim rules and has not adopted final cost-of-service rules, the Company has not determined to what extent it will be able to utilize cost-of-service showings to justify rates.[145]

Not only have the rules contributed to uncertainty in the private sector, the regulatory regime has been inordinately complicated for municipal governments. Designated as FCC partners in setting rates for basic services in the 1992 Cable Act, only a small fraction of the franchise authorities eligible to participate applied for the FCC certification necessary to do so.[146] The vast majority of cities have simply deferred to the federal agency, presumably because the complexity of the rules (and potential liability as a defendant in a lawsuit brought by a cable operator) outweighs the advantages of asserting local control. Even more striking among those cities that have elected to be part of the regulatory solution, perhaps, is the regularity with which outside experts are hired to help city officials figure out the regulations. Industry consultants have become *pro forma* assistants to municipal governments that step into the regulatory fray, and the need for their costly assistance is another reason why most jurisdictions routinely opt out.

The ineffectiveness of regulation in suppressing cable rates in quality-adjusted terms does not mean that regulation is without meaning or impact. In reacting to controls by repackaging and creating new, unregulated revenue streams, firms utilize real resources and sacrifice valuable (if unseen) opportunities. Suppliers expend significant sums in contesting the process whereby Congress creates legislation and the FCC and municipal authorities then implement it and in reworking business decisions in response to new regulatory realities. To the extent that those expenditures do not increase output in terms of either quality or quantity, we may properly think of them as socially wasteful rent seeking.

---

145. ADELPHIA CABLE COMMUNICATIONS, 1995 ANNUAL REPORT (1996), at 23.

146. "So far, only 5,823 franchising authorities out of 33,000—some 18 percent—have certified their authority to regulate basic cable rates with the FCC." Vincente Pasdeloup, *Cities Hit "Hold" Button on FCC Rules,* CABLE WORLD, Apr. 18, 1994, at 1, 37.

As is usually the case, reliable estimates of the magnitude of such expenditures are extraordinarily difficult to come by. Accounting practices do not separate out rent-seeking expenses, nor do government agencies diligently estimate wasteful social costs they have mandated or encouraged. Yet some hints of the scale of compliance (or evasion) costs are observable. In TCI's December 1993 10-K filing with the Securities and Exchange Commission, the firm reported spending $21 million in "one-time direct expense in connection with the implementation of the FCC's regulations."[147] In that TCI served about one in five U.S. cable subscribers, a linear extrapolation across all firms would suggest over $100 million in compliance costs for 1993.[148] Those costs, of course, do not include inefficiencies created in the marketing of different services, including those changes brought about by a scaled-back capital investment program.[149] It is unclear whether they include legal fees, lobbying expense, or both.

The FCC has also recorded a partial accounting of the government's costs associated with rate regulation of cable operators. In a document sent to the Office of Management and Budget in April 1994, the commission projected that its employees would expend 224,000 hours annually to respond to consumer rate complaints; that it would process 11,200 forms from cable operators listing their compliance with regulated benchmarks, and that each such filing would take the FCC twenty hours to process; that it would receive 14,000 requests from cable operators for assistance in filling out the commission's forms; that 2,100 systems would file cost-of-service showings, and that it would take eighty hours for the FCC to process each of those. Those activities total 616,000 hours plus however long the FCC staff spends handling the 14,000 cable operator requests for assistance. At $35 per hour, that amounts to $21.56 million. Those compliance costs would likely be matched or exceeded by the 6,000 local governments participating in the rate control process.

---

147. TELE-COMMUNICATIONS, INC., FORM 10-K (Mar. 28, 1994), at II-5.

148. InterMedia, an MSO serving about 750,000 subscribers, reported spending sixty cents per subscriber, or $450,000, just to fill out FCC "benchmark" forms to determine its rates during the 1994 re-reregulation. "And the extra workload appears to be benefiting accountants. 'I can't tell you one of the top-eight accounting firms that hasn't been retained to work on this,' said Leo Hindery, general managing partner of InterMedia." ELECTRONIC MEDIA, June 20, 1994, at 8.

149. In May 1994, TCI's 10-Q report to the Securities and Exchange Commission noted that the firm had suspended $500 million of its $1.2 billion capital budget "pending further clarification of the Federal Communications Commission's . . . February 22, 1994 revised benchmark regulations." TELE-COMMUNICATIONS, INC., FORM 10-Q FOR THE QUARTERLY PERIOD ENDED MARCH 31, 1994 (May 1994), at I-18.

As sketchy as those numbers are, it is apparent that the process of adjustment involves a nontrivial cost for both private and public sectors. The confusion over what the regulations really mean, after they are produced, also produces costs for operators. A TCI executive exclaimed at the May 1994 cable convention: "We're trying very hard to fully comply with the law. But we're making decisions at the same time the FCC is changing them. The FCC has changed its definition of what a subscriber is three times so far. We're trying to comply with the law and they can't figure out what a subscriber is."[150]

The hidden costs that result from regulation-inspired disorder are almost certainly dominant; the real expense to society involves lost surplus from the services not sold, the program services not begun, and the infrastructure not built. Those costs are virtually impossible to quantify. The social costs imposed by complying with—or evading—rate regulation are surely substantial.

---

150. Comments of Barry Marshall, Chief Operating Officer, Tele-Communications, Inc., *quoted in* K. C. Neel, *NCTA Show Buoys Spirits,* CABLE WORLD, May 30, 1994, at 65.

7

Political Coalitions and the 1992 Cable Act

IT IS PERHAPS easiest to gauge the impact of cable reregulation from the positions interested parties have taken on the issue. We employ the dual assumptions that financially vested entities expend substantial resources to discover the likely economic effects of various policy courses and then loyally assert public positions consistent with maximizing profit.[1] Examining the positions key industries have taken in the debate on cable rate regulation can thus shed light on the predictable effects of the law.

LOBBYING FOR PASSAGE

James Mooney, chairman of the National Cable Television Association, made revealing comments about the passage of the Cable Television Consumer Protection and Competition Act of 1992:

> "We started out with a controversy over rates and customer service, which, no matter the merits, was nonetheless a real controversy, and created an adverse grassroots political problem," Mooney said. "This problem festered and did not go away over time."
> A coalition against the cable industry was formed with "many of them (coalition members) seeking to use the consumer issue as a vehicle for realizing their own agenda vis-à-vis cable," he said.

---

1. Certainly, those are the operative assumptions driving Becker's classic formulation of political equilibria. The model relies on the belief that pressure groups reliably and intelligently lobby for public policies that advance their economic welfare. Gary Becker, *A Theory of Competition Among Pressure Groups for Political Influence,* 98 Q.J. ECON. 371 (1983).

The coalition included most of the broadcast industry, labor unions, consumer groups, wireless cable operators, rural electric cooperatives, independent telephone companies and companies interested in direct broadcast satellite services.

"Against this coalition, we were essentially alone," Mooney said.

The Motion Picture Association of America sided with cable only after Congress passed the conference report on S. 12, and the Bush Administration didn't commit to the fight until the very end, according to Mooney.[2]

Although the coalition that formed in favor of the bill included the participants Mooney lists, it is clear that the labor unions and consumer groups served as public relations agents, with industry interests applying the muscle to advance the legislation. Most important were the broadcasters, followed by certain telephone companies (which intensified their efforts in favor of stringent cable rate controls as the 1992 act was being implemented), and a host of potential competitors to cable. Those competitors, including wireless cable and DBS hopefuls, were primarily concerned with program access, a provision in the 1992 act to allow firms other than the local cable monopoly to purchase cable programming networks such as HBO, ESPN and TNT. Owing to their fledgling status, those new entrants had only marginal political clout.[3] On the other side, cable operators were joined in opposition to the act by programmers. The motion picture industry was the only one Mooney explicitly listed, but the NCTA itself included cable satellite networks, which strongly opposed the 1992 act. There is much to learn about the economic impact of cable reregulation from the positioning of those interest groups.

Cable Operators

That cable operators vigorously opposed the 1992 Cable Act is no surprise.[4] But their opposition does not necessarily imply, as some have as-

2. Vincente Pasdeloup, *Post-Mortem: Rereg Powered by Coalition,* CABLE WORLD, Oct. 12, 1992, at 1, 76.

3. To the extent that those new competitors exercised greater clout, were concerned with more than the program access portions of the bill, or both, the rent-seeking analysis of this section is strengthened. That competitors should seek—or not object to—price controls is evidence that market participants do not expect such controls to "work." That is, if prices for a substitute product are effectively lowered, the rival's subscriber base rises, and residual demand for a firm's output declines.

4. The evidence for that is overwhelming. Cable operator efforts to oppose the 1992 Cable Act were widely observed—particularly in the national advertising campaign urging cable customers to oppose the measure on the grounds it would raise their rates.

serted, that the 1992 Cable Act would result in lower quality-adjusted prices for consumers.[5] Cable interests would reliably oppose any added constraints that did not provide offsetting (protectionist) benefits.[6] Constraining profits via price controls, however, does not necessarily transfer surplus to consumers. If cable systems lower quality by a sufficient degree, rate regulation can lower both consumer surplus and (regulated) industry profits.[7] The evidence is clear that the cable industry did oppose rate regulation, and went so far as to conduct a national advertising campaign claiming that reregulation would raise consumers' rates.[8] Still, that tells us little about the impact of controls on consumers.

NTIA Defends Cable Bill Assessment as Conferees Meet, 12 Comm. Daily, Sept. 10, 1992, at 1–2; Mary Lu Carnevale, *Cable TV Industry Mounts an Ad Blitz Against Measure to Curb Rate Increases,* Wall St. J., Sept. 9, 1992, at B7; Vincente Pasdeloup & Kathy Clayton, *Cable Industry Launches Ad Blitz to Block Rereg,* Cable World, Aug. 31, 1992, at 1, 51.

5. Kathleen A. Carroll & Douglas J. Lamdin, *Measuring Market Response to Regulation of the Cable TV Industry,* 5 J. Reg. Econ. 385 (1993).

6. An industry may even try to enact hostile legislation if it is helpful *at the margin.* Indeed, cable lobbyists actually attempted to have a "reregulation" bill resuscitated and passed into law in October 1990. As described in the trade press, Sen. Timothy Wirth (D-CO), a cable-friendly legislator, narrowly failed to work out a last-minute compromise with then-Sen. Al Gore (D-TN) after the legislation had been given up for dead. The cable industry rationale was that it was in its interests to have a weak reregulation measure pass, rather than have the issue hanging over their heads; cable companies wanted to calm fears that the ban on telephone company competition (codified in the 1984 act) would be removed. In September 1990 a cable industry newsletter considered the key trade-off involved in blocking reregulation legislation: "Congress is serving notice that if cable doesn't swallow its pill this year, harsher medication may be dished out next year in the form of telco entry. Rep. Ed Markey (D-MA) plans telco-cable hearings next year." Paul Kagan Associates, SMATV News, Sept. 25, 1990, at 2.

7. Stigler's "capture theory" creates some confusion. Because economists, following Stigler, see regulation as typically sought by the regulated industry itself, they have sometimes been careless about distinguishing the precise nature of the regulations sought. The defining characteristic of proindustry (as opposed to proefficiency) regulation involves raising rivals' costs, making new entry more difficult. That an industry resists regulation that constrains the ability of incumbents to maximize profit is not evidence against regulatory capture, particularly if rival firms seeking to constrain interindustry competition are advancing such rules.

8. "The NCTA [National Cable Television Association] last week began mailing fliers to millions of cable subscribers warning of big price hikes if the bill [the 1992 Cable Act] becomes law." Paul Farhi, *House Probes Cable TV Cost Data,* Wash. Post, Aug. 29, 1992, at A7.

Cable Programmers

Far more interesting is the position taken on rate regulation by the owners of cable programming. If the commission's rules were likely to squeeze price-cost margins and expand output, then programmers—firms supplying inputs to retail distributors—should profit as their sales volumes increase. That is theoretically true, in that upstream suppliers desire downstream complements to be competitively priced, thereby raising consumer demand for their inputs. It is also easily observed from an accounting perspective: because cable networks are paid a per-subscriber licensing fee and sell commercials to advertisers on the basis of audience size, both sources of revenue will unambiguously increase with the higher penetration that would result from lower retail prices, all else constant.[9]

As a group, cable programmers argued vociferously that rate reregulation under the 1992 Cable Act would negatively affect basic networks. New networks, such as the Sci-Fi Channel, were particularly fearful of rate regulation,[10] but established channels, such as Discovery, were also strong lobbyists against it—particularly if they had begun new network ventures.[11] New "launches" were especially vulnerable to suppliers' reactions to price controls, either from being pushed off basic into à la carte status, or by failing to gain carriage at all. The actual program producers, represented by the Motion Picture Association of America, were also public opponents of reregulation.[12] The widespread belief in the video pro-

---

9. The USA Network, for instance, charges twenty-nine cents per subscriber per month for carriage and receives an average of twenty-three cents per subscriber per month in ad revenues. PAUL KAGAN ASSOCIATES, MARKETING NEW MEDIA, June 20, 1994, at 3.

10. Richard Turner, *Sci-Fi Channel Encounters a Hard Sell Due to Competition, Reregulation Threat,* WALL ST. J., May 24, 1990, at B1, B5.

11. "John Hendricks, the founder and chairman of the Discovery Channel, said that Discovery was able to surmount its initial financial problems because cable was de-regulated in 1984. With reregulation, he said, his new channel, the Learning Channel, will face an uncertain future." Bill Carter, *Now or in 1993, Cable TV Meets the Regulators,* N.Y. TIMES, Mar. 8, 1992, at 2E.

12. Edmund L. Andrews, *Cable's Big Ally on Capitol Hill: Hollywood,* N.Y. TIMES, Jan. 6, 1992, at D8. "Mr. Valenti [president of the MPAA] will not discuss his lobbying strategy, but he has not been shy about his distaste for the cable bill. 'We are opposed to rate regulation of our products in any form,' he said. 'That's a matter of principle.'" The trick here, of course, is that the cable bill attempted to control not the price of movies but rather the price of movie distribution services. Normally, if distribution costs fall, demand (or imputed demand) for a product increases. The article also noted that Hollywood was disgruntled with the 1992 Cable Act because of its retransmission consent provisions.

gramming sector was that reregulation was bad for business even before day 1: "The Cable Act of 1992 has already adversely impacted cable operators. It is causing a virtual freeze in new programming decisions. Cable operators are proceeding very cautiously when it comes to adding new services like the Cartoon Channel and the Sci-Fi Channel because it may prove difficult, if not impossible, to recoup the investment."[13]

Television Broadcasters

Also illuminating is the position taken by the broadcasters. Long in a competitive position vis-à-vis cable and erstwhile beneficiaries of anticable rules enforced by the FCC in the 1960s and 1970s, the broadcast industry was keenly interested in the Cable Act of 1992. Indeed, the broadcasters were the chief sponsors of the legislation. The industry had long pushed cable rate regulation, arguing forcefully for it in a 1990 FCC proceeding where no other issues (such as "must-carry" and retransmission consent) were involved.[14] The National Association of Broadcasters (NAB), which would have an economic interest in low-priced limited basic tiers and *high-priced* cable programming tiers in a world in which rate regulation effectively lowered prices, expressed a distinct interest in its FCC filing:

> The intent of the [1984] Cable Act is that, until such competition develops, franchise authorities should have the option of regulating rates for basic service to protect the public from monopolistic practices, and NAB believes the entire video industry suffers from the effects of excess revenue diversion to cable.[15]
>
> . . . .
>
> Finally, the Commission solicited comment . . . on measures it could take or recommend to avoid cable systems retiering their basic service to frustrate rate regulation. NAB agrees this poses a serious problem. Under the ACLU decision, however, the Commission lacks discretion to revise the statutory definition of basic service, which is the only service tier for which the Cable Act [of 1984] permits regulation. NAB suggests that the Commission recommend that Congress amend the Cable Act to include within the definition of basic cable service all tiers which carry local broadcast channels or services which carry advertising.[16]

---

13. Paul Kagan Associates, Cable TV Law Reporter, Nov. 30, 1992, at 1.

14. National Association of Broadcasters, Comments, In the Matter of Reexamination of the Effective Competition Standard for the Regulation of Cable Television Basic Service Rates, MM Dkt. No. 90-4 (Apr. 6, 1990).

15. *Id.* at 28–29.

16. *Id.* at 37.

The NAB thus endorsed ambitious rate regulation of all basic cable tiers. That position is key to understanding the economic logic of the broadcasters' interest in cable rate controls. Should rates for basic cable networks be constrained by regulators, the optimal situation for broadcasters would involve widespread cable system evasion of controls via retiering. That would leave the limited basic package, essentially including only broadcast signals, at a low price, with cable programming on higher-priced tiers beyond the reach of the regulations. In advocating policies, including new congressional action, to ensure that *all* basic cable programming would be covered by rate controls, the NAB exposes its belief that such controls will not effectively lower subscription prices.

In the competition for viewing audiences, any real reduction of cable prices would expand cable viewership—at the direct cost of broadcast advertising revenues. It is assuredly curious that the NAB endorses measures to stop what it claims to be the diversion of "excess revenue to cable." As a competitor, it benefits from such alleged high-price policies. In that broadcasters have been losing substantial market share to cable programmers throughout the past decade (see table 5-12), whatever monopolistic power cable operators exploit should work to ease the competitive crunch. Broadcasters evidently believed that, once transactions costs were accounted for, quality-adjusted rates were likely to be higher under cable rate regulation.[17]

Even well in advance of the legislation, broadcasters were generous in their support of cable reregulation, underwriting various advertising campaigns asking for public support for the policy. One broadcaster-financed newspaper ad appeared in August 1991, claiming, "If Cable Wins, Consumers Lose." The ad noted that cable rates had risen 56 percent in four years according to the General Accounting Office and warned, "And now the cable monopoly is threatening to raise your rates again."[18] In his treatise on network television, Ken Auletta writes that part of the strategic corporate rate plan common to each of the three broadcast networks in the early 1990s was to hamstring the cable industry with reregulation.[19] The cable industry

---

17. As we saw in chapter 6, their forecast was immediately proved correct: the decade-long rise in basic cable viewing share essentially ended in 1993, the first year of reregulation.

18. *NAB Pushing Cable Regulation in Print Ads,* Daily Variety, Aug. 30, 1991, at 22. *See also NAB Vows to Continue Push for Cable Regulation,* Daily Variety, Oct. 10, 1991, at 3. See also "Fed Up with Cable TV's High Rates and Poor Service? You're Not Alone" ad (among the signatories were both the National Association of Broadcasters and the Association of Independent Television Stations), Wash. Post, Apr. 30, 1992, at A15.

19. Ken Auletta, Three Blind Mice (Random House 1991).

readily shared that view, and industry insiders bluntly asserted, "The push for legislation is from broadcasters."[20] When the FCC released a study in 1991 that described the long decline in broadcast viewing shares in painful detail,[21] a broadcasting trade journal wishfully editorialized, "Congress . . . may well be inclined to follow the report's lead by putting the brakes on cable's expansion—by reregulation of the wired world while the FCC frees up the broadcast universe."[22]

LOBBYING FOR RE-REREGULATION, FEBRUARY 1994

Further political tensions are revealed by the FCC's rulemaking that dramatically tightened rate controls on February 22, 1994.

Telephone Companies

Like broadcasters, the local telephone exchange companies (LECs) view themselves as long-run competitors to cable television companies. Legally barred from direct entry into local video markets as full-fledged cable television suppliers until passage of the Telecommunications Act of 1996, local telephone exchange companies have been outspoken about their intention to overturn the telephone company–cable television cross-ownership ban, going so far as to file a series of First Amendment challenges to the law.

There is much evidence that telephone companies—also locked into long-run competition with cable for various telecommunications services—strongly supported the re-reregulation round at the FCC. As with the broadcasters, it would be anomalous for a competitive industry to want a substitute product to be priced more attractively. The telephone companies' push for tighter price controls reveals that they expected that such controls would lower quality enough to offset any nominal price reductions.

Leading telephone companies filed official documents supporting a tighter regulatory standard. They urged the FCC to revisit the question of the competitive price differential and argued that the 10 percent rate rollback based on that standard was excessively low. NYNEX lobbied the FCC on February 2, 1994, and again on February 4, 1994, arguing that cable

---

20. Comments of cable industry lawyer Frank Lloyd of Mintz, Levin, Cohn, Ferris, Glovsky & Popeo, CABLE TV LAW REPORTER, Mar. 19, 1992, at 1.

21. FLORENCE SETZER & JONATHAN LEVY, BROADCAST TELEVISION IN A MULTICHANNEL MARKETPLACE (Federal Communications Commission OPP Working Paper No. 26, June 1991).

22. Editorial, *But Words Can Never Hurt You?* BROADCASTING, July 1, 1991, at 78.

rates should be reduced by 28 percent, according to ex parte documents at the commission. NYNEX, Bell Atlantic, and GTE made a similar claim in their FCC joint filing in June 1993.[23] Moreover, Bell Atlantic sued the commission to overturn the first (10 percent) rate rollback on the grounds that it was too modest and *withdrew* its suit after announcing it would acquire TCI.[24]

According to industry analysts, the rationale for that anticable effort was straightforward:

> [W]hat temporarily handicaps cable gives competing technologies room to zoom. For the Baby Bells, cable re-regulation is a windfall. Nipped at on all sides by new competitors such as satellite and wireless, they now can play catch-up with the cable companies. Companies like Ameritech and Pacific Telesis look smart now. They avoided cable alliances and instead are spending billions to add video capability to their phone systems. "The FCC's decision buys the telephone companies at least another year to develop video capability," says analyst Fred Moran of Salomon Brothers. "That's a lot."[25]

Programmers

Cable programmers were as outspoken as cable operators about the inadvisability of the tightened FCC rate regulations. Programmer opposition to

---

23. Thomas Hazlett's expert affidavit was filed with the FCC as an exhibit to that filing. The affidavit did not endorse rate regulation or re-reregulation but argued that the likely magnitude of the price difference between competitive and monopoly systems was greater than 10 percent. Some of the logic (or evidence) contained in that affidavit was used in the FCC's February 1994 reconsideration.

24. *Cable Execs See Telco Fingerprints All over New FCC Rate Rollbacks,* CABLE WORLD, Feb. 28, 1994, at 1, 4. "Telco lobbyists denied the charges, but cable executives last week placed a large part of the blame for the FCC's latest cable rate rollbacks on lobbying efforts mounted by regional Bell operating companies in the market to buy— or compete against—cable systems. 'They were all over the FCC,' said one Washington, D.C. industry observer who requested anonymity. The source said only Bell Atlantic, U S West and Southwestern Bell, which have cut deals or wrapped up agreements with cable operators, didn't actively push the FCC to further rollback rates." *See also* Vincente Pasdeloup, *Bell Atlantic Seeking Cable Systems,* CABLE WORLD, Sept. 27, 1993, at 16.

25. Nancy Hass, *Full Speed Ahead—Maybe,* NEWSWEEK, Mar. 7, 1994, at 45. The same Salomon Brothers analyst commented to the *New York Times:* "'The playing field has tilted in favor of the regional Bells,' Mr. Moran said. 'By handicapping the cable industry's ability to upgrade their services, the Bells have essentially been given time to get into video and other related services.'" Kenneth N. Gilpin, *Market Place: A One-Two Combination Staggers the Cable Television Industry and Puts It on the Defensive,* N.Y. TIMES, Mar. 7, 1994, at C4.

price controls was driven by the chilling effect they had had on sales to cable systems. Although the February 1994 rules specifically allowed cable operators to pass on the cost of new basic channels (including a 7.5 percent profit markup), programmers petitioned the commission to allow much higher prices. Among their demands: either remove new channels from rate regulation altogether[26] or increase the 7.5 percent markup and allow cable operators to raise prices for new services immediately (rather than waiting six months for approval). That is remarkable, of course, because upstream manufacturers of programming were asking the commission to allow higher retail pricing of their (wholesale) output, a seemingly irrational response by profit-maximizing input suppliers.

By July 1994 several major programmers were petitioning the FCC to allow de facto free market pricing of new channels. Both Discovery and USA requested a commission rule change that would allow operators to raise monthly basic rates by the cost (or licensing fee) of the new channel plus twenty-five cents per subscriber per month. Because most new (and existing) networks are offered to cable systems at twenty-five cents per month or less, that rule would give operators at least a 100 percent markup on new basic cable channels.[27] Viacom, A&E, and ESPN proposed that operators be allowed to raise rates by the amount of the license fee plus the average (existing) profit margin in the relevant tier of programming. That plan was apparently designed to give the commission a face-saving path by which to beat a hasty retreat from binding price regulation.[28]

The programmers clearly saw price controls as depressing the demand for new programming.[29] An executive with Turner Broadcasting System, Inc., even asserted that if not for rate regulation, the current subscribership

---

26. That indicates that the incentive to add channels as a rate compliance tactic was not, on net, helping programmers.

27. Recall that Rubinovitz found that about one-half of price increases were attributed to cable's market power. Here, programmers advocated that the operator keep such margins as an incentive payment. That strikes a frontal blow to the view that 50 percent cash flow ratios were themselves evidence of the anticonsumer effect of deregulation. Robert N. Rubinovitz, *Market Power and Price Increases for Basic Cable Service Since Deregulation,* 24 RAND J. ECON. 1 (1993). Citations are to an earlier draft, ROBERT N. RUBINOVITZ, MARKET POWER AND PRICE INCREASES FOR BASIC CABLE SERVICE SINCE DEREGULATION (U.S. Dept. of Justice, Antitrust Division, Economic Analysis Group Discussion Paper No. 91-8, Aug. 6, 1991).

28. Vincente Pasdeloup, *FCC to Cable: Sit Tight on a la Carte,* CABLE WORLD, July 4, 1994, at 17.

29. Vincente Pasdeloup, *Programmers Ask for Net Incentives,* CABLE WORLD, Mar. 7, 1994, at 4.

of its Cartoon Channel, launched in October 1992, would be fifty million rather than just ten million.[30] Turner Classic Movies, a basic cable network that was scheduled to begin April 1994, "threw out its initial rate card and slashed proposed carriage fees by at least one-third to appease resistant system operators."[31] Such cuts put downward pressure on the rates of competing networks such as American Movie Classics.[32] System operators were reported hesitant to add programming in the wake of re-reregulation: "'I'd describe what we're doing as watchful waiting,' says John Clark, senior VP-marketing/programming at Crown Media Inc. Uncertainty over the impact of the FCC's new rate-regulation rules, he adds, has 'put a lot of new programming decisions on hold.'"[33]

In fact, the results of marketing efforts at the National Cable Television Association's annual convention in May 1994 were highly disappointing for new networks. "[W]hile the convention attracted 333 new exhibitors, no major programming or hardware deals were announced."[34] Industry analysts explained: "Operators have been reeling from a 17-percent rate rollback the FCC mandated in February. They've hesitated to add channels because there's no incentive to do so in the current rules, making life tenuous for the estimated 125 new networks hoping to launch on cable systems in the next 18 months."[35] A top executive with Viacom, owner of Showtime and MTV and one of the largest cable programmers, declared that "[w]e at Viacom are having more interesting conversations concerning new programming with the Chinese than we're having with anyone in the U.S."[36]

In an unusual step, the chief executives of two popular program services, A&E and C-SPAN, went public with complaints about the stifling nature of the price control regime. In an op-ed piece in the *Washington*

---

30. *Id.*

31. Alan Breznick, *Movie Wars: Operators Hit the "Hold" Button When It Comes to New Networks,* CABLE WORLD, Mar. 7, 1994, at 20.

32. *Id.*

33. *Id.*

34. K. C. Neel, *NCTA Show Buoys Spirits,* CABLE WORLD, May 30, 1994, at 65.

35. Vincente Pasdeloup, *Stressing the Positive,* CABLE WORLD, May 30, 1994, at 20. That was the conventional wisdom coming out of the 1994 cable convention. "Perhaps the most acute symptom of the industry's malaise is its sudden lack of interest in adding channels. . . . 'Let's see how many of those new channels are at the cable convention next year,' said Betty Cohen, the executive vice-president of Turner Broadcasting's Cartoon Network. Her channel, started in October 1992, is on cable systems serving about 10 million households, far fewer than what the channel had hoped." Bill Carter, *Cable TV Industry Shifts Approach as Growth Slows,* N.Y. TIMES, May 23, 1994, at 1.

36. Neel, *supra* note 34, at 65.

Post, Nickolas Davatzes, chief executive officer of A&E, argued that "the unintended victims of the FCC action are the cable programmers, who today find themselves confronting an uncertain and difficult future."[37] He specifically noted that new network investments were being derailed by cable systems that were reducing product quality:

> This fall, we are scheduled to launch a new programming service, the History Channel, which will feature historical documentaries, movies and miniseries. Independent research has indicated that among consumers the History Channel is the most eagerly awaited programming service on the horizon. Now, both the continued success of A&E and other established cable networks and the launching of new services such as the History Channel are at risk because [of] the latest set of government regulations on cable television.
>
> Like A&E, many cable programmers have seen their plans for improvement and expansion come to an abrupt halt as they wonder whether cable operators will still have the incentive to continue to add new networks to their channel lineups. Today it appears that the new cable regulations will actually discourage cable companies from offering consumers new channels.
>
> ... [T]hese new regulations may make it economically infeasible for cable companies to add new networks to their regulated package of service. This would be a tremendous blow to the 50 new program networks now underway, the History Channel among them. This is the bottom line: Without proper incentives for cable operators to expand their programming, we may have already seen the last new cable programming network of value. Should every exit on the information superhighway lead to home shopping?[38]

Brian Lamb, who as the inscrutable on-air host of C-SPAN never expresses a point of view, was surprisingly opinionated regarding the antiprogrammer effect of cable rate regulation. A *New Yorker* profile commented:

> A subject much on Lamb's mind at present is the recent decision of the Federal Communications Commission—implementing the Cable Consumer Protection and Competition Act of 1992—to cut cable rates by about seven percent, having already taken a bite out of the industry's revenues through a complex set of "must carry" rules that give broadcast stations the right to claim access to cable systems. Lamb sees this series of actions as a "baffling" and "incredibly punitive" assault on cable TV.[39]

---

37. Nickolas Davatzes, *Quality Cable at Risk,* WASH. POST, Apr. 27, 1994, at A23.
38. *Id.*
39. James Lardner, *The Anti-Network,* NEW YORKER, Mar. 14, 1994, at 50.

CROSS-SUBSIDIES UNDER REREGULATION

It is apparent that standard industry protectionism—for broadcasters and for other cable competitors—has been at the heart of the drive for rate regulation in cable. Similarly, there is no doubt that members of Congress were able to seize on a popular public issue in their vote for the 1992 Cable Act. But there is a standard view among economists that the rents created by legislation need to be distributed so as to bring additional coalitional support to those directly benefiting from the law in question.[40] Cable industry behavior since the 1992 Cable Act was enacted reveals that rate regulation did, indeed, produce "third dimensional" payoffs to various outside constituencies (not cable companies, not their competitors, not their customers).

In dealing with rate regulation after the 1992 act, cable industry strategists chose to focus on one of the "hot button" political concerns of our day: television violence.[41] Because cable operators have the option of shielding themselves with the First Amendment on that and similar issues, it is remarkable that the industry came forward with a self-censorship proposal that is far more compliant than anything offered by broadcasters—FCC licensees that enjoy much less protection under the First Amendment.[42] Adding to the irony is the cable industry's simultaneous aggressive assertion of its First Amendment rights in various courts in continuing efforts to have large parts of the 1992 Cable Act overturned.

---

40. Thomas W. Gilligan, William J. Marshall & Barry R. Weingast, *Regulation and the Theory of Legislative Choice: The Interstate Commerce Act of 1887,* 32 J.L. & ECON. 35 (1989).

41. Hollywood had been severely criticized for excessive violence in programming by President Bill Clinton, Attorney General Janet Reno, then–Senate Majority Leader Robert Dole, Senators Joseph Lieberman and Paul Simon, and former Education Secretary William Bennett, among others.

42. In NBC *v.* United States, 319 U.S. 190 (1943), the Supreme Court maintained that broadcasters were public trustees who, because of their use of "physically scarce" frequencies, could be regulated by government. That regulatory oversight included some control over program content. Although the decision has been convincingly attacked as error-prone in its economic logic (Ronald H. Coase, *The Federal Communications Commission,* 2 J.L. & ECON. 1 (1959)), in its historical analysis (Thomas W. Hazlett, *The Rationality of U.S. Regulation of the Broadcast Spectrum,* 33 J.L. & ECON. 133 (1990)), and in its legal interpretation (ITHIEL DE SOLA POOL, TECHNOLOGIES OF FREEDOM (Harvard University Press 1983); LUCAS A. POWE, JR., AMERICAN BROADCASTING AND THE FIRST AMENDMENT (University of California Press 1987); THOMAS G. KRATTENMAKER & LUCAS A. POWE, JR., REGULATING BROADCAST PROGRAMMING (MIT Press and AEI Press 1994)), its reasoning was reasserted in Red Lion Broadcasting *v.* FCC, 395 U.S. 367 (1969), and still defines the law governing regulation of the broadcast press.

Cable television companies responded to reregulation with a public rehabilitation campaign that did not focus on lower prices or higher-quality programming. Instead, the National Cable Television Association moved "to do some image-polishing and patch-up work after the pasting cable took in the last few years." The incentive to put something on the table for key regulatory policymakers was evident: "Certainly, the stakes have never been so high for the association: reregulation is taking its toll."[43] An industry analysis defined one key element in that effort:

> Case in point: The cable industry tackled the issue of TV violence this spring while broadcasters appeared to be dragging their feet.
>
> Indeed, cable's "Voices Against Violence" initiative, backed by the NCTA, let cable programmers grab the media spotlight on Capitol Hill and in the media. It also won the praise of U.S. Rep. Ed Markey (D-Mass.), a prime 1992 Cable Act backer, and U.S. Sen. Paul Simon (D-Ill.), a key sponsor of legislation to curb TV violence.[44]

The results of two rival studies released in 1995 and early 1996 vividly showed the degree to which the cable companies committed themselves to the issue of violence on television. "Both NCTA's and the networks' studies," reported the Associated Press, "were prompted by threats from Congress to intervene if the TV industry failed to take steps to stem violence in their programs."[45] But while the public demand to "do something" about the issue evidently drove Congress to show an interest and led the rival industry groups to "do something" in response, the substance of the two responses differed greatly.

The broadcasters' study, sponsored by ABC, CBS, NBC, and Fox, was conducted by researchers at the University of California, Los Angeles. It reported, in September 1995, that there were "promising signs" in the manner in which broadcasters were presenting violence in their programs. In essence, that analysis represented a modest, scholarly defense of current practices.

The cable-funded study, released in February 1996, was conducted by researchers from the University of North Carolina, the University of Texas, the University of Wisconsin, and the University of California, Santa Barbara. Its conclusions were far harsher: "The world of television is not only violent—it also consistently sanctions its violence." The report found that television viewing was associated with substantial harmful social effects,

---

43. Vincente Pasdeloup, *The New NCTA,* CABLE WORLD, May 23, 1994, at 28.

44. *Id.*

45. *Violent Acts on TV Go Unpunished,* AP ONLINE SERVICE, Feb. 6, 1996.

including the desensitization of attitudes toward wrongdoing, the provocation of fear of victimization, and the encouragement of aggressive behavior. Interestingly, the study pinpointed premium cable television channels as the most violent and determined that broadcast networks were airing somewhat less violent shows than were other television outlets.[46]

All in all, it is evident that the cable industry, in providing $1.5 million to fund a study that would, essentially, characterize cable systems as fueling a raging social problem, was far more responsive to the political demands of policymakers than were broadcasters.[47] The seriousness of the cable industry's efforts in complying with the demands of regulators could be portrayed as simply good citizenship, but that would leave unanswered the questions of why the industry waited until that time to conduct such research, why the broadcasters are any less "public spirited," and why the cable companies—if so obeisant to public interests—have, by their own study, the most violent programming. Given that the industry has frequently characterized its efforts to deal with program violence as part of its public relations campaign to relax rate controls,[48] it is more probable that the disparity in the broadcaster and cable studies is related to the political interests of each group in the wake of the 1992 Cable Act, when those studies were commissioned.[49]

46. *Id.*

47. It is true that $1.5 million constitutes a trivial cross-subsidy expense when amortized over the national cable television industry. What the cable operators are really expending, however, is their political (or programming) independence and, indeed, their First Amendment protections. Rather than refuse to compromise their rights as "electronic publishers" and risk further rate regulation grief, the industry elects to discuss the issue of political concern in a friendly, reasonable manner. That may be worth a lot to policymakers, because it creates the public impression that regulators are sternly dealing with an issue of importance to voters and are making some headway in gaining the cooperation of cable television companies.

48. Alan Breznick, *Programmers, Operators Line up Against Violence,* CABLE WORLD, Mar. 13, 1995, at 1, 51. That article reported that cable interests were funding a company called Mediascope to supervise the television violence study at a cost of $3.3 million, more than twice the published figure when the study was released. We do not know the reason for the disparity.

49. Those interests could well be changing. Because the 1996 Telecommunications Act again deregulates cable television rates, the cable companies now have less interest in playing the public interest card (that is, in being so generous with cross-subsidies). But because the issue of auctioning high-definition television licenses (worth $11 billion to $70 billion, according to FCC estimates) was not resolved in the 1996 act and is still a matter of debate in Washington, D.C., broadcasters have become relatively more interested in the harmful effects of violence (including what they consider armed rob-

That is not likely the sole dimension in which cable television operators became more willing to pursue political compromise, or cross-subsidies, in the wake of cable reregulation, although it is, perhaps, the most visible. Cable industry strategists posit that such rent sharing went a long way toward loosening the constraints imposed in the FCC's February 1994 rate control rulemaking, although the capital markets' reaction to the imposition of such controls also had a significant impact.[50] The cable companies' television violence campaign should be taken as a window on the political dynamics fundamentally at work.

The rebounding political fortunes of the cable industry in late 1994 and in 1995 also bear comment. In both the failed telecommunications legislation authored by Senator Ernest Hollings (D-SC) in 1994 and in the telecommunications bills passed by both houses of the Republican Congress in 1995,[51] cable operators had a surprising degree of legislative success—what one report called "an audacious comeback."[52]

The legislative victories are of two varieties, the first being the terms on which local telephone exchange companies are allowed to enter cable television markets, the second relating to rate deregulation (essentially repealing the rate control portion of the 1992 Cable Act). Although only the Republican Congress entertained (and enacted) the latter, cable interests did very well on the first count in both the 1994 and the 1995 legislation.

The industry privately gloats about its public policy successes after recovering from the depths of despair it found itself in around February 1994—a time when, as we have seen, the de facto industry leader and TCI chair John Malone declared that the best thing the administration could do to assist cable in constructing the information superhighway was to "Shoot [FCC chairman] Hundt!"[53]

Industry insiders boast of their lobbying efforts to put cable on better terms with key policymakers by cooperating with influential constituencies in Washington, D.C. *Cable World* identified the third-biggest cable industry story in 1994 as "NCTA Shifts":

---

bery in the form of competitive bidding for FCC licenses) if that will help them reach a compromise with policymakers on license auctions.

50. Vincente Pasdeloup, *An FCC Olive Branch?* CABLE WORLD, May 30, 1994, at 2. "The [FCC] concessions were the latest sign that the FCC may be moderating some reregulation policies which have come under fire from the industry and Congress."

51. Those became the Telecommunications Act of 1996.

52. Kirk Victor, *Cable's Comeback,* NAT'L J., Dec. 17, 1994, at 2962.

53. David Cline, *Infobahn Warrior,* WIRED, July 1994, at 131.

Decker Anstrom assumed the presidency of the NCTA, mending fences on Capitol Hill and within the cable industry after Jim Mooney's fractious last years. Anstrom even managed to place cable "on the side of the angels," as one observer put it—a not-small task after the cable industry took a beating in the 1992 Cable Act debate. Under Anstrom's direction, the cable industry won some kudos on Capitol Hill for crafting an ambitious anti-violence initiative and throwing its weight behind telecoms-reform legislation.[54]

As the author notes, cable gained points simply by cooperating with the legislative effort launched by Senator Hollings in 1994.[55] Interestingly, a secret of cable's success in the 1995 congressional drive to lift controls was silence. According to the *New York Times,* cable lobbyists were almost nonexistent in the telecommunications reform debates but emerged clear winners in the bills that were passed: "Cable operators managed to gain all this while lying low because of Congressional misgivings about the mixed results of the 1992 attempt to regulate prices."[56]

What is significant is that even that lack of assertion by an industry that has strong views as an interested party to legislation can best be seen as a constraint imposed by regulation. Although cross-subsidies are not directly targeted to constituent groups at the behest of legislators, the visible acquiescence of industry spokespersons itself reflects the greater responsiveness of the regulated entity to policymakers' demands.

THE POLITICAL ECONOMY OF RATE REGULATION

The very manner in which cable rate regulation came into existence should reveal unlikely prospects for consumer success. The 1992 Cable Act was heavily lobbied for by cable's direct competitors, most ominously the broadcasting sector—which had worked to impose rate controls on cable long before the Cable Act became law. Telephone companies joined the push for cable rate controls most heavily after the act was law. Those companies sought to intensify the constraint supplied by rate regulation and were fearless of the market share advances cable would make if the rules served to entice new subscribers.

Programmers, in contrast, bitterly fought both the 1992 Cable Act and the tightening of controls that the FCC imposed in February 1994. That

---

54. Vincente Pasdeloup, *Busy Times in D.C.,* CABLE WORLD, Jan. 2, 1995, at 7. The first- and second-biggest events of 1994 were identified as "rate cuts" and "going-forward rules."

55. *See also* Kirk Victor, *Cable's Comeback,* NAT'L J., Dec. 17, 1994, at 2962–66.

56. Mark Landler, *Cable TV's Quiet Victory,* N.Y. TIMES, Aug. 14, 1995, at C1, C6.

pressure eventually moved the commission to back away from rate regulation with its going-forward rules announced November 10, 1994. The *New
York Times* reported: "Today's veer back towards the industry's side comes
in response to complaints from developers of new cable programming that
the price controls had made it almost impossible to sell new cable networks. Operators, they said, had placed a virtual freeze on new channels
since the regulations were adopted."[57]

That input suppliers should push the regulatory authority to raise rates
is most revealing. But their analysis of the situation was well articulated by
Tim Brooks, a senior vice president of USA Networks, who told *Daily
Variety* in April 1994: "The biggest threat to cable networks is that government regulation could lead to the sucking sound of money being pulled out
of the industry. That could dry up the investment money we'd need to create
new series and original movies and specials."[58] Clearly, operators' response
to rate controls—as revealed by such expert witnesses in the programming
sector—was to lower quality (from trend) by failing to add channels as fast
as they had under deregulated conditions. And the FCC, implicitly conced-
ing that, crafted a solution: to permit cable operators to raise rates substantially in excess of marginal costs. The reaction to regulation by programmers
and, ultimately, the FCC strongly supports the hypothesis that rate regulation lowered cable program quality and did not lower quality-adjusted cable
rates.

---

57. Edmund L. Andrews, *F.C.C. Approves New Rate Rises for Cable TV,* N.Y. TIMES,
Nov. 11, 1994, at C1, C17.

58. John Dempsey, *Ad-Fed Cablers Unfazed After No-Growth 1993,* DAILY VARIETY,
Apr. 29, 1994, at 21.

8

New Competitive Realities in Video Delivery

> The cable TV industry is going to have to work harder over the next 10 years to grow the same amount it did over the past seven. Welcome to the colliding worlds of cable TV, DBS, MMDS and telephony, where competing on new turf with new technologies will be a fact of life for the next decade.
>
> —*Cable TV Investor,* May 31, 1995

WHILE CABLE REREGULATION has been front and center, the specter of competition has been lurking in the background.[1] In 1993–1994, the economic viability of the most immediately threatening cross-technology competitors to traditional cable television systems—direct broadcast satellite (DBS) and "wireless cable"—increased substantially.[2] The capital markets are the first to signal changes in expectations regarding market realities, and both technologies received huge financial lifts in the months following the passage of the 1992 Cable Act.

The infusion of about $1 billion of financial capital into direct broadcast satellite[3] was sufficient to launch the first two successful competing ventures, Direct Satellite Service (DSS) and Primestar. One of the partners

---

1. Epigraph: *When Cable/Telco Worlds Collide: Offense, Defense, Survival,* PAUL KAGAN ASSOCIATES, CABLE TV INVESTOR, May 31, 1995, at 6.

2. Cellular television should also be included in this listing, but it has been stalled in an FCC rulemaking since 1992. On the viability of that technology, see Edmund Andrews, *A New Microwave System Poses Threat to Cable TV,* N.Y. TIMES, Dec. 11, 1992, at A1; Michael Antonoff, *Wireless Cellular Cable,* POPULAR SCI., Nov. 1993, at 42.

3. Nikhil Hutheesing, *Kamikaze Satellites?* FORBES, July 4, 1994, at 126.

in DSS had applied for an FCC satellite license as early as 1981.[4] Indeed, in the early 1980s, Comcast lost $300 million in a failed direct broadcast satellite venture. The market appears far more promising today. In its first year of operation (beginning July 1994), DirecTV (a partner in DSS) achieved subscribership of 600,000 households, about half of which reside in homes passed by cable systems.[5] Excitement reigns within the sector, with analysts hailing DBS as "the biggest hit in consumer electronics since the VCR."[6] DBS subscribership was estimated to be 6.35 million at year-end 1996, with net new DBS subscribers in 1996 outpacing cable subscriber gains by nearly 2–1 (see table 8-1). Industry forecasters were predicting that, by the year 2000, cable's principal competitors—DBS, wireless cable, and telephone company overbuilders—would account for some 19.2 million subscribers, nearly one-third of cable's projected total.[7]

Prospects are also bullish in the wireless cable television (MMDS) business. Long stalled by regulatory uncertainty and anemic market performance, serious investment in wireless cable—while technically available as a video delivery system since the sixties[8]—materialized only in 1993. That year saw the first public offering of a wireless cable stock; it was highly successful and several others soon followed. A frenzy to buy up wireless cable systems developed when the local exchange companies joined the bidding. Pacific Bell's April 1995 purchase of the 42,500-subscriber Cross Country system operating in a 700,000-home market east of Los Angeles was followed within two weeks by a $100 million investment in CAI Wireless Cable by NYNEX–Bell Atlantic.[9] The Cross Country price,

---

4. K. C. Neel, *Sky High on DBS,* CABLE WORLD, June 26, 1995, at 60.

5. Christopher Stern, *DBS and Cable Square off at the FCC,* BROADCASTING & CABLE, July 10, 1995, at 42.

6. *Id.*

7. PAUL KAGAN ASSOCIATES, MARKETING NEW MEDIA, Sept. 16, 1996, at 1. The subscriber breakdown: cable = 64.3 million; DBS = 11.5 million; wireless cable = 4.1 million; telephone company cable = 3.6 million.

8. "This is not a new technology. The Federal Communications Commission began allocating spectrum for wireless cable channels in 1963. To date a total of 33 channels per market have been allocated, albeit in highly convoluted fashion. Licenses for 20 channels are restricted to educational institutions; the rest are awarded in a series of lotteries, with no one person being allowed to apply for more than 4 channels per market. Channel ownership can, however, be consolidated after the lotteries by buying, selling or leasing channels." Fleming Meeks, *The Wireless Wonder,* FORBES, Feb. 19, 1990, at 57.

9. K. C. Neel, *Tracking Cable's Savviest Competitors—PacTel's Wireless Tab: $175M for Calif. Systems,* CABLE WORLD, Apr. 24, 1995, at 1, 80.

Table 8-1
Direct Broadcast Satellite Subscribership (thousands), 1994–1996

	1994	1995	1996[a]
DirecTV	320	1,215	2,550
PrimeStar	225	1,000	2,000
USSB	119	629	1,400
EchoStar	—	—	400
Total DBS	664	2,844	6,350
Net new DBS	664	2,180	3,506
Net new CATV	2,500	2,400	1,900
Net new DBS/Net new CATV	.27	.91	1.85

a. As predicted by Paul Kagan Associates.

Sources: Paul Kagan Associates, *Cable TV Investor,* June 30, 1995, p. 5, May 21, 1996, p. 5; Paul Kagan Associates, *Marketing New Media,* July 15, 1996; *Cable World* insert, July 15, 1996.

$175 million (or nearly $4,150 per subscriber) signaled capital markets that competitive entry was economically viable. That was a shocking turnaround: "In 1991 . . . an investor could have bought the whole industry for $35–50 million. . . . We were told point blank it would never work."[10]

Hovering at about 200,000 subscribers until 1992,[11] MMDS suppliers now count about 700,000 households as customers,[12] and project that by the year 2000 some four million subscribers will be served.[13] The optimism of the capital markets is driven by that growth trend and by the prospect that digital compression technology will render wireless cable's largest drawback—its 33-channel capacity—a far less binding constraint.[14]

The resources now being devoted to new market entry have not eliminated the market power of incumbent cable systems, which are still capitalized at well above the replacement cost of tangible capital. Yet the newcomers

---

10. Comments of Eric Singer of Gerard Klauer Mattison & Co. *in* Rich Brown, *MMDS (Wireless Cable): A Capital Idea,* Broadcasting & Cable, May 1, 1995, at 16, 18.

11. Paul Kagan Associates, Cable TV Financial Databook, June 1993, at 10.

12. *Cable TV: A Crisis Looms,* Business Wk., Oct. 14, 1996, at 105.

13. Jennifer Pendleton, *Staking out the Competition,* Cable World, May 8, 1995, at 78, 80.

14. Harry A. Jessell, *Wireless Cable Is Going Digital . . . or at Least Is Trying to,* Broadcasting & Cable, July 24, 1995, at 30.

have begun to affect long-term growth forecasts as well as current marketing strategies. One obvious example is the cable industry's television ad campaign attacking the advantages of direct broadcast satellite. The *New York Times* describes one commercial, which "opens with a man on a couch joined by his wife with a large bowl of popcorn. They snuggle in front of their TV set, hooked up to DBS. She is excited: 'So this is it?' She asks how much the satellite dish cost, and when her husband answers, 'About $850,' the excitement begins to wear off. 'There's no monthly fee,' she says. 'No more than cable,' he responds. When she says she wants to watch the news, he sheepishly says, 'Uh, can't get local news.'"[15]

The satellite providers have responded with ads of their own, and the war is on.[16] By the summer of 1995, dispatches from cable television trade shows revealed that while the regulatory structure imposed in the 1992 Cable Act was still challenging industry imagination to uncover "unregulated revenue streams" to regain financial momentum, the heaviest pressure was coming from the upstart competitors.[17] Even the search to evade FCC rate constraints was portrayed as increasingly difficult owing to the encroachment of cable's new rivals. One prominent industry planner described the current mood: "What's on people's minds is how do we continue to grow our businesses in a competitive environment and at the same time contend with the various difficult regulatory hurdles we have to climb over. Growing unregulated revenue streams in a very tough marketplace will continue to be on cable people's minds."[18]

---

15. Kevin Goldman, *Cable-TV Ads Fight Satellite-Dish Threat,* N.Y. TIMES, Feb. 6, 1995, at B8.

16. Cable companies are on the offense as well as the defense, announcing plans to invade monopolistic telephony turf with wireline telecommunications service and duopolistic cellular markets with personal communications services offerings. *Gauging the Competition,* CABLE WORLD, Sept. 4, 1995, at 1, 25.

17. "In the good old days—that is, before DBS, wireless cable and the telcos were marshaling their resources to try to take cable's customers away—just about all that most cable operators had to worry about was sustaining their relationships with local franchising authorities and managing debt levels. . . . Today, all that has changed." Pendleton, *supra* note 13. A similar report was filed from the major industry trade show with coverage that began: "Stormy. That's the best word to describe the competitive clouds hanging over cable operators at the 1995 National Cable TV Association Convention held here [Dallas] May 7–10." PAUL KAGAN ASSOCIATES, CABLE TV REGULATION, May 23, 1995, at 1.

18. Jim McConville, *CTAM Focuses on Cable Competition,* BROADCASTING & CABLE, July 17, 1995, at 34. *See also The Promise of Data Communications—Cable May Be on to Something in a More Competitive Environment,"* CABLE WORLD, June 26, 1995, at 42.

By 1996 the new marketplace realities were battering capital values of cable companies. An October 14, 1996, cover story in *Business Week* was entitled "Cable TV: The Looming Crisis." It pinpointed the industry's stock market woes: "[C]able's monopoly-like hold on 67% of U.S. households is being seriously threatened by an array of new competitors."[19] A headline in a cable industry newsletter concluded that the industry was a victim of pathological behavior: "Wall Street's Competition Mania Drives Discounts." The story noted that "fears of what DBS will do to cable have kept operator stocks down since early March."[20]

The emerging rivalry in the multichannel video marketplace raises at least three major issues important to the analysis of regulation. First, because the prevailing assumptions of natural monopoly are, to a large degree, hostage to status quo conditions in a marketplace, competition is more viable than it may appear. That is not surprising: where should analysts go for information about efficient market structures if not to the currently prevailing structures? Yet a monopolized market is a hostile environment in which to hunt for evidence regarding the counterfactual, to discover what might prevail were rules or assumptions to shift. Virtually all those participants with intimate knowledge of the monopoly status quo have come to be comfortable with it. Both business interests and government regulators are far more able to manufacture reasons explaining why the market is inevitably organized the way it is than to imagine what is not observed. We see billions of investment dollars currently betting on competition not only as vindication of skepticism about the assertion that cable is a natural monopoly, but also as evidence that the outsider inevitably shakes the status quo—even as the cable industry still argues (to itself) that competition will not work.[21] At the same time, Wall Street analysts are now lecturing the industry to face up to competitive realities it would rather ignore.[22]

Second, the presence of competitive rivals is already affecting the operations of cable companies. Although competition has only marginally af-

19. *Cable TV, supra* note 12, at 101.

20. PAUL KAGAN ASSOCIATES, CABLE TV INVESTOR, Oct. 21, 1996, at 4.

21. Paul Kagan writes: "No matter which technology is used, overbuilds hold little promise for victory for either side." CABLE TV FINANCIAL DATABOOK, July 1995, at 5. *See also Prevailing Cable View: Overbuilds Don't Work*, CABLE TV INVESTOR, May 31, 1995, at 11; Alan Breznick, *Will Overbuilds Ever Work?* CABLE WORLD, Sept. 16, 1996, at 1, 53.

22. "The age of competition in cable has begun," according to an industry analyst at Morgan Stanley, and DBS is "a dangerous phenomenon that the [cable] industry has way over pooh-poohed." Reported in Alan Breznick & Will Workman, *Online News—CNN Interactive Debuts Web Site; DBS Poses Biggest Threat to Cable*, CABLE WORLD, Sept. 4, 1995, at 14.

fected the market power of incumbent operators, their marketing and investment strategies are already beginning to change. What we might call "leading indicators" of competitive rivalry are already visible on the horizon. Hence, the market—even when not entirely freed of the constraints of rate regulation—has begun drifting into a more competitive, postregulation period where the threat of entry drives strategic decision making. One incident highlighting that emerging market reality was TCI's September 1994 announcement that it would massively upgrade its pay-per-view offerings:

> Tele-Communications Inc. plans to dedicate a staggering 625 additional channels [on its systems in aggregate] to pay-per-view in a move that will double the average system's PPV [pay-per-view] shelf space and try to protect rural systems from DBS and wireless competition.
>
> The move, mapped out as TCI and most MSOs wrap up their 1995 budget-planning exercises, starkly points up the conflict cable operators face between their need to push unregulated revenue streams while keeping a tight rein on capital expenditures. . . .
>
> Right now, TCI systems average about 2.5 channels of PPV. And many of its smaller systems, typically in rural areas, have none. . . . Those systems are considered most vulnerable to competition from direct broadcast satellite and wireless cable operators.[23]

On a more general level, firms manufacturing the physical infrastructure for supplying telecommunications services saw large increases in equity values in 1994, when "equipment stocks soared more than 50% in anticipation of manufacturers arming the cable and telephone competitors for battle."[24] The August 1995 announcement that Jones Intercable would upgrade its Alexandria, Virginia, cable system to carry seventy-eight channels of regular programming plus nine of pay-per-view was instantly greeted by the trade press as a reaction to Bell Atlantic's threatened overbuild of that market.[25] Although tracing actual changes in operating data to the emerging competition is difficult, competition may already be affecting variables such as rates and subscriber penetration. With wireless competitors' adding approximately twice the number added by traditional cable systems, competitive constraints on current cable industry conduct begin to bind. We

---

23. *TCI Pumping up PPV Muscle as Industry Plots '95 Course,* CABLE WORLD, Sept. 19, 1994, at 1, 77.

24. Paul Kagan, *The Public Market,* CABLE TV FINANCIAL DATABOOK, July 1995, at 54.

25. Alexandria is the market where Bell Atlantic pressed, and won, its First Amendment claim to compete in local video markets. Carl Weinschenk, *Jones, Century Unveil Ambitious Rebuilds,* CABLE WORLD, Sept. 4, 1995, at 1.

suspect that competition is now eclipsing rate regulation as the predominant outside influence on cable operators' behavior.

The final point is that the emerging competition in video delivery is timed perfectly to render a verdict on the effectiveness of rate regulation. Were controls to suppress cable company prices to competitive, or cost-based, levels, new entrants would be severely handicapped. An incumbent's limiting prices (or even credibly threatening to limit prices in the future) to no more than the entrant's cost of providing service (or a minute amount less) deters competitive rivalry for a very logical reason: the incentive to compete tends to evaporate when the firm already in the market shows a willingness to supply customers for merely a competitive rate of return.

The economic rationale for applying rate controls is that the government may improve the situation for consumers by imposing a competitively priced outcome where the market is itself unable to entice rivals to provide the requisite pricing constraint. Rate regulation should thus deter competition, just as does limit pricing. In cable television, however, potential entrants who had been stalled for years or decades were visibly boosted at the very instant that government-mandated rate rollbacks were being enforced. The coincidence is startling. By all textbook logic, that should have been the most unlikely moment for new competition to emerge.

Industry experts are unanimous in the opinion that reregulation had far from an adverse impact on competitors to cable: "Indeed, the U.S. wireless cable industry has grown substantially in the last few years, thanks in part to the 1992 Cable Act, which gave wireless operators access to all cable programming. . . . After the favorable 1992 Cable Act was passed, Wall Street began to lend money to the fledgling industry, while several companies began to successfully sell stock to the public for the first time."[26]

The specific clause in the 1992 Cable Act targeted to assist competitors was the rule opening up access to program services, a provision we believe contained the only genuinely procompetitive substance in the measure. But the universal acclaim that is heaped on the antidiscrimination provision completely dwarfs what should be an offsetting effect: rate regulation. It is noteworthy that investors putting up significant sums to compete in video markets do not complain that the rate controls imposed in the 1992 Cable Act will hurt their chances.

In fact, one hears just the reverse. To prepare its annual assessment of competitive forces in the video distribution market (an obligation imposed by the 1992 Cable Act), the FCC invited comments from all parties (inter-

---

26. K. C. Neel, *Wireless Operators Go to Washington,* CABLE WORLD, July 17, 1995, at 4.

ested or otherwise) on the prevailing state of competition in cable markets in mid-1995. In the official comments submitted by DirecTV, the FCC was petitioned to keep its rate regulations in place on the grounds that cable television operators still enjoy de facto monopolies in the markets they serve. We do not quarrel with DirecTV's empirical assertion. What is pertinent here, however, is the corporate interest revealed: if the direct cable competitor had believed that rate regulation was lowering quality-adjusted cable prices and harming its effort to steal market share, it would surely have petitioned the commission to lift its rate controls, on the legal premise that "effective competition" had arrived—just as the National Cable Television Association had done in the same proceeding.[27] The revealed preference of the competitor to go head-to-head with a rate-regulated rival is powerful testimony that the scheme in place does not improve the package offered real customers in real markets.[28]

Even more powerful is the verdict rendered on cable television rate regulation by the regulated industry itself. In a revealing episode, an independent cable firm, FiberVision, was organized to compete in four major areas of Connecticut, and the state's Department of Public Utility Control sought to issue franchises to the entrant during the 1993–1995 period.[29] The area's largest cable television franchisees, including Tele-Communications, Inc., bitterly opposed the franchising effort. In contesting the award the applicant requested, TCI raised a number of issues, after which it declared its fallback position: if the state insisted upon granting a license to FiberVision-Hartford (FVH), it should at least impose the franchise obligation that the entrant be subject to federal rate regulation. "The Department should take into account and require," wrote TCI in a filing with the depart-

---

27. Christopher Stern, *DBS and Cable Square off at the FCC,* Broadcasting & Cable, July 10, 1995, at 42.

28. In another FCC proceeding, DirecTV argued against lifting rate controls in a "social contract" bargain with cable systems without safeguards maintaining program access for cable competitors. That offers a somewhat more complex picture, yet still underlines how little threatened cable rivals are by the continuation of rate regulation (on cable). *See* DirecTV, Comments, In the Matter of Implementation of the Cable Television Consumer Protection and Competition Act of 1992—Annual Assessment of the Status of Competition in the Market for the Delivery of Video Programming, CS Dkt. No. 95-61 (June 30, 1995).

29. FiberVision proposed building a $94 million system to compete with established operators but has been unsuccessful in procuring franchises in a timely fashion. Thomas W. Hazlett & George S. Ford, The Fallacy of Regulatory Symmetry: An Economic Analysis of the "Level Playing Field" in State Cable TV Franchising Statutes (paper presented at the meetings of the Southern Economic Association, Nov. 1995).

ment, "as a condition of an award to FVH, that FVH agree to be subject to some form of rate regulation, until such time as TCI is no longer subject to rate regulation."[30]

The logic that rate control lowers prices and increases penetration does not seem to be operative, as revealed in the actions of those agents with expert knowledge of the subject matter. Should regulation be expected to lower quality-adjusted prices to customers, then that regulatory constraint either would have been nonbinding (if duopoly pricing was at or below rate-regulated levels) or would have acted to increase the entrant's market share. Yet TCI, endowed with the experience gleaned from regulatory compliance in hundreds of local cable markets, believed that imposing rate regulation on a direct, head-to-head competitor would buttress the *incumbent's* market share. TCI signals that rate regulation, instead of reducing prices to consumers, is anticipated to hamstring suppliers and lessen their ability to compete for subscribers. The implication is that the practical effect of rate controls on cable television operators is not to advance the interests of consumers.

The entry of DBS at a price structure substantially higher than that of cable also undercuts the essential rationale of the rate regulation scheme. The question arises, How can cable rates require regulating when new entrants offer rate schedules considerably more inflated than cable's?[31] The instant answer is that the service menus are altogether different—an indisputably correct response that is too clever by half. For the regulator's problem is to discern precisely that quality difference; the fact is that administrators will have very poor tools with which to judge the apples of DBS against the oranges of cable television against the nectarines of MMDS and so on through the video orchard. Note, for example, the price and service comparison between cable and two competing DBS services made in a consumer magazine story, summarized in table 8-2.

The various news reports configure the relative packages somewhat differently; there is disagreement over what the rival suppliers offer even at that simple level. But even ignoring that, and assuming a high level of expertise in the regulatory authority investigating and ranking the various service menus by choice and quality, we must ask how the task of rating the competitive services can be achieved in any comprehensible manner. Clearly,

---

30. TCI, Reply Brief, Re: Application of the FiberVision Corporation of Greater Hartford for a CATV Certificate, Conn. Dep't of Public Utility Control, Dkt. No. 93-07-04 (Nov. 10, 1993), at 26.

31. Many in the cable television industry, including John Mansell, a senior analyst with Paul Kagan Associates, argue that this shows rate regulation to be outmoded.

Table 8-2
Cable Television versus DBS: Prices and Services

Delivery Mode	Average Month Fee ($)	Basic Channels	Installation Cost ($)
Traditional cable television	30	40–50	20–50
DBS-DSS	55	100	849–1,748
DBS-Primestar	34	35	200

Source: Steven T. Goldberg, "TV: The Next Generation," *Kiplinger's Personal Finance Magazine,* May 1995, p. 121.

DBS is more expensive than traditional cable service: "No matter how you slice it, you'll spend more money on satellite-dish TV than on cable."[32] It is also clear that DBS has at least one significant drawback: local broadcast affiliates are typically unavailable to its subscribers. On the plus side for DBS, however, are its higher picture and audio resolution, wider arrays of pay-per-view programming, more premium sports including an NFL season pass for $139.95 and an NBA season pass for $149.95 (both carrying virtually every regular season game), and more sophisticated programmability with the remote control including a blocking feature keeping R- or PG-rated movies out of a child's reach.

The market will give consumers a choice, and we shall soon see how the game plays out. That, of course, is the very argument for competition— the future is plagued with uncertainties and only in a consumer-driven process of trial and error can we discover the best ways of providing service for the public. But such a process is exactly what rate regulation overrules in favor of mandated prices. The "optimal" rate schedule is imposed from above, and the cable operator then makes a series of moves to adjust package quality within the legal parameters set. That is a hugely complex task, and it is difficult for the regulator to beat even the unregulated monopoly outcome.

32. Steven T. Goldberg, *TV: The Next Generation,* KIPLINGER'S PERS. FIN. MAG., May 1995, at 121.

9

Conclusion

This [rate regulation] should lead to more sales, which should lead to more growth, which should lead to more jobs.

—Reed Hundt, November 1993

These noxious FCC rules are not going to be able to constrain the economics in entertainment for very long. What's gonna happen is there'll be a shift from basic to à la carte services. . . . We'll continue to diversify away from the regulated government-attacked core.

—John Malone, July 1994

WE END WHERE we began, with competing visions of economic regulation.[1] In one, market power is a necessary and sufficient precondition for successful rate controls. The announced object of such a scheme is to constrain the seller to a price closer to what would obtain in the competitive marketplace; that is, a price approximating the long-run average cost of production. In the cable television marketplace, the evidence that such market power abounds is overwhelming.

The FCC itself has adduced much of that evidence. In a report issued in September 1994, not only did the commission show that local monopolies dominated the cable television market, but it delivered a decisive verdict on cable rate regulation. Proof of the market power hypothesis came

---

1. Epigraphs: Reed Hundt, *quoted in* Bill Carter, *Cable TV Industry Shifts Approach as Growth Slows,* N.Y. TIMES, May 23, 1994, at C9; John Malone, *quoted in* David Cline, *Infobahn Warrior,* WIRED, July 1994, at 90.

largely from the FCC's summary of data revealing that market values of cable systems were, even after the full imposition of rate regulation,[2] about four to five times the replacement cost of tangible capital. The very evidence used to show that market competition is ineffectual in constraining monopoly pricing by cable systems can be seen as simultaneously condemning the imposed constraints of regulators as ineffectual.[3]

In table 9-1, comparing the FCC's calculation of 1994 q-ratios with 1989 levels estimated by Paul MacAvoy, the degree of market power actually rose in three of five measures.[4] That is all the more remarkable when we recall that 1989 was the very height of the boom in cable television system values; the restriction on highly leveraged transactions in October 1989 brought asset prices tumbling down, and the lengthy credit crunch and recession kept them there. In 1995, in fact, cable analysts talked about the industry emerging from its post-1989 slump.[5] About the best the FCC can conclude from those data is that "the current q ratios suggest that, overall, cable television operators possess substantial market power." Rate regulation evidently failed to tame the cable monopoly beast.

But the story of rate regulation, deregulation, and reregulation in the cable television industry is considerably more illuminating than most tales

---

2. Although the market value data series was terminated before the official end of the second FCC-mandated rollbacks in July 1994, the rollbacks had been fully publicized and anticipated during the first half of 1994. The FCC data covered that period. Indeed, favorable regulatory announcements later in 1994 drove capital asset prices higher at year-end.

3. Regulation's inability to drive q-ratios to 1 could be a product of market anticipation that, although current rules constrain operators to some degree, future regulations will not be so successful. The condemnation of controls rendered by the capital market evidence is of the regulatory regime most broadly construed. Likewise, it would not be true that success in driving q-ratios to unity would prove consumer benefits from controls. Regulations that transferred rents from, or simply imposed costs upon, cable system owners would have such an effect. Still, q-ratios above 3 are clear evidence that controls have not come close to eliminating monopoly power. Low (or, at least, lowered) q-ratios are necessary, if insufficient, for rate controls to be considered successful.

4. FCC, Annual Assessment of the Status of Competition in the Market for the Delivery of Video Programming, First Report, CS Dkt. No. 94-48, 9 F.C.C. Rcd. 7442 (Sept. 28, 1994); Paul W. MacAvoy, Tobin's q and the Cable Industry, Attachment to Comments of the United States Telephone Association to the Federal Communications Commission, MM Dkt. No. 89-600 (Feb. 28, 1990).

5. "Life in cable TV's fast lane on the information superhighway has been characterized by fear and oppression in recent years. But as I write this on May 29, 1995 the road signs are changing. Financial and regulatory barriers introduce the word 'recovery' into the cable lexicon for the first time in years. It all started in October 1989." Paul Kagan, *Publisher's Letter,* CABLE TV FINANCIAL DATABOOK, July 1995, at 4.

Table 9-1
Estimated q-Ratios for the Cable Industry

Method	FCC 1994 q Estimates	MacAvoy 1989 q Estimates
Public market value/adjusted book value (Current, four firms; MacAvoy, five firms)	4.47	4.3
Public market value/adjusted book value (For two firms common to both samples)	4.52	4.17
Public market value/median construction cost (Current, four firms; MacAvoy, five firms)	5.23	4.56
Private market value (1993 transactions)/ median construction cost	4.11	6.2
Private market value (some 1994 transactions)/ median construction cost	3.95	6.2

Sources: FCC, Annual Assessment of the Status of Competition in the Market for the Delivery of Video Programming, First Report, CS Dkt. No. 94-48, 9 F.C.C. Rcd. 7442 (Sept. 28, 1994) ¶ 211. Paul W. MacAvoy, "Tobin's q and the Cable Industry's Market Power," Attachment to Comments of United States Telephone Association to the Federal Communications Commission, MM Dkt. No. 89-600 (Feb. 28, 1990).

of regulatory failure. The complexity of even a seemingly easy task—lowering rates in a demonstrably monopolistic business—quickly spirals. In cable the private system operator's ultimate right to regulate investment flows, to shift marketing efforts, and to control the programmed content of what is offered on the basic cable package compounds the regulator's burden beyond whatever general difficulties arise in monitoring and regulating service quality. The task quickly becomes unworkable. That is the alternative vision of price regulation.

In a 1995 case before the D.C. Circuit Court of Appeals,[6] one of us (TWH) was quoted as having written, in a previous article, that "consumers cannot be worse off than under an unregulated monopoly."[7] Although the

6. Time Warner Entertainment Co. v. Federal Communications Commission, 1995 WL 330928 (D.C. Cir.).

7. Id. at 21 (quoting Thomas W. Hazlett, Duopolistic Competition in Cable Television: Implications for Public Policy, 7 YALE J. ON REG. 65, 86 (1990)).

context of the earlier article was distinct, dealing with the question of whether franchising authorities should permit a second entrant to compete in an unregulated cable TV market, the lesson teaches us to be more careful. It *is* theoretically possible for rate regulation of a monopolist to impose such social costs and distorting incentives that consumers are worse off than under unregulated monopoly, a position Milton Friedman takes in a passage quoted at the beginning of chapter 1.

Indeed, the ironic result of this analysis of rate controls is that deregulation of cable TV rates in the 1984 Cable Act appeared to lower quality-adjusted rates and increase penetration and viewership of cable programming, whereas reregulation pursuant to the 1992 Cable Act appears to have achieved just the reverse. As inefficient as unregulated monopoly is, it has outperformed the regulated alternative, as evidenced by consumer behavior in that market.

The major dilemma for cable rate regulators is that whatever price level an administrative order sets, cable operators have the next move. They may respond in countless dimensions: retiering basic program services, lowering their demand price for programming, shifting to home shopping networks (and others) that pay for carriage, promoting infomercials over costly productions, investing in nonvideo service technologies, enhancing efforts in marketing pay and unregulated services such as advertising (taking the resources away from regulated services), or reducing costs by measures that range from work force reductions to billing customers quarterly—in advance—rather than monthly. In addition, cable operators are not passive reactors to regulation; they will predictably mount a sophisticated, extravagant, multifront offensive in the legal and political worlds in an attempt to reconfigure each specific regulatory constraint. When the reregulation dust had settled sometime in 1994, the effects appeared to be much the reverse of deregulation: subscribership growth slowed and viewer ratings languished.

The penetration of basic cable programming, not only into U.S. households but onto U.S. television sets, is a fundamental output measure in the sector. In figure 6-1 we can see the trend in all-day viewer shares for basic cable television channels, taken as a package, across deregulation and reregulation. The pattern seems to be clear and devastating for the hypothesis that regulation works: deregulation during the 1987–1992 period saw huge growth in basic cable television service, with audience gains averaging 18.5 percent compounded annually. Reregulation in 1993–94 saw trendline growth stop dead in its tracks, with audience gains of an anemic 3.4 percent.

The cable rate series (figure 9-1) shows some of the dynamics at work. The revenue per subscriber and rate-generated revenue per subscriber se-

Figure 9-1
U.S. Cable Rate Growth, 1977–1994

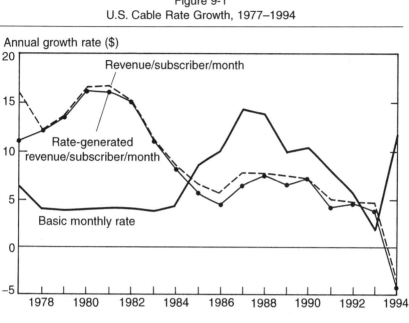

Source: Paul Kagan Associates, *Cable TV Investor,* Mar. 31, 1994, p. 9; June 30, 1995, p. 5.

ries show that the cost of the cable package increases modestly during the years following deregulation.[8] It does so over time, as new services are added and as quality improves. That accounts for the increasing rate of subscriber growth and strong audience gains following deregulation. Rates and program quality are increasing together, yielding the otherwise counterintuitive result that price and quantity demanded are both rising. But beginning in 1991 the rate of price increase slows markedly, owing to recession, impending regulatory clouds, or both; Congress came within a whisker of passing cable reregulation in October 1990. And reregulation

---

8. The basic rate, meanwhile, experiences much more severe gyrations, increasing dramatically in response to both deregulation and reregulation. The latter phenomenon has been attributed to a reporting quirk: reregulation caused many systems to collapse expanded tiers and raise the "basic rate." PAUL KAGAN ASSOCIATES, CABLE TV INVESTOR, June 30, 1995, at 5. That the regulated price—the basic rate—demonstrates such a different profile from the overall package price paid by consumers reveals a primary difficulty in enacting cable television rate controls.

stayed on the agenda (we can say with the benefit of hindsight), leading eventually to enactment in October 1992. That anxiety caused investments in program quality to slip and stemmed the tide of rate increases. As the industry was staggered by the break in cash flow gains inflicted by rate regulation, finally binding in 1994, it looked back and saw just this picture: "[T]he industry experienced its first decline in total revenue per sub/mo.— probably in its entire 45-year history—with a 3.7% drop in 1994. But, as our data show, the annual change had already fallen precipitously in 1991, long before the toughest rate regulation [or the Cable Act] was imposed. This was the beginning of the industry's pullback on new programming, the dark side of rate reg that the Democratic Congress failed to recognize."[9]

The quality issue has been elusive for regulators. FCC rulemakings have countered network "migration" and other obvious tactics used to evade rate controls—an indication that the agency has taken its mission seriously. Yet, far more subtle issues concerning service quality have gone unaddressed, because they cannot be regulated: both the "bounded rationality" of 200 Cable Services Bureau administrative personnel and the First Amendment place substantial barriers between video content and regulators.

Of further importance is that the regulatory agency is not "exogenous." The FCC has been alert and sensitive to political realities, as any theory of rational behavior would predict. Official agency positions on the practice and effects of rate regulation have frequently had to shift in response to changing political equilibria. In May 1994, when the tough rules of February 1994 were having a sharp impact on reducing basic cable's growth rate, FCC chairman Reed Hundt defended rate regulation with these words: "The industry is not in any way ruined. They're just going through a period of flatness."[10] Then, following the Republican congressional victories, the agency adopted a new approach in January 1995: "[I]t is particularly remarkable that during the reregulation period . . . the numbers indicate that there has been a significant increase in basic subscriber growth. An article from November 28, 1994 in *Cable World* called it the 'best basic subscriber growth in recent memory.' This is confirmed by the Kagan study, which indicates a subscriber growth increase from 3.1% to 5.2% between September 1993 and September 1994."[11]

---

9. Paul Kagan Associates, Cable TV Investor, June 30, 1995, at 4.

10. Reed Hundt, *quoted in* Bill Carter, *Cable TV Industry Shifts Approach as Growth Slows,* N.Y. Times, May 23, 1994, at C9.

11. Letter from Blair Levin, Chief of Staff, Office of the Chairman, Federal Communications Commission, to Adam Thierer, Heritage Foundation, Jan. 31, 1995.

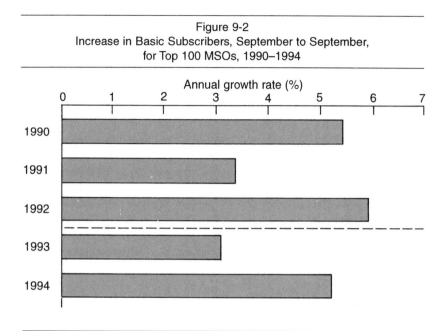

Figure 9-2
Increase in Basic Subscribers, September to September,
for Top 100 MSOs, 1990–1994

Source: Paul Kagan Associates, 1995.

Although an increase in subscriber growth from the first year of rate controls to the second does not reveal much about the effectiveness of regulation, the actual data series cited is interesting. When extended to the few years preceding rate regulation (see figure 9-2), it shows that subscriber growth had slowed in 1993–1994, despite macroeconomic recovery.

The going-forward rules, of course, were an explicit retreat from rate regulation; they allowed immediate rate increases without any cost justification and were incentive payments to encourage cable systems to insert new channels on regulated basic tiers. That they had a sharp impact on bringing new programming services to market, services that had been stalled during years of uncertainty before and after the 1992 Cable Act, is direct testimony of the ability of rate regulation to depress program quality. The commission soon observed its success in relaxing controls in response to its policies: "The Going Forward rules are already providing relief to programmers by giving them access to millions of new subscribers. . . . The new rules are also benefiting cable operators, who can expect to see healthy gains in cash flow as a direct result of the Going Forward regulations."[12]

---

12. FCC, 1 CABLE INDUSTRY TRENDS, no. 2 (Mar. 15, 1995), at 3.

In the end, the FCC broadly retreated with a measured deregulation of cable rates—measured so as not to be politically embarrassing. Rates for the entire cable package began rising at twice that of inflation during the October 1994–May 1995 interval, and with the going-forward rules, 3 percent annual inflation increases, and allowable price hikes in unregulated (à la carte) services, cash flow per subscriber growth was set to regain pre-1991 levels of 7 percent according to commission projections.[13]

By mid-1995, the only real debate at the commission was whether the deregulation was full and complete. Cable operators, believing that they may have had the votes to turn the going-forward rate increases into annual events, attempted in May 1995 to gain further incentives for introducing new program services. Chairman Reed Hundt's office held that the going-forward rules were the last regulatory loopholes to be opened; every other commissioner issued a statement that further relief was necessary. Hundt's spokesman, chief of staff Blair Levin, issued a revealing defense of the no-more-deregulation position. Noting that cost-based rate increases were too difficult for the FCC to administer, he suggested that further rate relief was not "a top priority with cable lobbyists." After each of the other commissioners' representatives took issue with that position, Levin fell back to the following: "Let's be very candid. If you look at the $1.50 for going forward, inflation and external cost pass-throughs, you're not far from the maximum [rate] of where you [cable operators] want to be."[14]

The FCC's advice to cable operators had become: you're already deregulated, so just keep quiet about it. Indeed, large parts of the industry were explicitly released from the 1993–1994 rate rules, both for administrative convenience and as a sop to economic reality. Just before the May 1995 convention of the National Cable Television Association, held in Dallas, the commission released rules allowing any small cable system (fewer than 15,000 subscribers, with fewer than 400,000 belonging to the system operator in total) to escape from rate regulation if its rates were below $1.25 per channel.[15] That is a very high price ceiling: it allows the average limited basic package of twenty channels (as per the February 1994 FCC survey) to charge $25 per month, with the average full basic package of forty-one channels (in the same survey) to be sold for over $50. That deregulation was bestowed upon "close to two-thirds of all systems and 12% of all subscribers."[16]

---

13. PAUL KAGAN ASSOCIATES, CABLE TV INVESTOR, June 30, 1995, at 4.

14. PAUL KAGAN ASSOCIATES, CABLE TV REGULATION, May 23, 1995, at 5.

15. Such rates would be presumptively reasonable; a city alleging such rates were unreasonable would assume the burden of proof.

16. PAUL KAGAN ASSOCIATES, CABLE TV REGULATION, May 23, 1995, at 1.

Further deregulation was embodied in the "social contract" deal struck with Continental Cablevision in April 1995. The country's third-largest MSO, with 3.1 million subscribers, was essentially freed of the regulatory regime imposed on other operators by agreeing to invest 120 percent of the firm's 1990–1994 capital budget on system upgrades over the 1995–2000 period.[17] Because the base period chosen was one wracked by capital rationing within the industry, and because the large cable operators were preparing their systems to deliver expanded products and digital telecommunications services to vie with both telephone companies and wireless competitors, the capital expenditure condition was likely nonbinding.[18] The MSO agreed to rebate some $9.5 million to customers (roughly $3 per subscriber), but not necessarily in cash (the firm could offer in-kind payments, such as a free pay-per-view movie, instead) and to offer a low-priced limited basic service (15 percent below FCC benchmark rates). But the company could then raise rates by 15 percent on expanded basic tiers, and gained the freedom to shift popular services from lower tiers to expanded basic (called "migration").[19] Those alterations would put expanded basic, for all intents and purposes, at unregulated levels.

The Continental "contract" included settlement of some 350 rate complaints pending against the company and deregulation for the great majority of its subscribers. It is difficult to see the deal as anything but window dressing for a favorable verdict in the regulated firm's favor. Indeed, the cable industry has long sought—in the 1990 cable reregulation debate, in the 1992 cable reregulation debate, in the 1993 and 1994 rate regulation rulemakings at the FCC, and even in early versions of the Telecommunications Act of 1996—to have rate regulation bind only on the lifeline service tier. Both municipal regulators and the cable industry have certainly viewed the "social contract" as virtually an unconditional surrender by the FCC.[20]

---

17. PAUL KAGAN ASSOCIATES, CABLE TV LAW REPORTER, Apr. 30, 1995, at 4.

18. That is the optimal industrial policy. The "social contract" affords political cover, however, wherein lies its true importance.

19. Vincente Pasdeloup, *Continental's FCC Deal the Dawn of a New Regulatory Day?* CABLE WORLD, Apr. 10, 1995, at 1, 52.

20. In a May 22, 1995, filing with the FCC protesting the "social contract" with Continental, three Florida cities wrote: "The purported benefit to consumers of refunds and upgrades is a sham. With respect to upgrades, Continental is promising no more than the cable operator would have to do in order to remain viable in a competitive marketplace." *New Takes on Continental's "Social Contract,"* CABLE WORLD, May 29, 1995, at 8. The cable operator's view was summed up succinctly: "FCC Chairman Reed Hundt sent the cable industry mixed signals, giving with one hand and taking with the other. On the plus side, cable ops are looking at social contracts and small system de-

Such accommodations and retreats remind one of the Mark Russell line about the California state legislature, which he compared to professional wrestling: "A bunch of overweight white guys pretending to hurt each other." The "social contract" with Continental allowed a quiet deregulation, which keeps lifeline rates in check by, perversely, limiting channels provided consumers: "Ironically, the pact actually prohibits Continental from adding channels to [limited] basic. Apparently, the FCC fears such a move might lead to embarrassing rate hikes, exposing the agency's regulatory regime to further ridicule."[21] And Continental's counsel freely conceded that the capital expenditure figure was nonbinding: "[Robert] Sachs said Continental already had been planning to spend more than $1 billion this year on rebuilds and upgrades. The deal with the FCC merely put it down on paper in exchange for some clear rate-regulation guidelines."[22] That bargain, lowering risk premiums on the capital raised, was created via a face-saving deal that made it look as though the cable MSO were being regulated. The trick was instantly popular: "Sachs said the deal had already struck a chord last week with quite a few MSOs, whose attorneys and bankers called him seeking information—not surprising considering the fact that the U.S. financial community has expressed quite a bit of frustration over the lack of regulatory certainty in the cable industry."[23]

By the end of 1995, "social contracts" had come to dominate the regulatory landscape, as other MSOs entered into special bargains with the FCC. Those deals, like Continental's, gave companies wide latitude to determine future price hikes. In return, the commission was able to dispose of huge numbers of rate control petitions submitted by individuals and municipalities, to announce millions of dollars worth of "rebates" to customers, and to claim credit for cable infrastructure investments running to the billions of dollars. Driven by the changing political winds and overwhelmed by the sheer size of the administrative task of regulating 11,000 cable television systems, the enforcement agency (not illogically) strove for "peace with honor." In January 1996 substantial rate hikes in systems owned by operators striking "social contract" bargains (for example, 11–13 percent basic rate increases for the Time Warner systems in New York, San Diego, Austin, and Portland) seemed to signal the public burial of cable rate regulation:

---

regulation. On the minus side, there's telco entry, digital standards, and an adverse DBS ruling." Paul Kagan Associates, Cable TV Regulation, May 23, 1995, at 1.

21. Paul Kagan Associates, Cable TV Law Reporter, Apr. 30, 1995, at 5.

22. Pasdeloup, *supra* note 19, at 52.

23. *Id.*

> Cities and towns around the U.S. are up in arms over a recent wave of special deals between Washington regulators and big cable companies that have sent some cable rates suddenly jumping by double-digits.
>
> The outcry follows a push by the Federal Communications Commission, overflowing with thousands of cable complaints, to dispose of them by crafting a single settlement for each cable operator. The FCC started announcing the deals late last year, some under the benevolent-sounding epithet "social contract."[24]

Finally, in an act of supreme political irony, the U.S. Department of Commerce announced that it would launch a special investigation of rising cable TV rates in June 1996. That placed one Clinton administration department in the position of attempting to regulate the regulators—regulators appointed to the FCC by the same administration.[25]

Even in retreat, the terms of surrender are negotiated in the currency of cross-subsidy: the ostensible rationale for ceding greater rate-setting authority to the cable company is the operator's promise to invest in socially worthy endeavors such as upgrading network infrastructure and wiring schools for broadband access. The cynical view is that ninety-nine cents of each such capital dollar would be expended exactly the same way in the absence of any agreement, but that perspective still leaves open the door for an important—if inexpensive—"public interest" defense of the settlements. Some public agencies have endorsed the "social contract" approach, and the deregulation has proceeded without generating sufficient political backlash to undermine the process.

Cable rate regulation has proven unsuccessful in the dynamic marketplace. The initial success—and limits—of the DBS market rivalry to cable make that plain. The entrant has descended upon the monopolized multichannel video market with a substitute product that is considerably more expensive than the cable package (regulated or unregulated). That price premium is apparent both in the monthly fees charged and in the initial capital expenditure required. To offset that price disadvantage, satellite television delivers a much wider array of services via digital transmissions. The subscriber's television picture and audio are much clearer, and programming choices are vastly expanded.[26]

---

24. Mark Robichaux, *FCC's "Social Contract" for Cable Companies Draws Ire: Double-Digit Rate Increases Prompt Angry Complaints Against the Agency,* WALL ST. J., Jan. 29, 1996, at B4.

25. *Commerce Division Begins Policy Analysis of Cable-TV Rates,* WALL ST. J., June 18, 1996, at B8.

26. That competitive trade-off between cable and DBS remains, even as DBS dish prices have fallen precipitously.

The existence of a higher-priced competitive alternative casts a dark shadow on rate regulation. It demonstrates the underlying importance of product quality and suggests just how definitionally elusive a product the cable television package is. As telephone companies gain the right to compete in video markets, they too will have to offer preferred forms of news, information, and entertainment; already, major telephone companies have aligned with Disney and Sony and other great program creators to produce the software that will be a crucial piece of their competitive arsenal. No one in the business can think that lower rates alone are sufficient competitive enticements; as Alfred Kahn suggests, price is just a ratio.

We return to the Stigler-Friedland question: What *can* regulators regulate?[27] It is apparent that quality-adjusted cable rates are one item they cannot effectively regulate in the U.S. economy. Yet regulators regulate for reasons, and some benefits—to some parties—result from cable rate regulation. Certainly a lively interindustry competition has dominated the public policy developments here, and cable's competitors believe they are better off with rate regulation than without. The evidence points relentlessly to regulatory capture, even as the primary industry beneficiaries of regulation have switched: the winning coalition in the 1984 Cable Act, led by cable interests, gave way to a new coalition, dominated by anticable interests, that secured passage of the Cable Act of 1992.

The surprising result is that unregulated monopoly can be superior to regulated monopoly for consumers, even in the presence of legal entry barriers. When escape is convenient, rate regulation encourages transactions costs and rent-seeking behavior that may be so unproductive that they make the net impact of controls negative, even under "optimal" (franchise monopoly) conditions. Just as Stigler and Friedland raised eyebrows by doubting that regulated prices might not be below unregulated rates for electric power,[28] the cable market offers a powerful lesson concerning the efficacy of price regulation.

---

27. George J. Stigler & Claire Friedland, *What Can Regulators Regulate? The Case of Electricity,* 5 J.L. & Econ. 1 (1962).

28. In the end, that skepticism won the day, rather than any particular empirical findings about electricity regulation. Although a methodological breakthrough had been achieved, and economists began furiously studying the actual effects of regulation as opposed to its announced objectives, the Stigler and Friedland case study turned out to be error-prone. First, there were mathematical mistakes in the regression analysis; when done properly, electricity charges in states with public utility regulation were about one-fourth lower and output about 50 percent higher (Sam Peltzman, *George Stigler's Contribution to the Economic Analysis of Regulation,* 101 J. Pol. Econ. 818 (1993)). Second, the difference in the policy regimes was not, as argued, "unregulated" versus

In fact, we arrive at a stronger result than that broached by Stigler and Friedland: unregulated cable monopoly works better for consumers than regulated monopoly even in the face of anticompetitive barriers (yielding substantial market power) and during relatively brief adjustment periods. Whereas both George Stigler and Milton Friedman interpreted the evidence on regulation to suggest that the dynamic aspects of market competition would outperform regulated monopoly markets in the long run, the regulatory changes examined in this book have all been observed in the short to medium run. Dynamic aspects of the regulatory dilemma, wherein technological change renders existing structures obsolete, would no doubt have further undermined regulatory effectiveness—had rate reregulation regime survived to see the long run. It has become crystal clear, at a minimum, that rate control is far easier in the abstract than it is in practice. A journalist surveying the wreckage of predictions made by various political, public interest, and corporate lobbyists on the effects of 1992 rate regulation bill commented: "Welcome to the world of overblown expectations."[29]

To discover that price controls have underperformed unregulated franchise-protected monopoly is sobering. A new and starchy wrinkle is added to the choice among policy evils. The challenge to those who would reinvent rate regulation is significant. Whereas price competition has demonstrably led to increased consumer satisfaction in those cable markets where it has flourished, the market failure of price controls should inform the debate over regulation more generally. The evidence suggests that the burden of proof be shifted: whatever difficulties are involved in promoting competition in the near term, it is rate regulation that must prove its viability, even as an interim substitute. Through the experiment of deregulation in the 1980s and the reverse experiment of reregulation in the 1990s, rate regulation of cable television systems has yet to do so.

"regulated." In fact, all electric companies in the sample were regulated by either a state commission or a municipal government. It is very difficult to interpret the price and output data—regardless of what they show—as implying anything about government regulation per se.

29. Kirk Victor, *Beware the Soothsayers,* NAT'L J., Dec. 4, 1993, at 2912.

Appendix: Estimates of Consumer Savings from the 1992 Cable Act

Date	Estimated Savings	Source of of Estimate	Citation
Sept. 1992	$6 billion annually	Consumer Federation of America	"Lawmakers routinely try to claim the moral high ground by invoking the Consumer Federation of America, and they frequently quote its estimate that the measure will save cable consumers $6 billion a year." —Edmund Andrews, "Cable Bill Advocate Divides and Conquers," *New York Times,* Sept. 28, 1992, at D6
Apr. 1993	$1 billion annually	Federal Communications Commission	"Citing FCC's additional funding, Rep. Markey (D.-Mass.), chmn. of House Telecom Subcommittee, said last week that delay until Oct. 1 would cost consumers $250 million: 'It is important that the Commission act

Date	Estimated Savings	Source of of Estimate	Citation
			swiftly, decisively and unequivocally' to save cable subscribers the $1 billion FCC had promised in April." —"Unpaid Furloughs Out at FCC as Supplemental Arrives," *Television Digest,* July 12, 1993 "FCC officials said the action should produce $1 billion in rate cuts for consumers, but they refused to estimate how much average rates might drop per cable system. By some estimates, however, an average monthly rate of $20 last fall could drop as low as $18 by this fall. The commission says two-thirds to three-fourths of all cable subscribers and companies will be affected." —Jeanne Saddler and Mark Robichaux, "FCC Angers Cable Firms, Aids Networks with Rate Move," *Dow Jones News Service–Edited Wall Street Journal Stories,* Apr. 2, 1993
Sept. 1993	$1 billion annually	Federal Communications Commission	"Quello, the chairman of the FCC, said yesterday, 'There has been too much of an expectation that all rates will go down.' He said he still expects consumers will save about $1 billion from the reregulation of the cable

Date	Estimated Savings	Source of of Estimate	Citation
			industry, 'or we'll do re-regulation or [Congress] will have to do some legislation.'" —Cindy Skrzycki, "Lawmakers Lean on FCC over New Cable Rules; Rising Rates Spur Complaint," *Washington Post,* Sept. 25, 1993, at C1
Feb. 1994	$3 billion annually	Federal Communications Commission	"Nevertheless, FCC Chairman Reed E. Hundt, asserting that the government has finally 'broken the back of cable price increases,' claimed the new rules will save consumers $3 billion a year and will be backed by tough enforcement measures against violators. "'This is the greatest consumer savings in the history of American business regulation,' Hundt said." —Jube Shiver, Jr., and Amy Harmon, "Cable Rates Cut Again, Consumers: The 7% Reduction, the FCC's Second in Less than a Year, Follows Complaints That First Rollback Was Ineffective," *Los Angeles Times,* Feb. 23, 1994, at D1
Nov. 1994	$3 billion	Federal Communications Commission	"In a phone interview Friday, Hundt said the FCC's action would do nothing to jeopardize the estimated $3 billion in consumer savings under cable rate regulations, and

Date	Estimated Savings	Source of of Estimate	Citation
			that consumer bills would rise modestly—about 2.5 percent—when new channels are added to regulated tiers." —Ted Hearn, "Cable Disappointed as FCC Goes Forward," *Multichannel News,* Nov. 14, 1994
Mar. 1995	$2.5 billion	Consumers Union of the United States *(Consumer Reports)*	"Carrying out the bill's mandates, the FCC required cable companies to cut their rates by as much as 17 percent last year. The reduction totaled roughly $2.5 billion, said Gene Kimmelman of Consumers Union of the United States, a consumer-advocacy group that publishes *Consumer Reports.*" —Jon Healey, "Republican's Cable Plan Strikes a Nerve," *CQ*, Mar. 11, 1995, at 749
Mar. 1995	$2.8 billion total	Federal Communications Commission	Testimony of Reed Hundt, Chairman, Federal Communications Commission, on FY 1996 Budget Estimates before the Subcommittee on Commerce, Justice, and State, the Judiciary and Related Agencies, Committee on Appropriations, U.S. House of Representatives, March 22, 1995. Chairman Hundt stated that the Commission's regulation of cable has "promoted competition, improved service, stopped

Date	Estimated Savings	Source of of Estimate	Citation
			hyperinflation of prices, increased the number of subscribers, and promoted new programming."
Apr. 1995	$3 billion total	Federal Communications Commission	"The FCC points to recent auctions for wireless communications licenses that have raised more than $7 billion for the Treasury, and recent cable industry rate rollbacks that the agency claims have saved consumers as much as $3 billion." —Mike Mills and Paul Farhi, "Republicans Map Out an Assault on FCC's Powers," *Washington Post,* Apr. 13, 1995, at D12
May 1995	$3.5 billion total	Federal Communications Commission	"Since rate regulation took effect in September 1993, cable customers have saved $3.5 billion, or $4 a month per customer on average, according to the Federal Communications Commission. The regulations apply to most of the country's 11,000 cable systems." —"Panel Set to Free Cable Rates," *Associated Press,* May 17, 1995

Source: 1995 Dow Jones text database.

Glossary

À la carte: Channels of programming sold individually, not in basic cable package. *See* Premium channels.

Addressable/addressability: Technology that makes it possible for cable systems to change program offerings to individual subscribers easily. Old-style systems deliver the same package of channels to each customer; newer, addressable systems can add or block specific channels to give households specialized packages.

Band/bandwidth: An allotment of radio spectrum. A standard television signal is delivered over a 6 megahertz band, for instance. Wires can create new conduits for bandwidth as "spectrum in a tube." Modern cable TV systems typically are equipped with 450–550 megahertz of bandwidth, although advanced 1 gigahertz systems are now being constructed.

Basic cable: The standard package of channels sold to the customer for a flat monthly fee; that is, cable service without premium channels or pay-per-view (which may be purchased in addition). Often defined as the tier of programming that includes retransmission of off-air broadcast television signals. *See* Limited basic and Expanded basic.

Broadband: Communications transmission facilities capable of delivering high-capacity signals, such as those necessary for full-motion video. As a rule, cable television wires into the home are deemed "broadband," while "twisted pair" telephone wires into the home are "narrowband."

Broadcaster: In television, a distributor of programming using over-the-air transmissions received by viewers via ordinary antennas. Stations do not charge customers directly for signal reception (which would require scrambling) but are supported by advertising (commercial) or a combination of donations and subsidies (public).

Cable deregulation: Generally refers to the relaxation of government controls on basic cable rates. (Has also been used to describe the abolition of federal controls on what sorts of programming could be offered on cable systems.) Does not typically refer to policies to open up cable markets to competition, a meaning with which the term is elsewhere associated.

Cable operators: Companies that deliver multichannel video service to household subscribers via a wireline system. Such firms serve both as transporters (owning the cable grid) and as editors who select the programming offered. Sometimes such systems own program networks or produce local programming as well. Compensation is largely in the form of subscriber fees, but advertising revenues and ancillary services such as burglar alarms or Internet access are anticipated to become more important over time.

Cable plant: The actual cable, or wire, that sends video signals to customers. Generally either coaxial cables (copper) or optical fiber (glass). Includes various electronic components to boost signals or translate communications from one medium to another. *See also* Fiber optics.

Cable programmers: Firms that distribute television shows to cable operators via satellite distribution. Basic cable networks generally accept advertising and charge a per-subscriber licensing fee to cable system operators; premium channels, being commercial-free, receive only the latter.

Cable television–telephone company cross-ownership ban: *See* Telephone company–cable television cross-ownership ban.

Cash flow: In cable, a common expression used to denote operating profits: revenues minus operating costs. The costs excluded are taxes, interest, amortization, and depreciation.

CATV: An acronym for "community antenna television," the now anachronistic terminology for a cable TV system. Historically, cable systems developed as, simply, community antennas, bringing in no additional (that is, cable-originated) programming other than broadcast signals.

Converter: The electronic box that transfers cable signals into the subscriber's television set. It controls the channel settings and any special features allowing for interactivity, addressability, or both.

Digital compression: Using digital technology to send more information over the same bandwidth.

Digital signals: Discrete transmission signals that allow for much greater computer control of electronic communications than the older analog technology.

Direct broadcast satellite: Reception of satellite television programming at home via a small (one to two feet in diameter) receiver dish. Two major new American ventures launched in 1994: Digital Satellite Service (a partnership between DirecTV and USSB) and Primestar (owned by cable operators). A third, EchoStar, launched in 1996.

Drop/dropline: The cable segment that connects a subscriber's television set to the cable network. May be underground or aerial.

Expanded basic: A cable package involving more than just retransmission of off-air broadcast signals, generally including twenty or more cable programming services such as CNN, ESPN, Discovery, and MTV.

Fiber optics: Glass strands capable of transporting very large quantities of electronic communications compared with copper wires. Used extensively in the "backbone" of cable systems, transporting video signals over relatively long distances to nodes or hubs (of, perhaps, a few hundred homes). The final distribution of signals to the customer is then achieved by coaxial cables, as the conversion of fiber-optic transmissions to individual television sets is still relatively expensive.

Franchise: In cable, a franchise refers to a license issued by the municipal government for operation of a cable television system. It allows a firm to use city streets and rights-of-way to construct a cable television distribution network and imposes certain obligations on the firm. Historically, local governments have preferred to give out just one (monopoly) franchise, although some governments have either issued multiple (competitive) franchises or, up to the 1984 Cable Act's mandate of local franchising, maintained a no-franchise-needed (open-entry) policy.

Head-end: The central receiving point of a cable television system, involving terrestrial antennas, microwave links, satellite dishes, electronic translation equipment, and computer controls to turn video inputs into cable output: signals sent over wires to subscribers.

Homes passed: The number of potential subscribers to a cable system; the number of homes that the plant comes close enough to connect via a drop.

Interactivity: Two-way messaging, as when there is direct communication from the subscriber to the cable system as well as vice versa. The ability to order pay-per-view on an addressable system is an example of interactivity. The individual customer is informing the network of a specific demand on the cable system's own network.

LECs: Local exchange carriers; telephone companies providing local exchange service. Specifically the suppliers of the dial tone that provides caller access to the telephone network. LECs interconnect with long-distance companies, sometimes called interexchange carriers. Within business districts, competition has already begun making inroads, with "bypass" or "competitive access providers" linking business phone traffic directly to long-distance connections. Residential area competition is just beginning to be seen.

Limited basic: A cable package including a bare-bones menu of off-air broadcast signals and local origination–public access programming (sometimes including C-SPAN).

Megahertz/MHz: Units of radio spectrum; a measure of transmission capacity. A 450 MHz cable television system is able to economically deliver sixty-four channels of video to customers; each signal is allotted 6 MHz, and some additional capacity is used for various communication services or electronic functions performed by the cable system itself. Digital compression will drastically increase the number of channels that such a cable grid will be able to deliver to subscribers economically.

Minipay: Low-priced premium channels introduced after reregulation. Often sold as a package on a "premium tier."

MMDS. Multichannel, multipoint distribution service. *See* Wireless cable.

MSO: Multiple system operator. A firm, such as Tele-Communications, Inc., or Time Warner Cable, that owns several cable systems.

Multiplex: Sending the same channel to the subscriber at different times, so that it is more convenient to tune in to particular programs. Also denotes the marketing practice of splitting up new program offerings into multiple channels; Encore refers to its new six-channel minipay lineup with varying genres of films as a multiplexed service. The increasing use of digital compression encourages that sort of channel addition because the new channels can be carried over the same frequency band used by one channel.

Must-carry rules: Rules that force cable operators to give free carriage to local television broadcast stations.

NAB: National Association of Broadcasters, the primary trade association of over-the-air television stations.

NCTA: National Cable Television Association, the primary trade association serving cable television operators.

Overbuilder: Industry jargon for a firm that competes in a local cable television market. An overbuilder gives individual households a choice between two different cable companies.

Pay channels. *See* Premium channels.

Pay-per-view: Programs for which there is an individual charge. They generally involve recently released movies or live events, such as concerts or prizefights. Generally available only on addressable systems.

PEG channels: Public, educational, and government channels typically required in the local cable franchise. Also known as public access/local origination.

Penetration: An important measure of output in the cable television industry. Defined as subscribers per homes passed. U.S. cable penetration in 1994 was about 65 percent.

Premium channels: Networks that the consumer pays for separately, not included in the basic (or expanded basic) service. Examples are HBO, Showtime, Disney, Cinemax, Playboy, and the Movie Channel.

Price caps: Rate regulations that are not specifically tied to costs, as is rate-of-return regulation. Rather, a maximum price is set, and the regulated firm is allowed to keep whatever profits are achievable as long as prices do not exceed that level. (Firms are sometimes allowed to keep only some, but not all, of the profits above a certain level.)

Retransmission consent: A broadcaster's property right in its signal; the rules governing whether cable operators must pay broadcasters when they put a broadcast signal on their basic cable package.

Saturation: A measure of cable availability throughout an area; specifically, the percentage of residents able to subscribe to cable. Formally defined as homes passed per homes in franchise area. Throughout the United States, the saturation rate in 1994 was 94 percent.

Scramble/descramble: Encoding transmissions for security purposes; scrambled signals require a decoding device. Since the mid-1980s, most cable satellite networks have been scrambled, so that owners of satellite dishes (TVROs) have had to pay a subscription fee for descrambling.

Spectrum: Short for "electromagnetic spectrum." Also called "radio waves." The nondepletable natural resource through which electronic communications (including sound waves and visible light) travel. Spectrum exists naturally in the atmosphere, providing the conduit for wireless technologies, or can be manufactured by the use of cables, sometimes called "spectrum in a tube."

Telephone company–cable television cross-ownership ban. Law prohibiting local exchange companies from supplying video service in their local telephone territories. Enacted by the FCC in 1970 and codified by Congress in the 1984 Cable Act. Repealed, subject to various FCC-monitored "safeguards," in Telecommunications Act of 1996.

Tiers: The packages offered to basic cable subscribers. Often cable systems offer more than one basic cable option, starting with limited basic and involving one or more tiers of expanded basic.

TVROs: Backyard satellite dishes, of which there are currently about two million in the United States. Stands for "television receive only." TVROs receive programming distinct from DBS subscribers.

Video-on-demand: Future technology that presumably will, through high-capacity (presumably fiber-optic) infrastructure, deliver customers specific shows as they are called up from an extensive menu. That would be the ultimate in pay-per-view.

Wireless cable: An oxymoron describing microwave television service, formally called MMDS (multichannel, multipoint distribution service). Involves a line-of-sight over-the-air transmission of television signals from a transmitting tower (linked to a traditional cable head-end) to a rooftop antenna. Owing to FCC regulation, wireless cable is limited to a maximum of thirty-three channels in any one market; in addition, MMDS signals can be combined with a standard television antenna to deliver subscribers locally available broadcast signals. There are about 900,000 U.S. wireless cable subscribers.

References

Adelphia Cable Communications, *1995 Annual Report* (1996).

Allard, Nicholas W., "The 1992 Cable Act: Just the Beginning," 15 *Hastings Communications and Entertainment Law Journal* 305 (1993).

Allard, Nicholas W., "Reinventing Rate Regulation," 46 *Federal Communications Law Journal* 63 (1993).

Allard, Nicholas W., and Theresa Lauerhass, "Debalkanizing the Telecommunications Marketplace," 28 *California Western Law Review* 231 (1991–1992).

Allen, D., and D. Kennedy, "Municipal Regulation of Cable Television in the Commonwealth of Pennsylvania," Pennsylvania State University, Institute of Public Administration, 1982.

Auletta, Ken, *Three Blind Mice* (Random House 1991).

Averch, Harvey, and Leland L. Johnson, "Behavior of the Firm under Regulatory Constraint," *52 American Economic Review* 1053 (1962).

Becker, Gary, "A Theory of Competition among Pressure Groups for Political Influence," 98 *Quarterly Journal of Economics* 371 (1983).

Besen, Stanley M., and Robert W. Crandall, "The Deregulation of Cable Television," 44 *Law and Contemporary Problems* 77 (1981).
Beutel, Philip, "City Objectives in Monopoly Franchising: The Case of Cable Television," 22 *Applied Economics* 1237 (1990).

Boudreaux, Donald J., and Robert B. Ekelund, "The Cable Television Consumer Protection and Competition Act of 1992: The Triumph of Private over Public Interest," 44 *Alabama Law Review* 355 (1993).

California Public Broadcasting Commission (CPBC), *The Impact of 699* (April 1982).

Carroll, Kathleen A., and Douglas J. Lamdin, "Measuring Market Response to Regulation of the Cable TV Industry," 5 *Journal of Regulatory Economics* 385 (1993).

Cheung, Steven N. S., "A Theory of Price Control," 17 *Journal of Law and Economics* 53 (1974).

Coase, Ronald, "The Federal Communications Commission," 2 *Journal of Law and Economics* 1 (1959).

Copple, Robert F., "Cable Television and the Allocation of Regulatory Power: A Study of Demarcation and Roles," 44 *Federal Communications Law Journal* 1 (1991).

Edwards, Peter D., "Cable Television Franchising: A Case Study of Minneapolis, Minnesota," Communications Media Center, New York Law School (1985).

Egan, Bruce L., *Information Superhighways: The Economics of Advanced Public Communication Networks* (Artech House 1991).

Egan, Bruce L., and Douglas A. Conn, "Capital Budgeting Alternatives for Residential Broadband Networks." In *Telephone Company and Cable Television Competition: Key Technical, Economic, Legal and Policy Issues,* 135 (Stuart Brotman ed., Artech House 1990).

Emmons, William M., III, Adam B. Jaffe, and Jonathan B. Taylor, *The Investment Consequences of the Re-Regulation of Cable Television* (Economics Resource Group, Inc. December 20, 1994).

Emmons, Willis, and Robin Prager, "The Effects of Market Structure and Ownership on Prices and Service Offerings in the U.S. Cable Television Industry," paper presented to the Western Economic Association 68th annual conference (June 22, 1993).

Fearing, Jennifer, and Charles Lubinsky, "Qualitative Differences in Competitive Cable Markets Prior to Rate Reregulation," paper delivered at the annual meetings of the Southern Economic Association (November 19, 1995).

Federal Communications Commission (FCC), *Cable Industry Trends* (various issues).

FCC, *FCC Cable Rate Survey Database* (Government Printing Office Feb. 24, 1993).

FCC, Cable Services Bureau, *FCC Cable Regulation Impact Survey, Changes in Cable Television Rates between April 5, 1993–September, 1, 1993: Report and Summary* (February 22, 1994).

Friedman, Milton, *Capitalism and Freedom* (University of Chicago Press 1962).

General Accounting Office (GAO), *Telecommunications: Follow-up National Survey of Cable Television Rates and Services* (GAO/RCED-90-199) (June 13, 1990).

GAO, *Telecommunications: National Survey of Cable Television Rates and Services* (GAO/RCED-89-193) (August 3, 1989).

GAO, *Telecommunications: 1991 Survey of Cable Television Rates and Services* (GAO/RCED-91-195) (July 17, 1991).

Gilligan, Thomas W., William J. Marshall, and Barry R. Weingast, "Regulation and the Theory of Legislative Choice: The Interstate Commerce Act of 1887," 32 *Journal of Law and Economics* 35 (1989).

Greenhut, M. L., George Norman, and Chao-Sun Hung, *The Economics of Imperfect Competition: A Spatial Approach* (Cambridge University Press 1987).

Hazlett, Thomas W., "Cable Reregulation: The Episodes You Didn't See on C-SPAN," 16 *Regulation* 45 (1993).

Hazlett, Thomas W., "Cabling America: Economic Forces in a Political World," in *Freedom in Broadcasting* 208 (C. Veljanovski ed., London Institute of Economic Affairs 1989).

Hazlett, Thomas W., "Competition vs. Franchise Monopoly in Cable Television," 4 *Contemporary Policy Issues* 80 (1986a).

Hazlett, Thomas W., "The Demand to Regulate Franchise Monopoly: Evidence from CATV Rate Deregulation in California," 29 *Economic Inquiry* 275 (1991).

Hazlett, Thomas W., "Duopolistic Competition in Cable Television: Implications for Public Policy," 7 *Yale Journal on Regulation* 65 (1990).

Hazlett, Thomas W., "Predation in Local TV Markets," 40 *Antitrust Bulletin* 609 (1995).

Hazlett, Thomas W., "Private Monopoly and the Public Interest: An Economic Analysis of the Cable Television Franchise," 134 *University of Pennsylvania Law Review* 1335 (1986b).

Hazlett, Thomas W., "Rate Regulation and the Quality of Cable Television," in William Lehr, ed., *Quality and Reliability of Telecommunications Infrastructure* (Lawrence Erlbaum Associates 1994).

Hazlett, Thomas W., "The Rationality of U.S. Regulation of the Broadcast Spectrum," 33 *Journal of Law and Economics* 133 (1990).

Hazlett, Thomas W., "A Reply to Regulation and Competition in Cable Television," 7 *Yale Journal on Regulation* 141 (1990).

Hazlett, Thomas W., "Telco Entry into Video," *Annual Review of Communications, 1994–95* 212 (1995).

Hazlett, Thomas W., and George S. Ford, "The Fallacy of Regulatory Symmetry: An Economic Analysis of the 'Level Playing Field' in State Cable TV Franchising Statutes," paper presented at the meetings of the Southern Economic Association (November 19, 1995).

Jaffe, Adam B., and David M. Kanter, "Market Power of Local Cable Television Franchises: Evidence from the Effects of Deregulation," 21 *RAND Journal of Economics* 226 (1990).

Johnson, Leland L., *Toward Competition in Cable Television* (MIT Press and AEI Press 1994).

Kahn, Alfred E., "Deregulation: Looking Backward and Looking Forward," 7 *Yale Journal on Regulation* 325 (1990).

Kahn, Alfred E., *The Economics of Regulation* (MIT Press 1988).

Katz, Lawrence F., and Lawrence H. Summers, "Industry Rents: Evidence and Implications," *Brookings Papers on Economic Activity: Microeconomics* 209 (1989).

Katz, Michael L., and Harvey S. Rosen, *Microeconomics* (Irwin 1991).

Krattenmaker, Thomas G., and Lucas A. Powe, Jr., *Regulating Broadcast Programming* (MIT Press and AEI Press 1994).

Leffler, Keith, "Ambiguous Changes in Product Quality," 72 *American Economic Review* 956 (1982).

Leibenstein, Harvey, "Allocative Efficiency vs. 'X-Efficiency,'" 56 *American Economic Review* 392 (1966).

Levin, Stanford L., and John B. Meisel, "Cable Television and Telecommunications: Theory, Evidence, and Policy," *Telecommunications Policy* 519 (1991).

Mayo, John W., and Yasuji Otsuka, "Demand, Pricing, and Regulation: Evidence from the Cable TV Industry," 22 *RAND Journal of Economics* 396 (1991).

Merline, John, "How to Get Better Cable TV at Lower Prices," *Consumer's Research* 10 (1990).

National Cable Television Association (NCTA), *Cable Television Developments* (various issues).

Noam, Eli M., "Towards an Integrated Communications Market: Overcoming the Local Monopoly of Cable Television," 34 *Federal Communications Law Journal* 209 (1982).

Noll, Roger G., "Comments and Discussion," *Brookings Papers on Economic Activity: Microeconomics* 48 (1989).

Otsuka, Yasuji, "The Effects of Regulation on Social Welfare: Evidence from the Cable TV Industry," paper presented at the meetings of the Southern Economic Association (November 1993).

Owen, Bruce M., and Steven S. Wildman, *Video Economics* (Harvard University Press 1992).

Paul Kagan Associates, *Cable TV Financial Databook* (various issues).

Paul Kagan Associates, *Cable TV Franchising* (various issues).

Paul Kagan Associates, *Cable TV Investor* (various issues).

Paul Kagan Associates, *Cable TV Law Reporter* (various issues).

Paul Kagan Associates, *Cable TV Regulation* (various issues).

Paul Kagan Associates, *Marketing New Media* (various issues).

Peltzman, Sam, "The Economic Theory of Regulation after a Decade of Deregulation," *Brookings Papers on Economic Activity: Microeconomics* 1 (1989).

Peltzman, Sam, "George Stigler's Contribution to the Economic Analysis of Regulation," 101 *Journal of Political Economy* 818 (1993).

Peltzman, Sam, "Towards a More General Theory of Regulation," 19 *Journal of Law and Economics* 211 (1976).

Pigou, Arthur Cecil, *The Economics of Welfare,* 4th ed. (Macmillan 1932, reprinted 1962).

Pool, Ithiel de Sola, *Technologies of Freedom* (Harvard University Press 1983).

Posner, Richard A., "Taxation by Regulation," 2 *Bell Journal of Economics and Management Science* 22 (1971).

Powe, Lucas A., Jr., *American Broadcasting and the First Amendment* (University of California Press 1987).

Prager, Robin, "The Effects of Deregulating Cable Television: Evidence from the Financial Markets," 4 *Journal of Regulatory Economics* 347 (1992).

Prager, Robin, "Firm Behavior in Franchise Monopoly Markets," 21 *RAND Journal of Economics* 211 (1990).

Robinson, Kenneth, "How Much Wood Would a Woodchuck Chuck, If a

Woodchuck Could Chuck Wood? The FCC, the New Congress, and Regulatory Spending," 11 *Telecommunications Policy Review* (Feb. 26, 1995).

Robinson, Kenneth, "Things Worth Remembering," 11 *Telecommunications Policy Review* (May 7, 1995).

Rubinovitz, Robert N., "Market Power and Price Increases for Basic Cable Service since Deregulation," 24 *RAND Journal of Economics* 1 (1993). Citations are to an earlier draft from the U.S. Department of Justice, Antitrust Division, Economic Analysis Group Discussion Paper No. 91-8 (August 6, 1991).

Setzer, Florence, and Jonathan Levy, "Broadcast Television in a Multichannel Marketplace," Federal Communications Commission OPP Working Paper No. 26 (June 1991).

Smiley, Albert K., "Direct Competition among Cable Television Systems," U.S. Department of Justice, Antitrust Division, Economic Analysis Group Discussion Paper No. 86-9 (June 5, 1986).

Stigler, George J., "The Theory of Economic Regulation," 2 *Bell Journal of Economics & Management Science* 3 (1971).

Stigler, George J., and Claire Friedland, "What Can Regulators Regulate? The Case of Electricity," 5 *Journal of Law and Economics* 1 (1962).

Tele-Communications, Inc. *Form 10-K* (March 28, 1994).

Tele-Communications, Inc. *Form 10-Q* (May 1994).

U.S. Department of Commerce, National Telecommunications and Information Administration (NTIA), *Video Program Distribution and Cable Television: Current Policy Issues and Recommendations* (Government Printing Office June 1988).

Webbink, Douglas, "The Impact of Regulation and Competition on Cable TV Service Prices, Channels, and Pay Tier," Bureau of Economics, Federal Trade Commission (May 2, 1985).

Williamson, Oliver E., "Franchise Bidding for Natural Monopoly—In General and with Respect to CATV," 7 *Bell Journal of Economics* 73 (1976).

Woodbury, John R., and Kenneth C. Baseman, "Assessing the Effect of Cable Rate Deregulation," paper presented at the American Enterprise Institute conference on network industries (October 10–11, 1990).

Woodward, Bob, *The Agenda* (Simon & Schuster 1994).

Zupan, Mark A., "The Efficacy of Franchise Bidding Schemes in the Case of Cable Television: Some Systematic Evidence," 32 *Journal of Law and Economics* 401 (1989).

Zupan, Mark A., "Non-price Concessions and the Effect of Franchise Bidding Schemes on Cable Company Costs," 21 *Applied Economics* 305 (1989).

Case and Regulatory Proceeding Index

Name Index

Subject Index

A. C. Nielsen data, 110–14, 125, 129, 130
A&E Television Networks, 48, 155, 186–88
ABC, 48, 190
Access to program services, 179, 201
Additional outlet charges, 31, 138, 141
Adelphia Cable Communications, 32n, 174–75
Advertising charges, 71, 80n, 137, 140n, 141, 181
Airline industry, 44n
Alabama, 32, 127n, 138–39
À la carte services, 223. *See also* Premium channels
Albertville, Alabama, 138–39
Alexandria, Virginia, 200
Alsea River Cable, 29
AMC, 140
American Movie Classics network, 187
American Telecasting, 168
Ameritech, 185
Ancillary markets, 145
Apartment market, 45
Appropriations Committee, House, 109n
Associated Press, 190
Association of Independent Television Stations, 183n
Austin, Texas, 214
"Authorized" subscribers defined, 20n

Basic cable, 48, 223
detiering, 91–94
"must-carry" rules, 57, 88, 140
retiering, 125–26, 138–39

tiers of service, 48–49
viewer ratings, 128–33
Bell Atlantic, 46, 196, 200
cable reregulation support, 185
TCI merger, 150, 159–60, 163, 165, 173, 185
Bell Cablemedia, 168
Blocking features, 204
Bond market, 163–69
The Box network, 144n
Broadcast television. *See* Television broadcasters
Bureau of Labor Statistics (BLS), 76n
CPI cable index, 70–76, 107–10
data tables, 110, 122
Bypass charges, 71

C-SPAN, 48, 140, 187, 188
Cable Communications Policy Act of 1984, 2
effective date, 69
interest politics, 10n, 14, 216
passage date, 71
See also Deregulation effects
Cable franchises. *See* Franchise agreements
Cable operators, 224
cash flows, 88–91, 133–35, 186n, 224
opposition to reregulation, 179–80
response to rate controls, 194
Cable programmers, 224
reregulation opposition, 2, 180–82, 185–88, 193–94
Cable satellite networks, 93, 95, 156–58

245

Cable Services Bureau, 107, 170, 171, 210
Cable subscribership data, 2, 20, 22, 87
  reregulation effects, 110–28, 210–11
Cable systems
  capital costs, 9, 21–24, 33n
  competitive market value, 33–35
  franchise data, 56n
  lifespan, 9
  selling prices per subscriber, 21, 23
  telephone companies cross-owner-ship ban, 56, 58, 61, 180n, 184, 228
Cable Telecommunications Policy Act of 1983, 10n
Cable Television Consumer Protection and Competition Act of 1992, 2, 68, 73, 75
  competition spurred by, 195, 198, 201
  exempt services, 48n
  impetus for regulation, 3–5, 8
  passage date, 71, 102
  service terms defined, 49
  See also Reregulation effects
Cable television package, 48–49
Cable TV Financial Databook, 20n
Cabletelevision Advertising Bureau, 135
Cablevision Systems, 142–43, 160–61
CAI Wireless Cable, 196
California, 29n, 214
  1979 rate deregulation, 13, 15, 50, 53–55, 79n
  1993 retiering, 138
California Cable Television Association, 53
California League of Cities, 15
California Public Broadcasting Commission, 15n
Capital costs, 9, 19, 21–24, 33n
Capital markets' response
  to cable regulation or deregulation, 16, 67, 150, 158–69, 192, 206n
  to cable system sales, 33–35

to new technologies, 195–201
to risk factors, 25
Capture theory, 180n, 216
Carriage charges, 155, 181n
Cartoon Network, 140, 154–56, 182, 187
Cash flows, 88–91, 133–35, 186n, 224
CBS, 48, 190
Cellular television, 195n
Channel substitution, 105
Churning, 113n
Chow test, 74
Cinemax, 147, 227
CNN, 48, 123, 124, 133n
CNN International, 155
Comcast, 196
Comedy Channel, 139
Commerce Department, 13n, 215
Commerce, Justice, and State, the Judiciary and Related Agencies Subcommittee, House, 109n
Commerce, Science, and Transportation Committee, Senate, 10n, 11n, 92
Communications Act of 1934, 59n
Communications Subcommittee, Senate, 3
Competition
  as preferred remedy to monopoly pricing, 4–5, 207–8, 217
  See also Market power
Compliance costs, 175–77
Computer services, 158
Comsat Corp., 161
Connecticut, 202
Consultant costs, 175
Consumer Federation of America, 5
Consumer groups, 179
Consumer welfare, 9, 13, 17–19, 24–25, 43, 216–17
  savings estimates, 5–7, 218–22 (table)
  See also Deregulation effects; Reregulation effects
Content regulation. *See* First Amendment rights
Continental Cablevision, 174, 213–14

Urban consumer price index, 71
USA Network, 48, 181n, 186n, 194
U.S. Conference of Mayors, 10n
User fees, 134n
USSB, 20n, 225

Value Vision, 141n
VH-1, 139
Viacom, 148, 186, 187
Video dialtone (VDT) systems, 58n, 156
Videotron Holdings, 168
Viewer ratings, 2, 128–33, 135, 157, 208
Viewing shares, 96–98

Violence in programming, 189–92
Virginia, 200

Waldport, Oregon, 29, 31
Weather Channel, 122
WGN, 139
Wireless cable, 59n, 168
    cable reregulation position, 179
    competitive pressure on cable, 156, 195–97, 200, 201, 203
    definition, 229
    penetration and subscribership, 20, 124
Wiring charges, 139